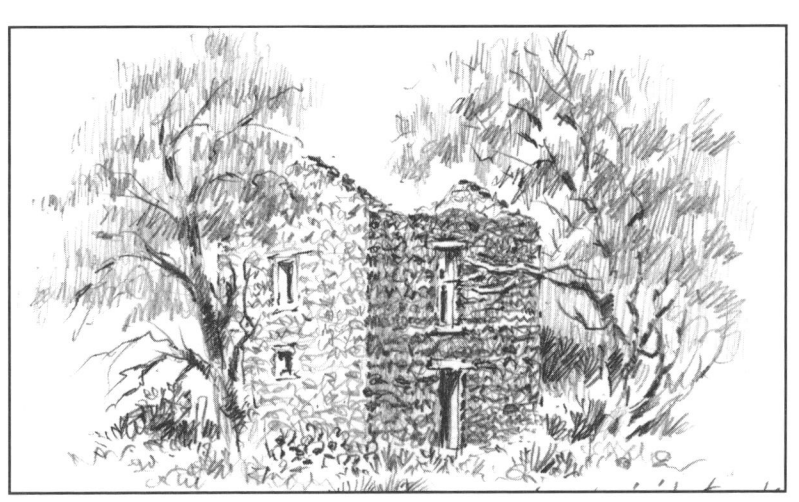

TRACES OF FORGOTTEN PLACES

TRACES

OF

FORGOTTEN

PLACES

An artist's thirty-year exploration and celebration of Texas, as it was

Don Collins

edited by T. Lindsay Baker

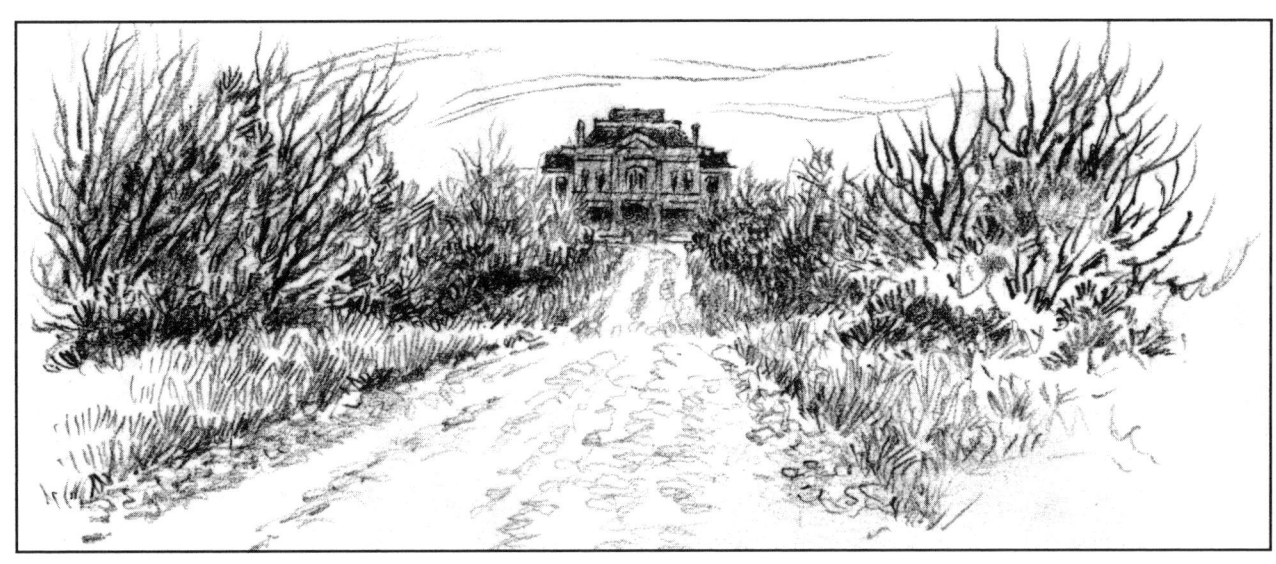

TCU Press / *Fort Worth*

Library of Congress Cataloging-in-Publication Data

Collins, Don.
  Traces of forgotten places : An artist's thirty-year exploration and
celebration of Texas, as it was / by Don Collins ; edited by T.
Lindsay Baker.
      p. cm.
  Selected from the almost four hundred illustrations made for the
Miller Blueprint calendars.
  ISBN 978-0-87565-361-7 (alk. paper)
  I. Collins, Don. 2. Texas--In art. I. Baker, T. Lindsay. II. Miller
Blue Print Company, Austin, Tex. III. Title.

NCI39.C593A4 2008
741'.092--dc22

                            2007041129

TCU Press
P. O. Box 298300
Fort Worth, TX 76129
817.257.7822
http://www.prs.tcu.edu
To order books; 800.826.8911

Designed by
Barbara Mathews Whitehead

To Robert Lambie Miller

Contents

Preface ix

Introduction by T. Lindsay Baker 1

PART ONE—Central Texas 7

PART TWO—South Texas 41

PART THREE—The Hill Country 57

PART FOUR—The Panhandle Plains 99

PART FIVE—West Texas 109

PART SIX—East Texas 125

PART SEVEN—North Central Texas 139

List of Plates 161

Preface

MY GRATEFUL THANKS go to Robert Miller for his 1977 idea for calendars. Robert's idea fit well with my lifelong enthusiasm to see and record what lies just around the next bend. After thousands of enjoyable back-road miles in search of subject matter, I remain astonished at how large and diverse is the state of Texas! I have barely scratched the surface. I have deliberately chosen to avoid the more celebrated subjects in favor of lesser known, more humble ones. As the years have gone by and population shifts have occurred, many of these images are all that remain. I have been encouraged in this effort by the Miller family, artist friends, responsive viewers, my wife Mary Linda, and a multitude of children and grandchildren. I hope the works are as pleasant to see as they were to do.

—Don Collins
Austin, Texas

Introduction

IN MANY WAYS Don Collins and I have trod the same fields—we have trespassed across pastures to inspect the same dilapidated farmhouses, we have drawn and photographed the same old mills, and we have stepped from floor joist to floor joist across the same rotted floors of abandoned courthouses, marveling that we didn't fall through.

"There is always a little leap, you know, a sudden expectation," he explained about his feelings when he discovers a "new" weathered-away hulk. The "Wow!" for him is the same excitement that a hunter experiences when he jumps a big buck deer. "I have a feeling of exhilaration. Immediately I start processing it. What's the best place to stand to encompass all of this? It's a good feeling." He is absolutely right, because this is precisely the same emotion that bubbles up for me as I clamber through someone's fence to head toward the latest "find."

Don came by his enthusiasm for the past honestly. He grew up on a small ranch in southeastern Parker County, Texas, with his mother, his older brother Neil, and three bachelor uncles. They lived in a large, tumbled-down old house in a beautiful area that his McGlinchey ancestors had occupied since the 1870s. He got to know this frame dwelling of hand-hewed oak sills intimately—really intimately. He crawled around beneath it to collect eggs from the laying hens, sometimes coming head-to-head with snakes that were looking for the same eggs. The ranch and dairy operation managed to support the family during the depths of the Great Depression. But since money was tight and the uncles unmotivated, "the house gradually fell apart around our ears . . . one of the porches even fell off."

After high school, Don attended North Texas Agricultural College, now the University of Texas at Arlington. "I went two years. Although art-minded from childhood, I didn't know anything about art as a profession. I wasn't sure you could make a living from art, and my family concurred." Summers and alternating semesters, he worked at the big Consolidated-Vultee bomber plant on the west side of Fort Worth, as well as a newspaper copy boy, grain harvester, fence builder, and soft-drink truck driver. Having saved some money, Don then returned to school, this time with a pre-law major at Texas Technical College in Lubbock. That did not last long, for shortly thereafter the Korean War turned critical.

Dissatisfied with the infantry and the ROTC program at the school, he withdrew and signed up to become an aviation cadet.

Don was not the only college student who wanted to fly for the air force during the early 1950s. There were so many others that the service disqualified many applicants for the slightest reasons. "In October 1951 they flunked me," he remembered, explaining, "They said I had a heart murmur. My doctor said, 'There's nothing wrong with you; they don't want you.'" Days before being drafted, the young man next signed up for the regular U.S. Army, receiving duty that even a Texan who grew up on a ranch could never have imagined. After training at the quartermaster school at Fort Lee, Virginia, Collins went to Fort Reno, a nineteenth-century cavalry post in Oklahoma, where the service was purchasing and quarantining large numbers of horses for the Turkish army, an ally in the Korean conflict. "They had three to four thousand horses there, and it was beautiful to see them run." Eventually Don, eight hundred horses, and a contingent of American soldiers boarded an old Victory Ship at New Orleans and sailed across the Atlantic and through the Mediterranean to a dock at Istanbul. There they unloaded the horses, explored Istanbul, stocked up on what food they could find in the local markets, and returned across the sea. They passed for over a week through a hurricane, and he remembers, "The sailors would be looking over the side of the boat at a reinforced iron band, because those ships had a reputation for breaking in half in storms, but it held together."

After his discharge from the army, Don went to work as a designer for a container company in Fort Worth, but he didn't like the corporate world. He resigned his job and returned to school, this time to the University of Texas at Austin, using his educational benefits as a veteran under the GI Bill. He completed study during the summer of 1956, but even before this Don entered an informal partnership with Jack Wilson, an Austin typesetter/designer. "It was a free-lance operation. He sought the work and I did it, and we divided the money. . . . We never had any contract. It was called The Art Studio." The working agreement lasted forty-nine-and-a-half years.

What a job this was for an enthusiastic young illustrator and graphic artist. Designers in Austin at that time had to be generalists, because there wasn't enough work to go around for specialists. "Whenever anyone came in and asked if I could do something, I would always say, 'yes,' and then figure out how to do it." He was always inclined towards architectural subjects, and happily many of the jobs at the time came from builders, contractors, and real estate salespeople for renderings of houses, stores, and other structures. "I think that I would have been an architect if I could have added and subtracted," Collins quipped. The Art Studio did work of all kinds, and Don for over a dozen years even prepared the artwork for Sunday school publications. In the 1960s the Steck Company in Austin commissioned him to prepare renderings of selected architectural works as background art for checks the firm printed. This job led to a thirty-year project for another client.

Robert Miller of the Miller Blueprint Company in Austin was a regular client of The Art Studio. One day in the shop he saw some of Don's renderings of buildings. For several years Miller had purchased ready-made calendars to distribute to his customers at year-end, but he wanted something different. In 1977 he asked, "Why don't we try a calendar?" Don collaborated with five colleagues in assembling a calendar with drawings depicting buildings around Austin. It produced a mixed result, so for the next twenty-nine years on his own he prepared the artwork for the subsequent Miller Blueprint calendars. The pieces became hits with Miller's main customers—architects, builders, contractors, and surveyors. Many of them even saved collections of them. "Robert let me choose my subjects. Every two or three years he might make some slight comments about something just to keep

his hand in," Don commented. Annually the artist began making two or three deliberate trips "just wandering across the state" looking for subject matter for the calendars.

After a while Don discovered that he was retracing his routes, so he bought a stack of county road maps. He marked the courses that he had taken so that he would be sure to see new country on subsequent forays. "I would seek out roads that followed the path of least resistance, often up a creek, as had the pioneers. I would follow them and frequently find an old structure." In time he expanded his geographical range to more distant parts of the state. "I wanted to go there and see what it's like."

In the field Don followed what became a time-tested procedure. He would spot his subject matter, often an old farmhouse or barn, pull over to the side of the road, and inspect his discovery more closely. "I get excited about it," he declared. While in the field Don sometimes makes a rough sketch on the spot and always shoots documentary photographs. "I take a roll of pictures to nail the detail," the artist explained, adding, "I have a gift to remember details anyway." He then returns to his studio to prepare the final drawing, even though he had decided in the field what approach he would take.

"It's not necessarily a literal rendering," Don stated. To improve the composition, he sometimes "cuts down some trees or moves something." Occasionally he combines elements of two locations into one work of art, as in his drawing in this book showing two abandoned trucks and a set of old barns. Don found the trucks in Oklahoma and the barns near LaGrange. "It's the artist's license," he declared. From the almost four hundred illustrations that he made for the Miller Blueprint calendars, Don has selected the seventy renderings that comprise this book. They show the forgotten traces of the past that dot the Texas landscape from the Panhandle to the Gulf Coast. His attraction to stone architecture and rural settings becomes obvious to all readers, though the selection of drawings encompasses almost every architectural form from fancy houses to industrial plants. These drawings provide a feast for the eye as well as stimulus for viewers to head out in their own cars to prowl the country lanes in search of more such places.

As Don created these works over three decades, his mind went time and again to the people who built and lived in the places he has drawn. As much as the shapes, textures, and combinations of geometric forms, Don has been attracted to these locations because emotionally he has connected with the people who occupied them. For him this feeling has been the trigger for creation. "You can imagine . . . the immense effort they went to . . . You wind up liking the people who did it even though they've been dead for a hundred years."

—T. Lindsay Baker
Tarleton State University

PART ONE

Central Texas

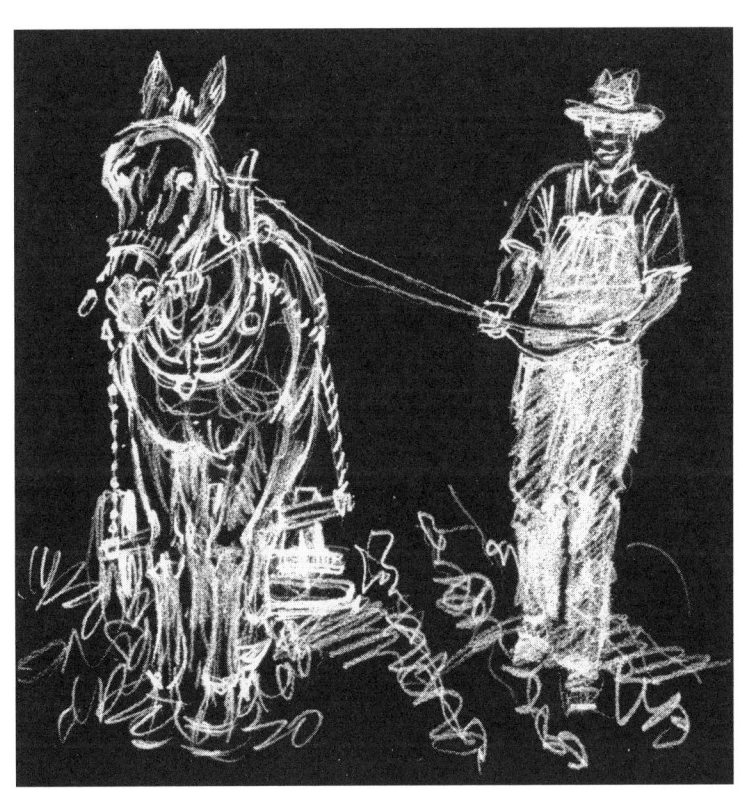

1. View of Waller Creek, Austin.

This is a view of Waller Creek that's not often seen by Austin citizens. It's down in the creek bottom right in the heart of the city between Sixth and Seventh streets. I was inspired by the fact that it has a little bit of a remote, rural look. I love the old house on the left-hand side and the Sixth Street Bridge. It is an interesting mix of an arched passageway, stonework, modern buildings, and some of the old, original limestone creek bed.

I had to step around several recumbent figures to get to where I did. It's not a place where people go on a daily basis, because it's a haven for the down and out.

I think it made a pretty nice picture. It's one of the most difficult sketches that I ever did. There's a lot going on in there. It took the time for three or four normal sketches. It's one of those things that at a certain point you ask yourself, "Why did I start this?"

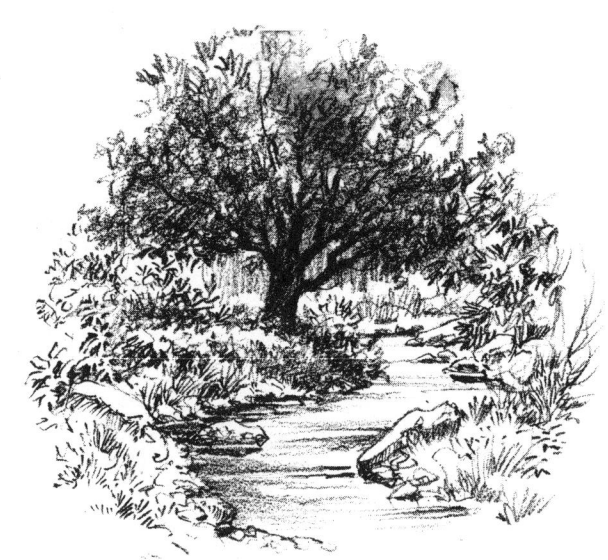

There are still small stretches of Waller creek nearby where you can almost forget being in the heart of a city.

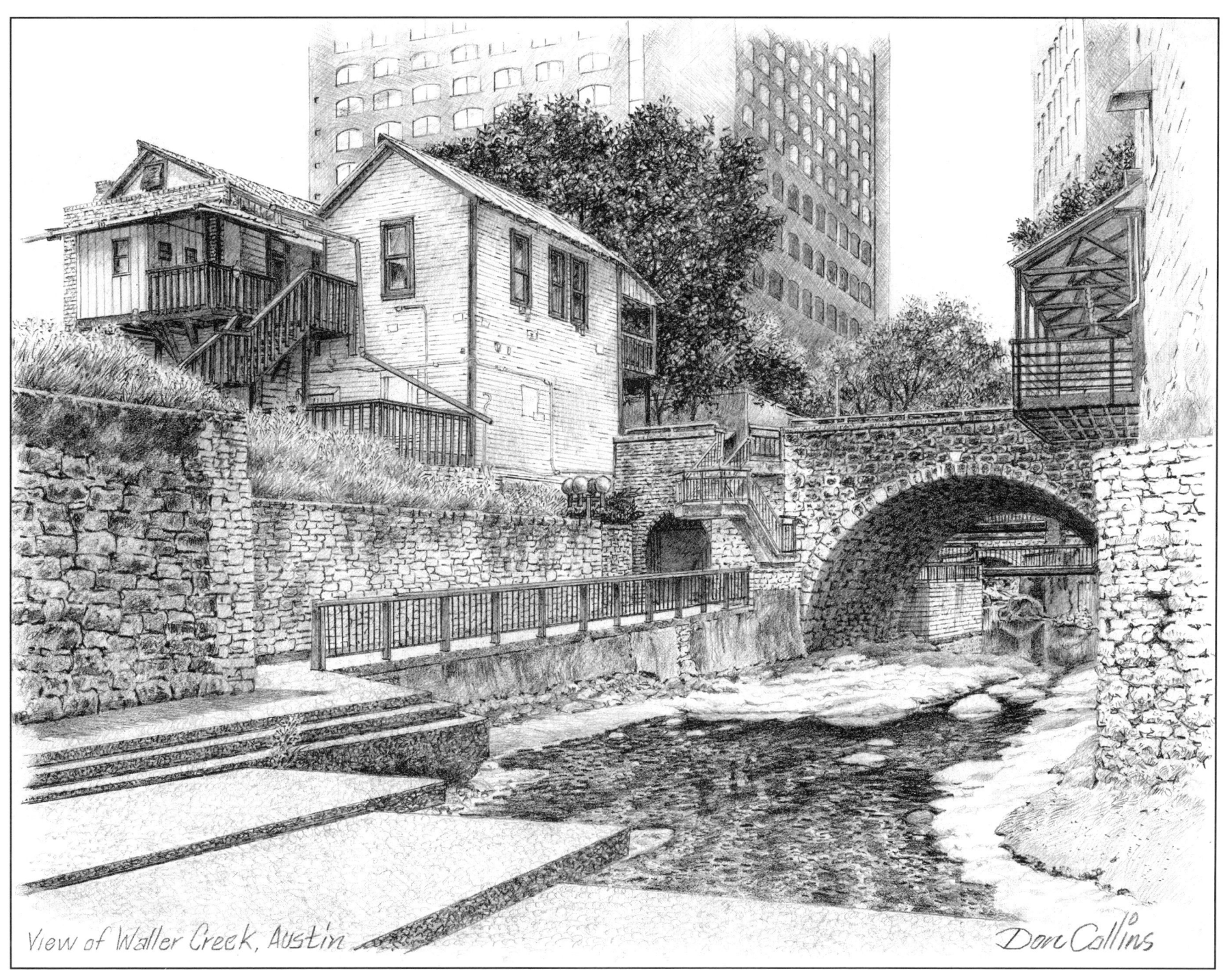

View of Waller Creek, Austin

Don Collins

2. Cottonseed Oil Mill, High Hill.

I just discovered this place while wandering down the road one day, a beautiful spring day as I recall. This enormous building came into view off Interstate 10. I didn't know what it was at the time, and there was nobody to ask. As things turned out, it was the cottonseed oil mill started at High Hill in Fayette County in 1867. It provides an interesting combination of architectural features: a big stone building that is stuccoed over, lean-to structures on either end, and collateral additions going off in all directions. There are geometric things occurring all over the face of it. And random piercings here and there for doors and windows. It is a very interesting piece of art.

I attracted a herd of cows, and I had to shoo them away, as I recall. That happens with some frequency. The cows are very interested in what you're doing. You can see the alert cow on the right checking me out.

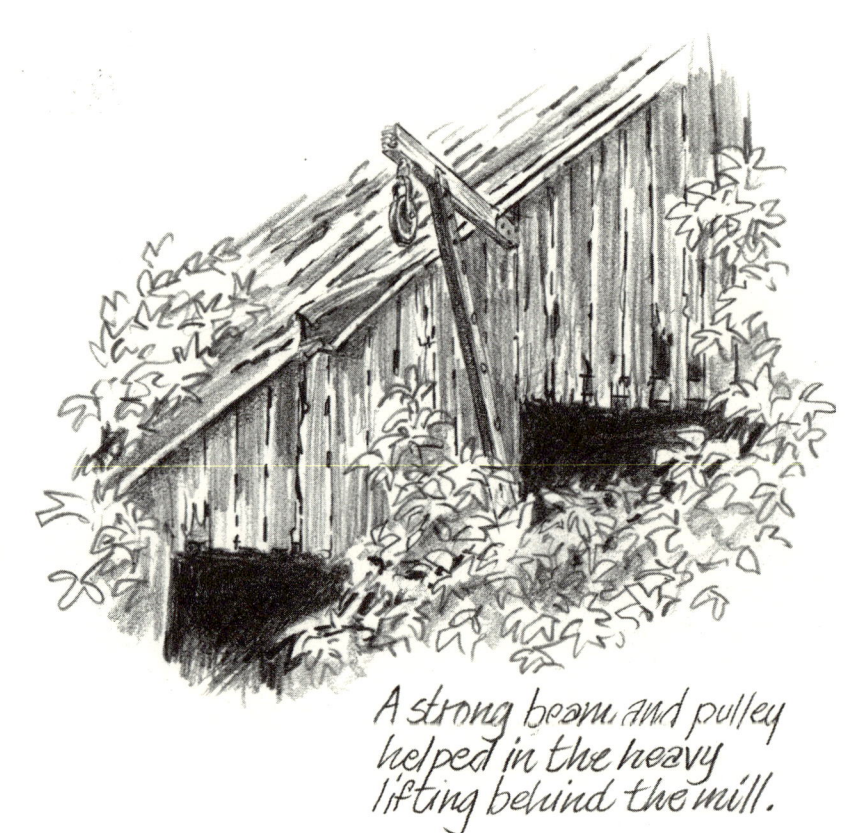

A strong beam and pulley helped in the heavy lifting behind the mill.

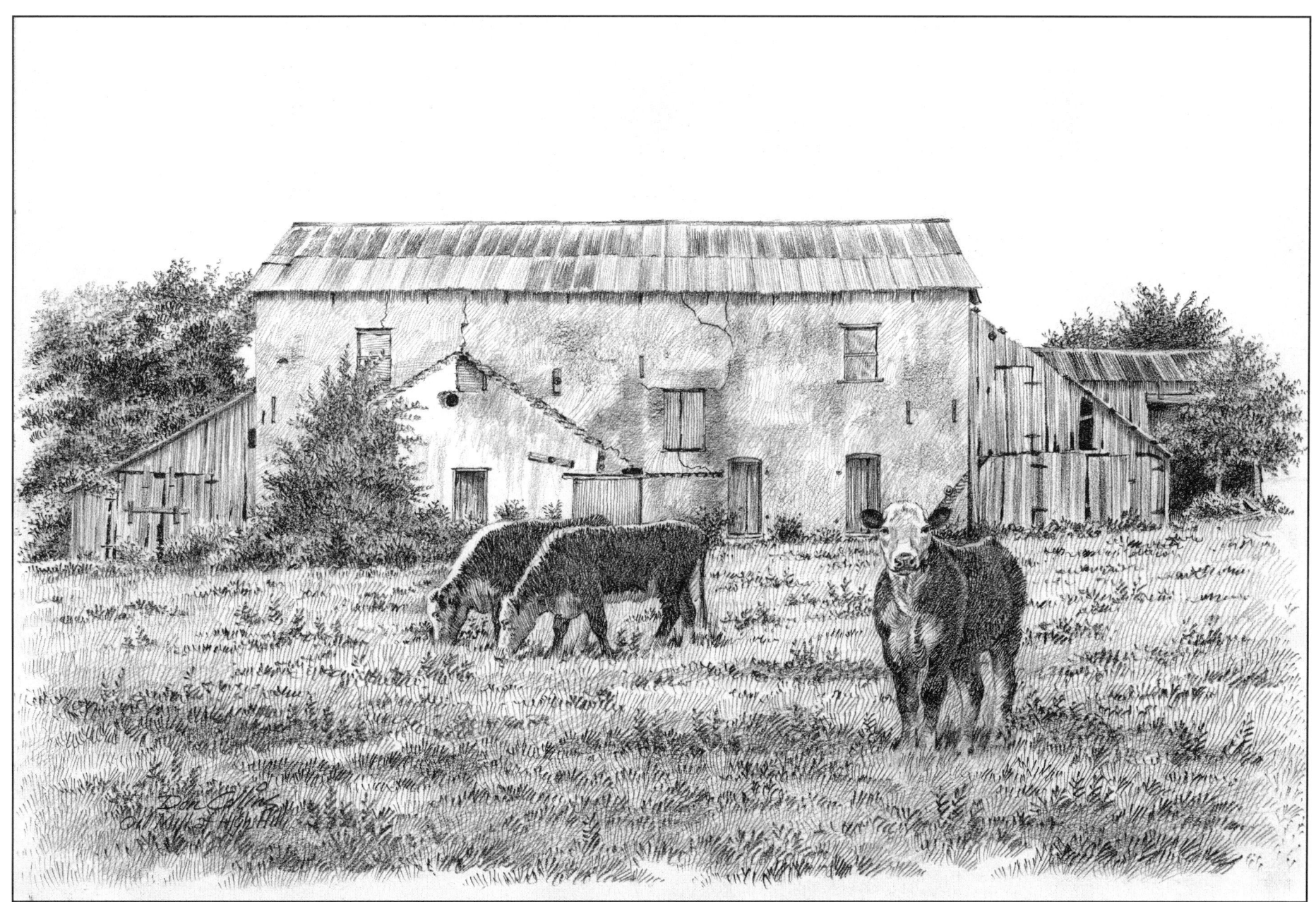

3. Ranch House near Evant.

I was going up Highway 281 many years ago. I just glanced over my left shoulder before proceeding up the big hill south of Evant and happened to see a structure over there. It set off alarms the way it always does when I see something in the distance that interests me. I worked my way over to it on a diagonal road. Made out of heavy limestone blocks, it is a pioneer structure that has some unusual features: a tapering chimney on each end, a very low upstairs, little windows that I'd never seen before, and a hipped roof.

It was in pretty bad repair. Much later, I learned that husband-and-wife architectural historians had bought the place and were in the process of restoring it. They did a lot of research on it and discovered that the little short upstairs was not original, that for unknown reasons the original owners had taken several feet off the top of the thing and lowered the roof. As it turned out, the house once belonged to Benjamin Franklin Gholson, who had been one of the party that rescued Indian captive Cynthia Ann Parker in 1860.

Anyway, I'm pleased to see that it is back in good condition now and will serve another hundred and fifty years.

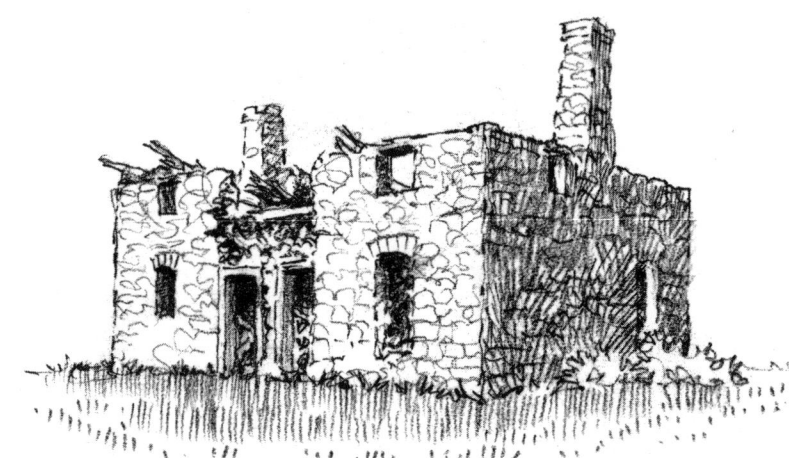

In the 18 year interval between my visits to this house, the roof structure had collapsed and the center section had virtually crumbled away. A timely restoration has reversed the damage.

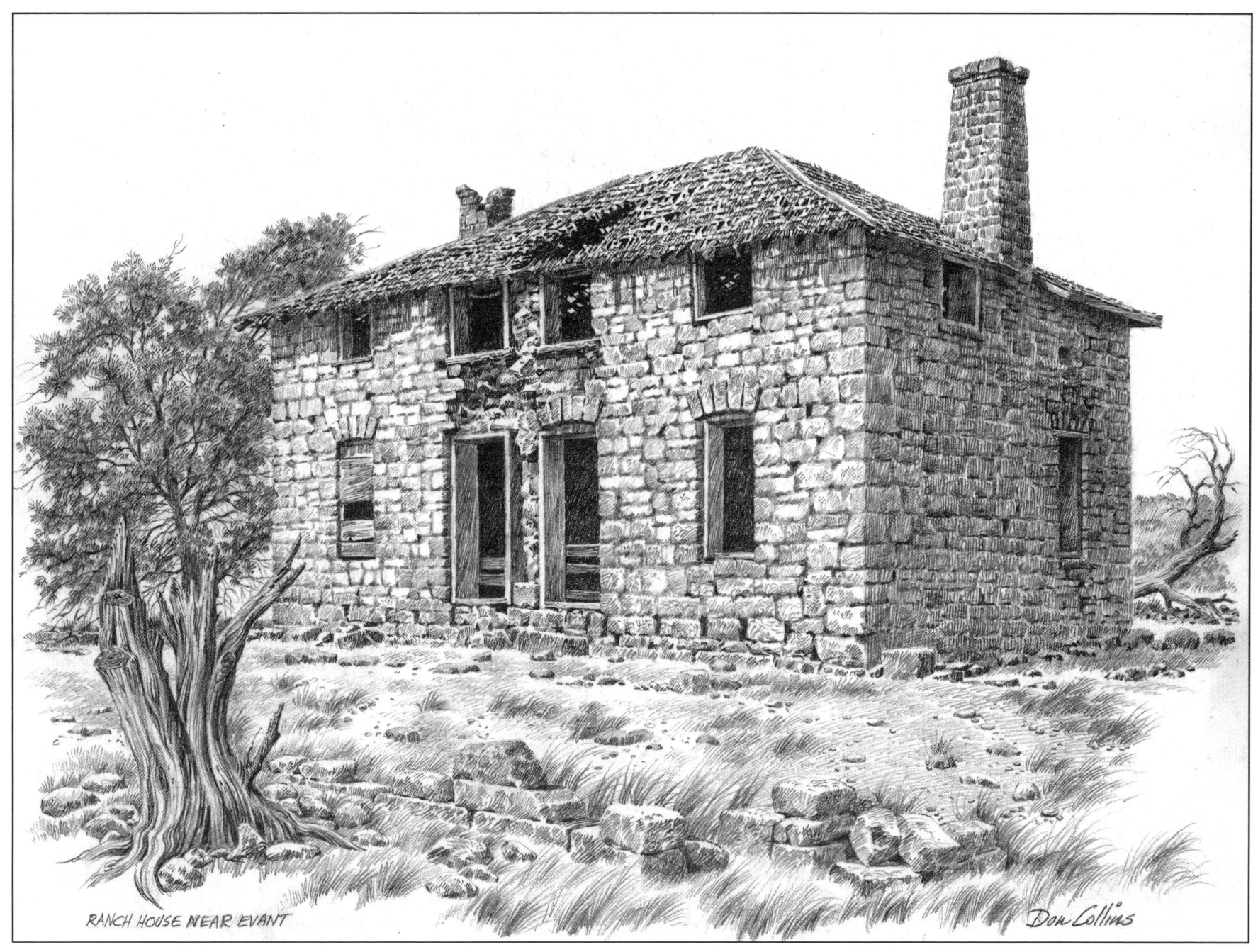

RANCH HOUSE NEAR EVANT

Don Collins

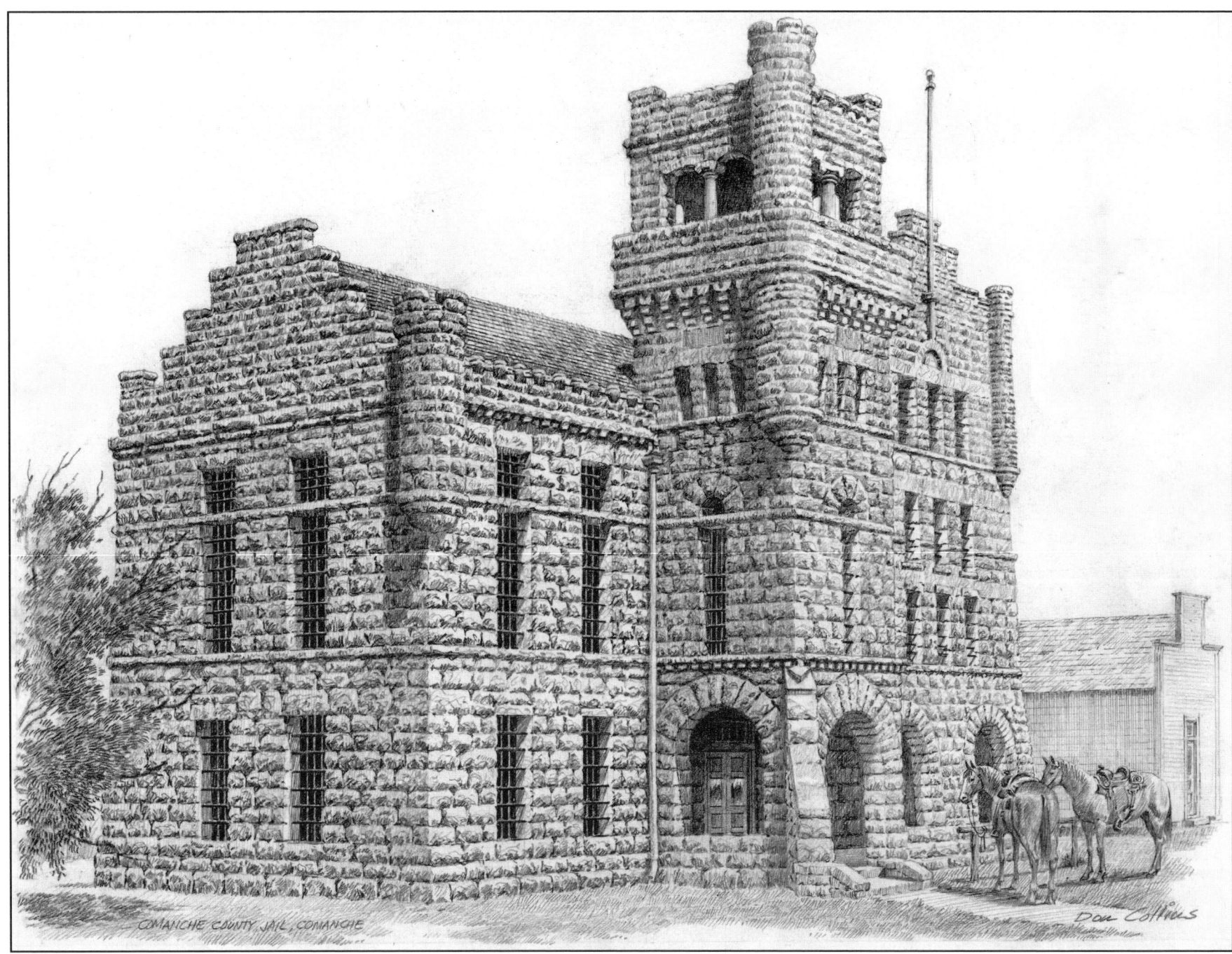

COMANCHE COUNTY JAIL, COMANCHE

Don Collins

4. Comanche County Jail, Comanche.

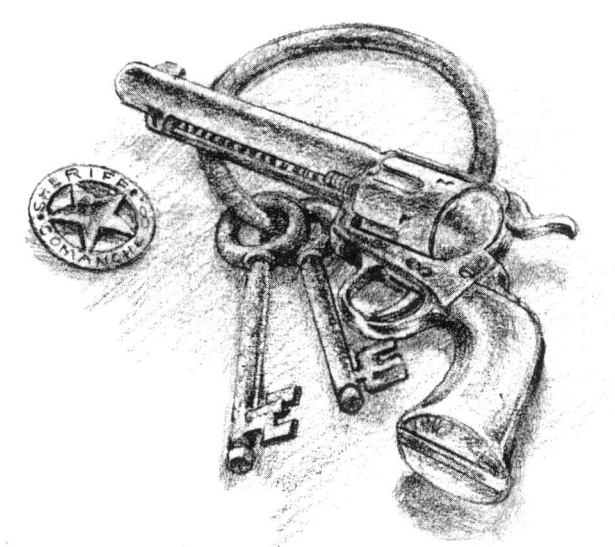

The 1903 Comanche County Jail is on a pattern of several others in Texas and looks like a medieval fortress to me. There's a jail in Brownwood that is almost precisely the same pattern, with some very minor variations in the decorations in the tower. This is a fine piece of stonework. I don't think you'd find anyone to do that now. An awful lot of things went onto that building that didn't serve any purpose, but it probably loomed over the town and inhibited wrongdoing in some way. An artist who likes to draw rocks feasts on this kind of thing, because it's nothing but stone. It's a great old building.

Unlike the bland warehouse-like look of modern jails, these old ones loudly announce their purpose... they are grim and forbidding, inside and out!

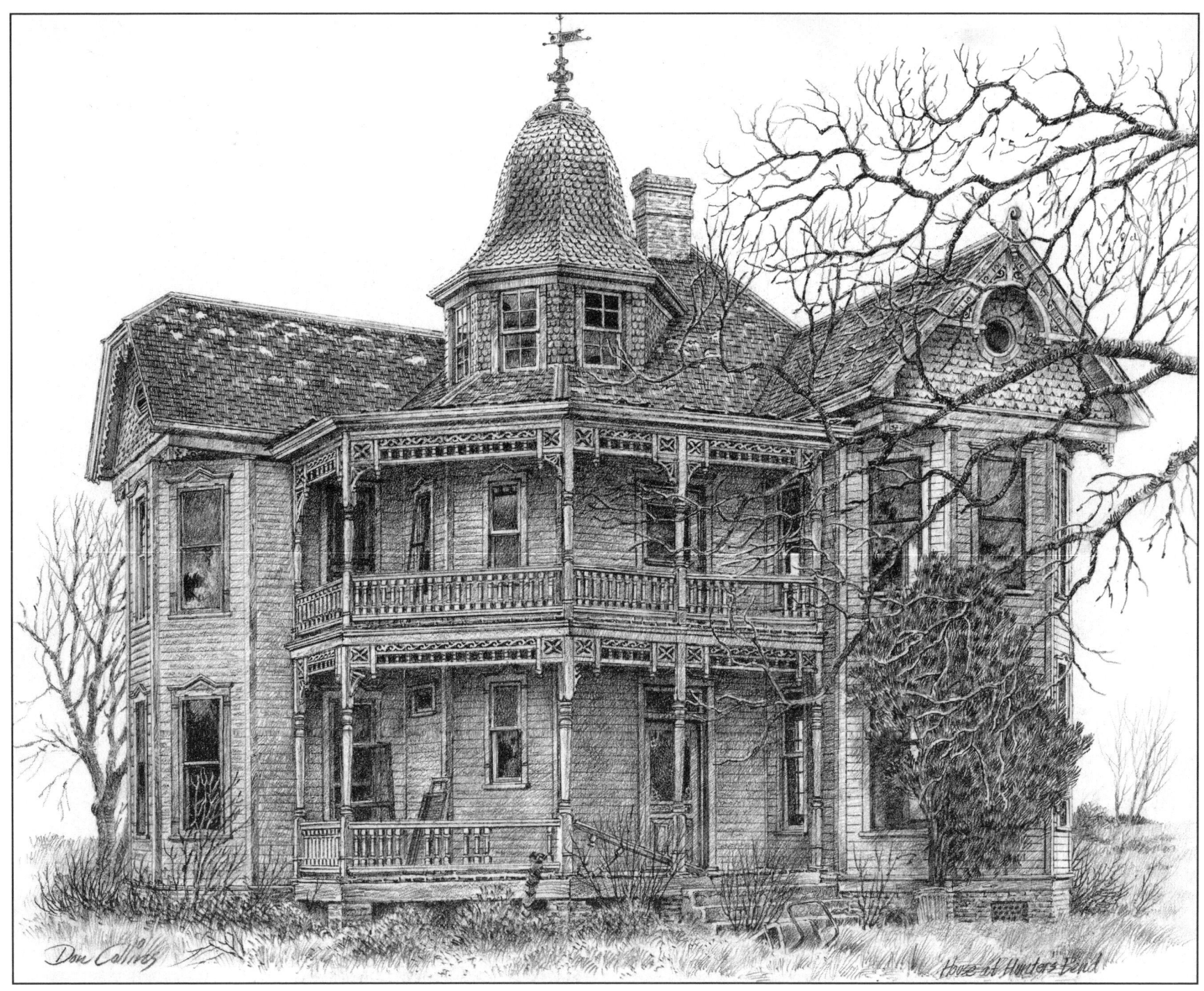

Don Collins   House at Hunters Bend

5. House at Hunter's Bend.

Istumbled onto this fine old Victorian house at Hunter's Bend on the Colorado River east of Austin as a consequence of a hunting trip. I was hunting ducks down in Southeast Texas and decided for some reason to take Farm Road 969 that parallels the Colorado from Bastrop back to Austin. It was late in the day and I was losing light, but I screeched to a halt when I saw this structure I had never seen before. I didn't think I could take pictures, but I did. I captured it.

It's just a fantastic Victorian house. And it was actually in pretty good condition. I believe it was being used at the time for storing hay. After I had gotten my photographs, two or three weeks later, perhaps, a big story appeared in the Austin paper about a fire at the house on Hunter's Bend. It burned to the ground. So I was lucky to get there in time to capture the image. And I don't know anything more about its history, but it was an exciting moment to be driving through the twilight and come upon something like that.

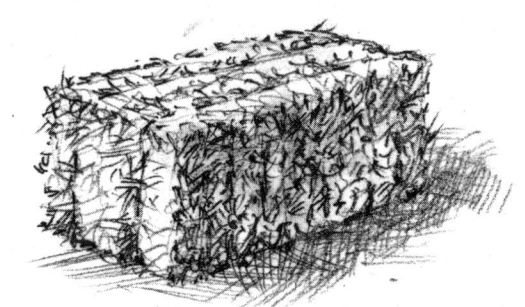

Tragically, it was reported that this grand old house was destroyed by spontaneous combustion of stored hay.

6. Gin at Burton.

I'd never been to Burton, but when I drove into the little Washington County town I saw this enormous pile of rusted metal in the distance. As you might expect, the view excited me and got me over there in a hurry. It has a tremendous amount of stuff going on there, and every angle is there for a purpose. They didn't worry about the cosmetics. They just built and built to accommodate the machinery they were using inside. When I got there the gin was totally abandoned and covered up with vines.

Since I made this drawing, the gin has been refurbished and been made much smaller. They've taken down a lot of stuff since I drew this picture. Even though it has been restored as original and now is going to survive, I kind of liked it the way it was in the first place.

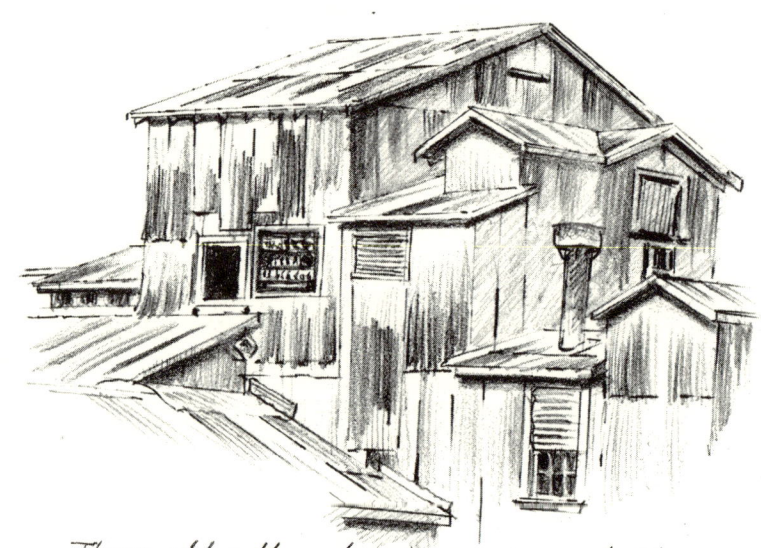

These old cotton gins have a remarkable amount going on visually in a very compact space.

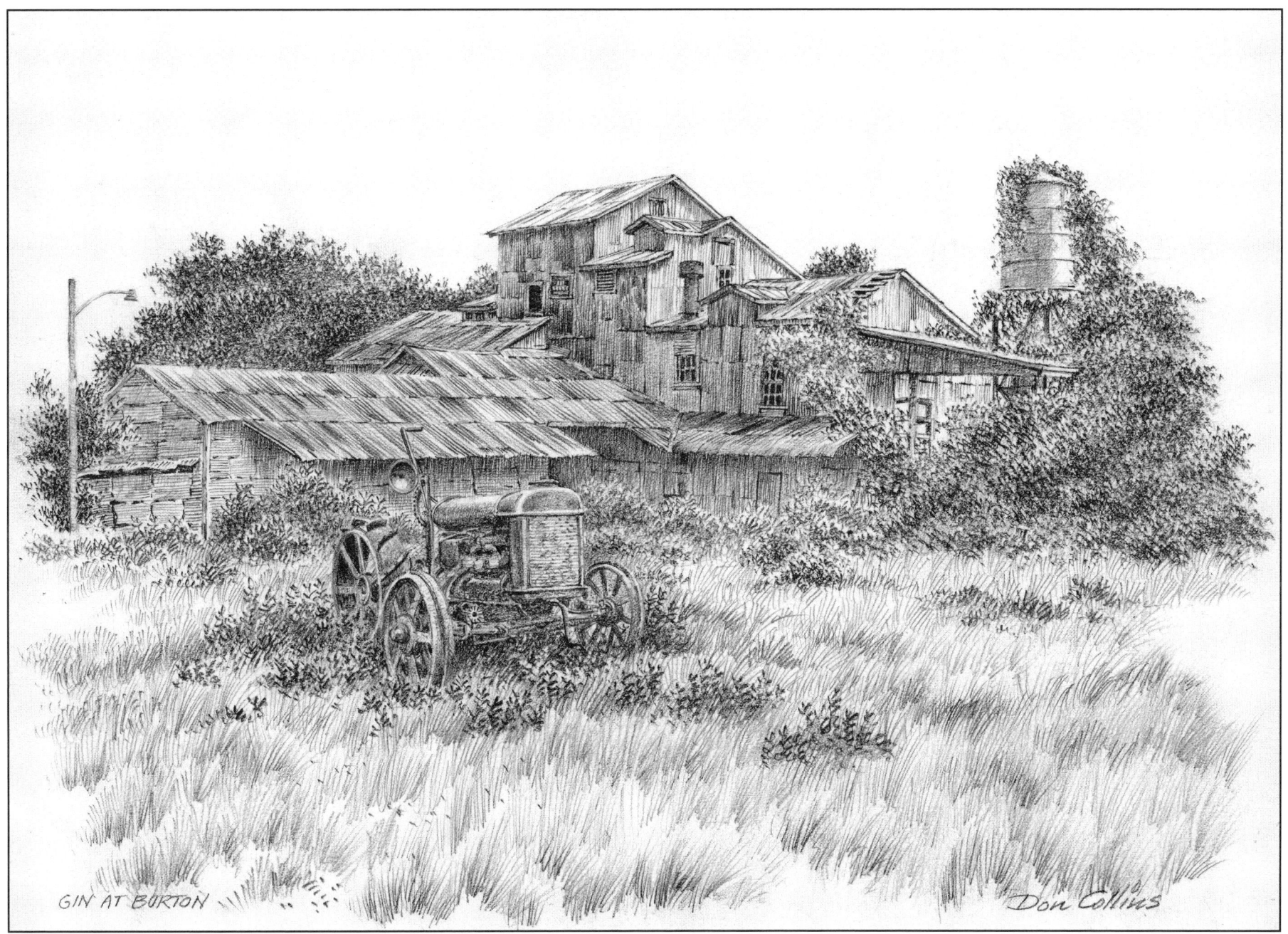

GIN AT BURTON

Don Collins

19

7. Possible Code Issues, Austin.

group of us old fellows have been going for lunch to El Azteca Café on East Seventh Street in Austin every Thursday for something on the order of thirty-five or forty years. It has been our habit occasionally to branch off and drive around East Austin on our way back to work, just because it's a very interesting place. It has an eclectic mix of architecture, with a monumental house standing next to a little shack. You never know what to expect. It's got rolling hills, beautiful vistas, and is actually a pretty area that perhaps has not been used as well as it might have been.

We came upon this house that is a conglomeration of everything you can probably think of. It's just a homemade house. Apparently the man brought home whatever he could find and stuck it up there. Otherwise it's unexplainable. The core seems to be a little stone house with an interesting arched entryway on the right-hand side. There's some wrought iron that the owner found someplace. He used every possible material that a human could use on a house. We were

charmed by that. And as in the case of the Hunter's Bend house, three or four weeks after I gathered my information on this, the city came along and bull-dozed it and it disappeared. So that's the end of that. Now all we have is the drawing.

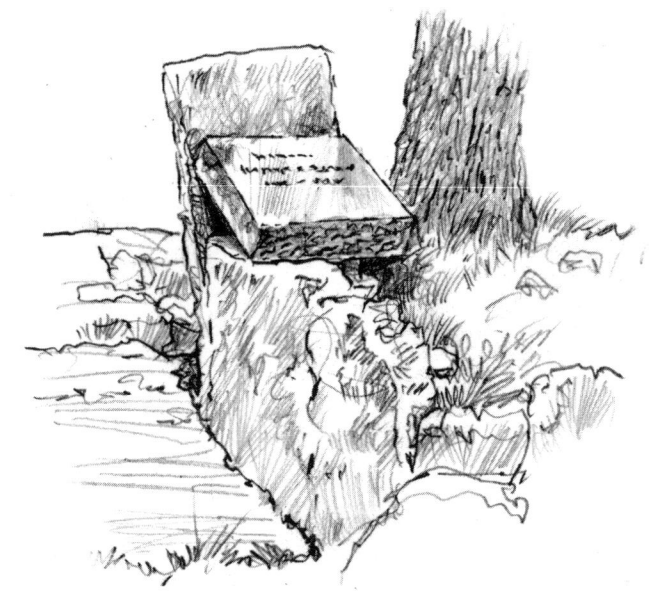

Resting on the retaining wall was a polished, inscribed slab of granite...a used tombstone?

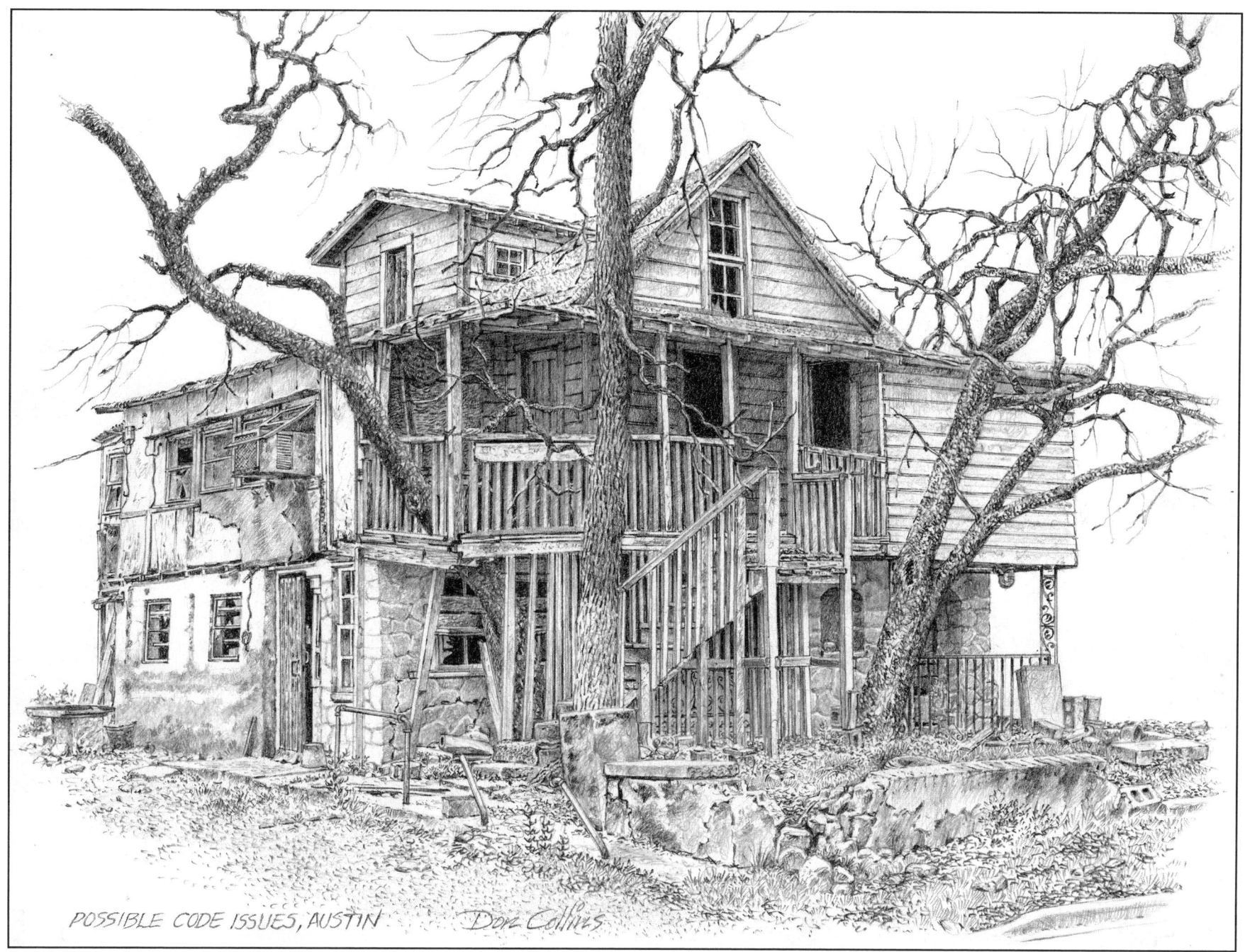

POSSIBLE CODE ISSUES, AUSTIN   Don Collins

8. Bastrop County Barn, with Privy.

I can't tell you what road I was on, but it was a sunny fall day with no leaves on the trees. The barn is not distinctive in any particular way, except that I have never seen one strung together lengthwise like that. I don't know whether the little sheds were for milking, but I was kind of charmed by the fact that he put his privy out on the end of the thing. I'd never seen that done. I believe that I retraced my steps there several years later and it was gone, so now I am glad I caught it.

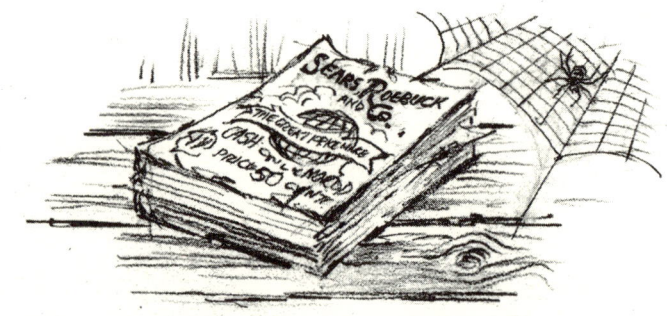

Viewers of a certain age and rural heritage will immediately grasp this.

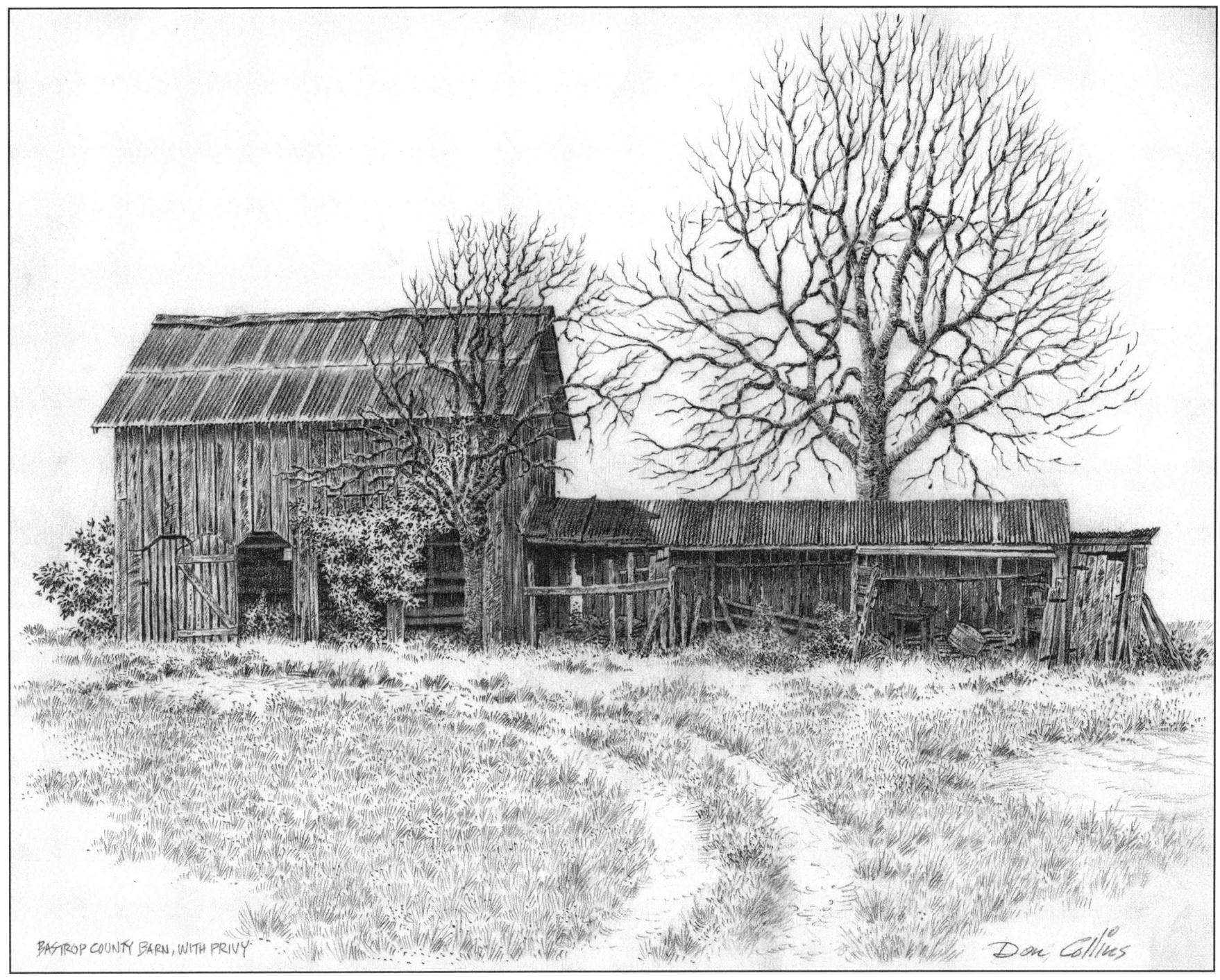

BASTROP COUNTY BARN, WITH PRIVY

Don Collins

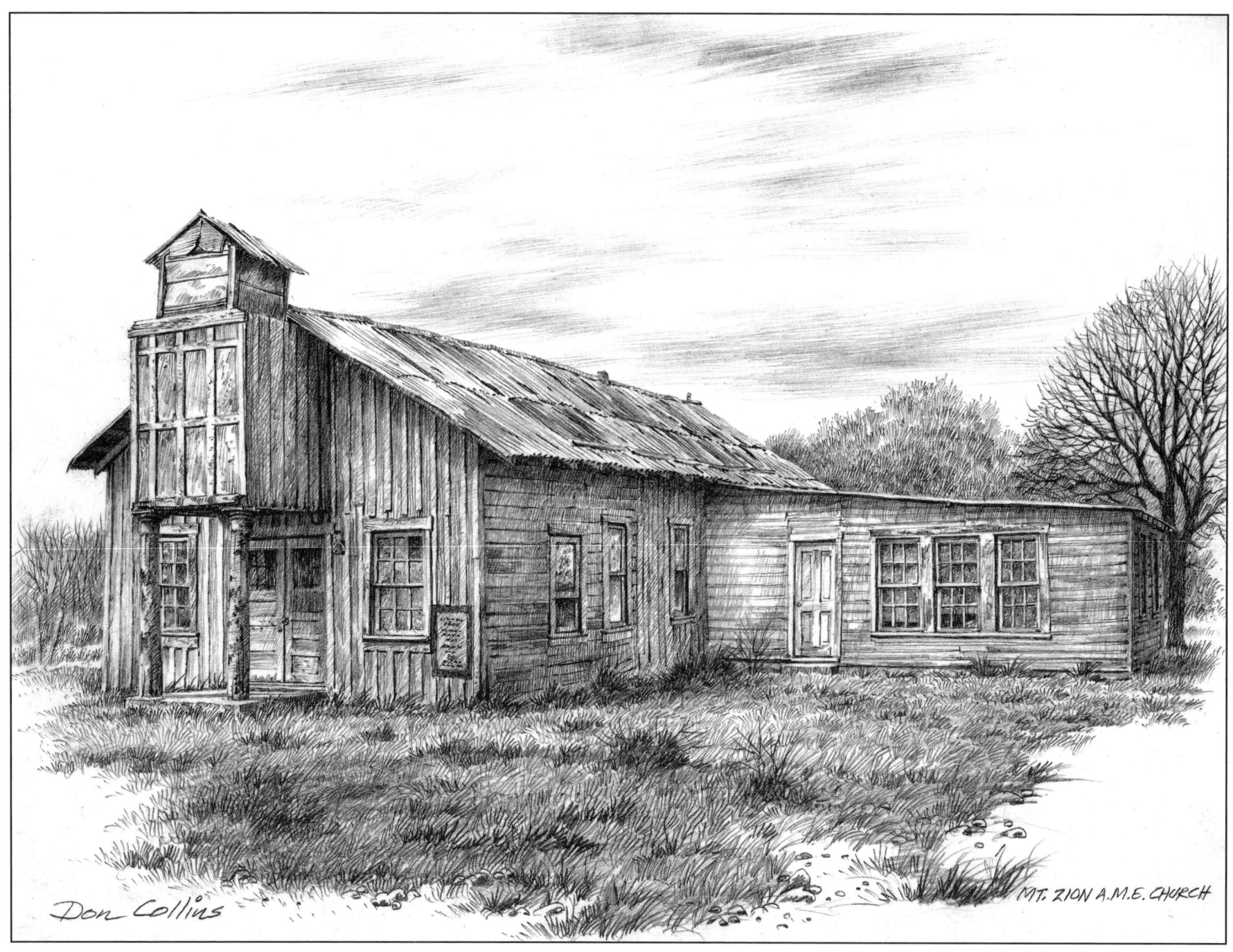

Don Collins

MT. ZION A.M.E. CHURCH

9. Mt. Zion African Methodist Episcopal Church.

Mt. Zion A.M.E. Church is an old building obviously put up a piece at a time by the congregation. It is east and not far out of Austin. I was intrigued by the log columns. They were pine logs that they'd gotten somewhere, and they'd used their axes to put a decorative capital on top of each one. And then there's this interesting boxlike structure above that is capped by a little doghouse-type thing to make a steeple. They got various sized windows here and there and just put them where they wanted them. The most interesting thing of all is the cornerstone inserted into the wooden wall in the right-hand corner of the entryway. It has the names of all the elders and the preacher. I just thought that it was a neat church. An obviously poor congregation had pulled it together, and I am sure they enjoyed it. It's the kind of thing I could not possibly drive by and ignore.

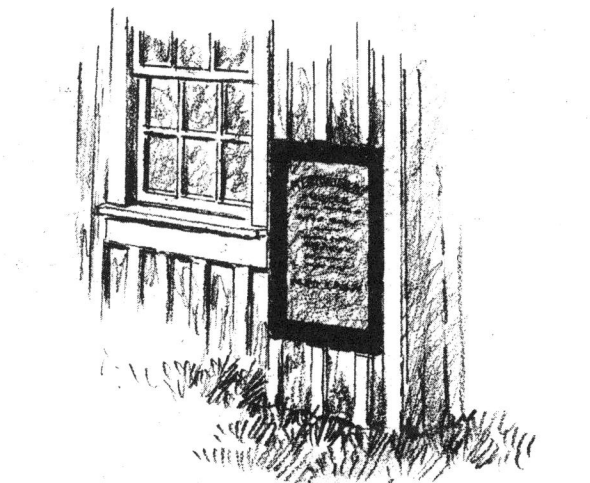

Reflecting both their poverty and their dedication, the congregation had this thin marble cornerstone set into the humble board and bat wall.

10. Austin Mansion.

The John Bremond House is the most promi-nent house out of several on the Bremond Block in Austin. All of them were built by a very important early Austin family. Each one of them had a fancy house. I guess there were four or five enor-mous homes there. You can see why someone would stop and take a look at it. It's got everything in the world going on and shows the very finest kind of craftsmanship.

This is the kind of drawing that an artist with time problems should never get near. It is by far more difficult than even the sketch of Waller Creek that I was complaining about. It is just terrible from the standpoint of trying to do it. I'm sure I spent three or four days rendering this.

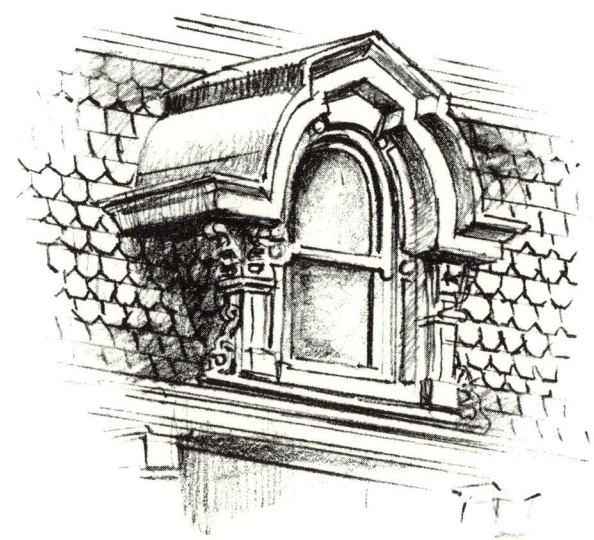

The Bremond mansion is a riot of shapes, colors, and textures — a feast for the eye, but *very* tough to draw!

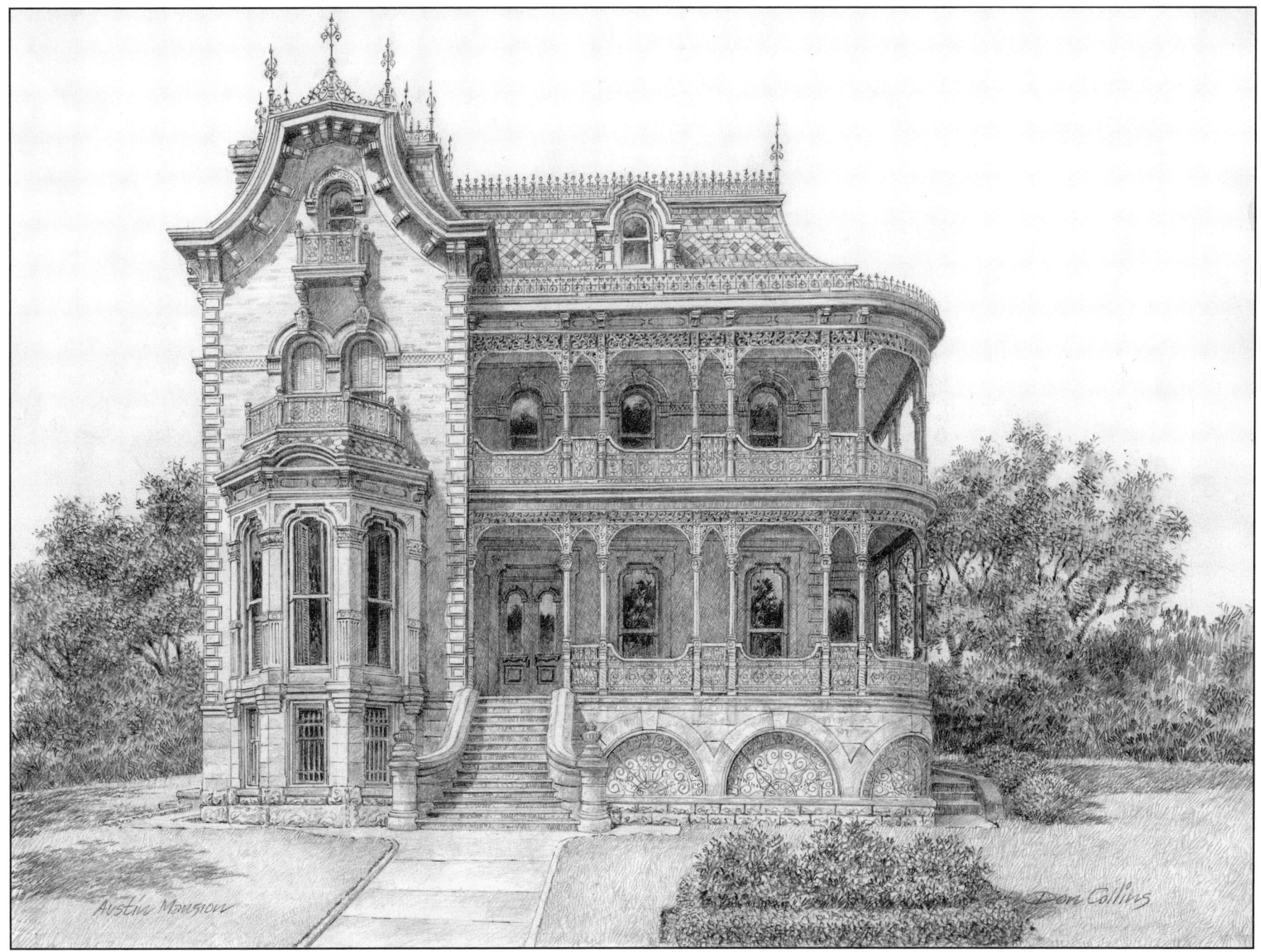

Austin Mansion

Don Collins

11. Dime Box Ferguson.

Well, I cheated a little on this. I was driving through Dime Box in Lee County many years ago. At that time there was a kind of a narrow little road that threaded its way through Dime Box, and this Ferguson tractor was almost in the way. You sort of had to steer around it. It is a tractor from the '20s I am sure, or maybe a little earlier. It's an attractive piece of old machinery, but I'm sure it must have been a terror to operate. It had been sinking into the ground at Dime Box for many, many years. I didn't appreciate the setting it had in Dime Box, so I created one by putting it in front of a tumbled-down house near Manor in Travis County. I liked the stark look of the old house—the totally abandoned and forlorn look of it out in the middle of a pasture—so I put the Dime Box tractor in front of it.

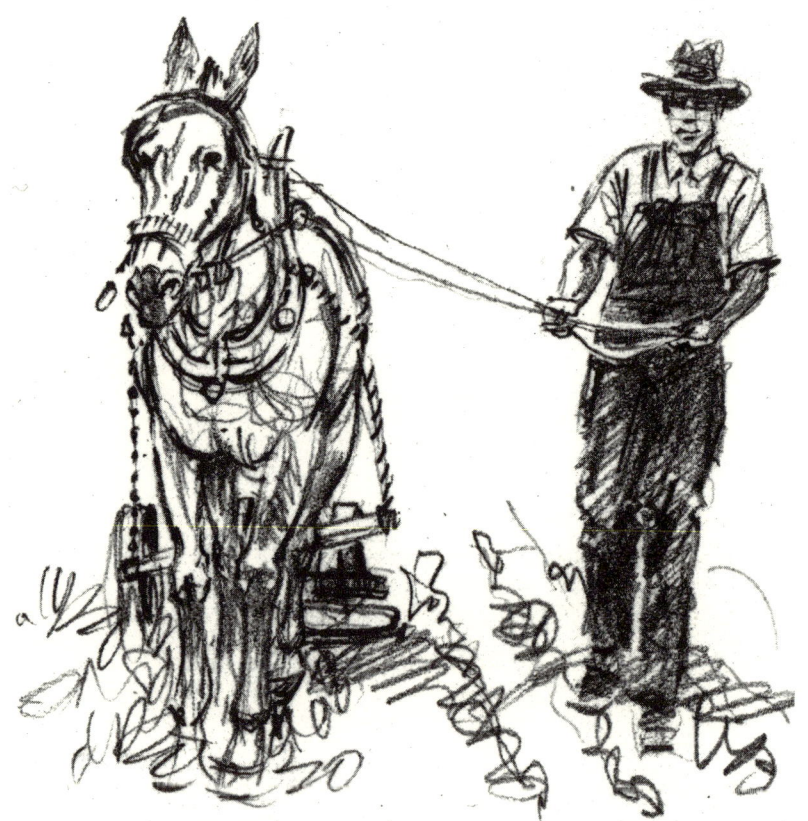

The tractor was crude, noisy, smelly, and inefficient, but on the other hand...

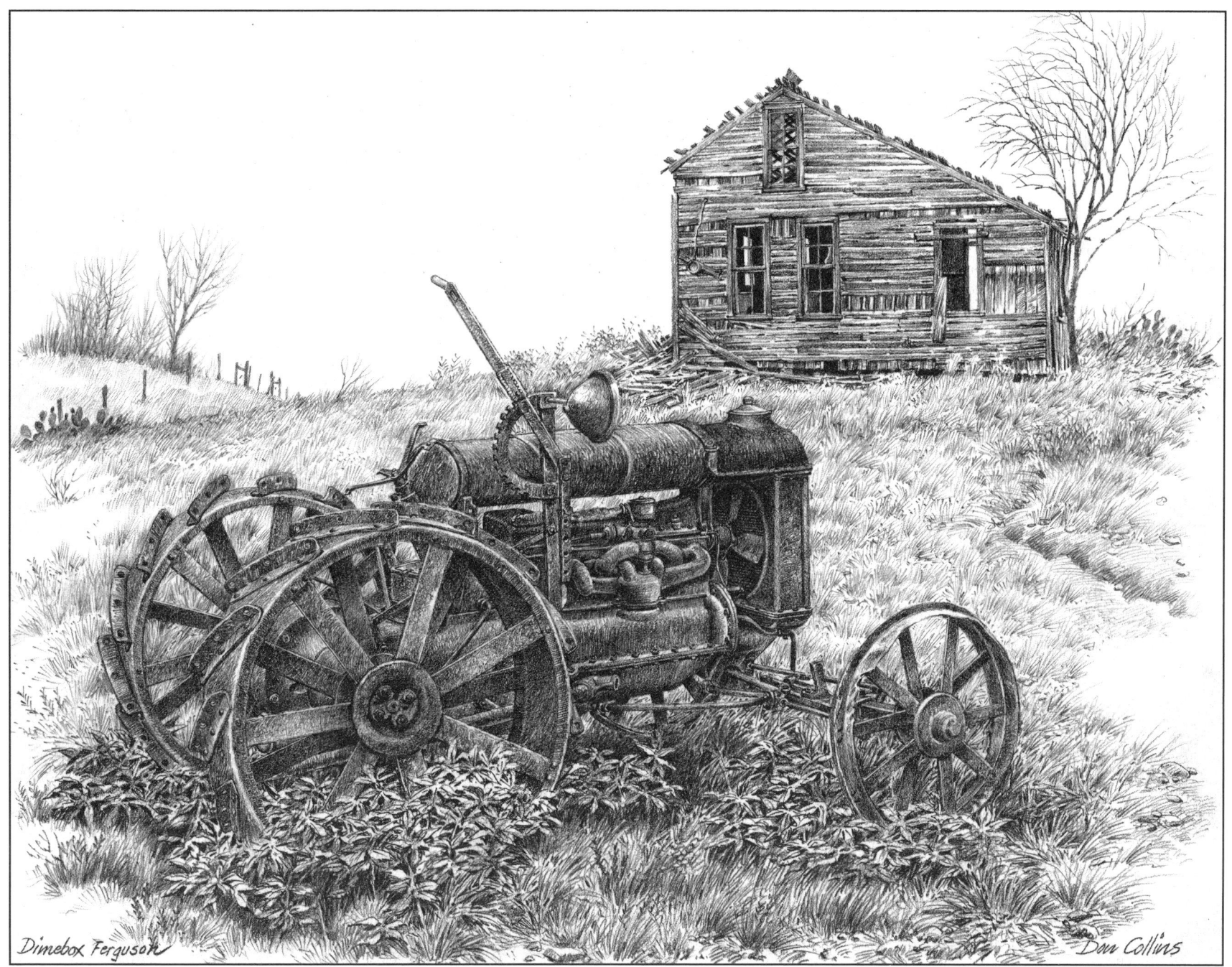

Dimebox Ferguson

Don Collins

29

12. LaGrange Jail House.

Part of the memory of this is taking my nine-year-old grandson, Hayden, with me. We decided we'd have a day of adventure on a bright, sunny summer afternoon. I had relatives in LaGrange, but we departed their place and decided to take a tour around the town to see what we could find. I had been in LaGrange many times, but I had never steered off the main street. This jail is a block or so south of the main highway. I was, again, stunned by the quality of the stonework. It is absolutely marvelous. This one does not have the looming, ominous quality of the Comanche jail. Instead there are more delicate touches, and work by stonemasons so long departed that you could not possibly duplicate it today. It's stone, and anything stone appeals to me. As a matter of fact, some of my fellow artists have dubbed me "the stone freak."

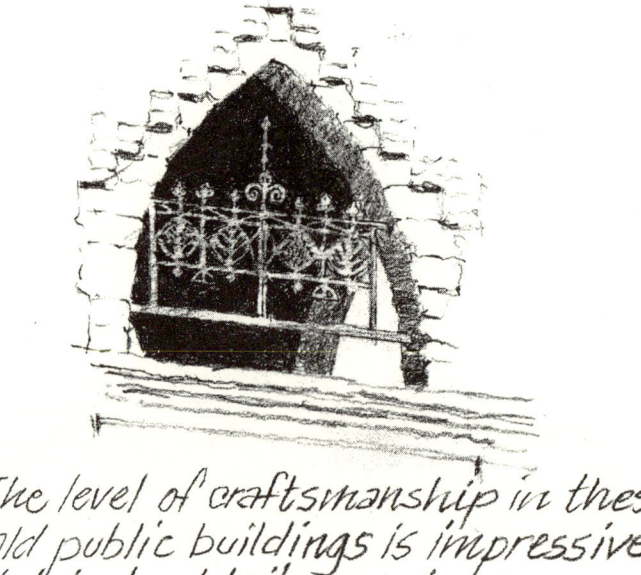

The level of craftsmanship in these old public buildings is impressive... intricate detail everywhere — even 60 feet up!

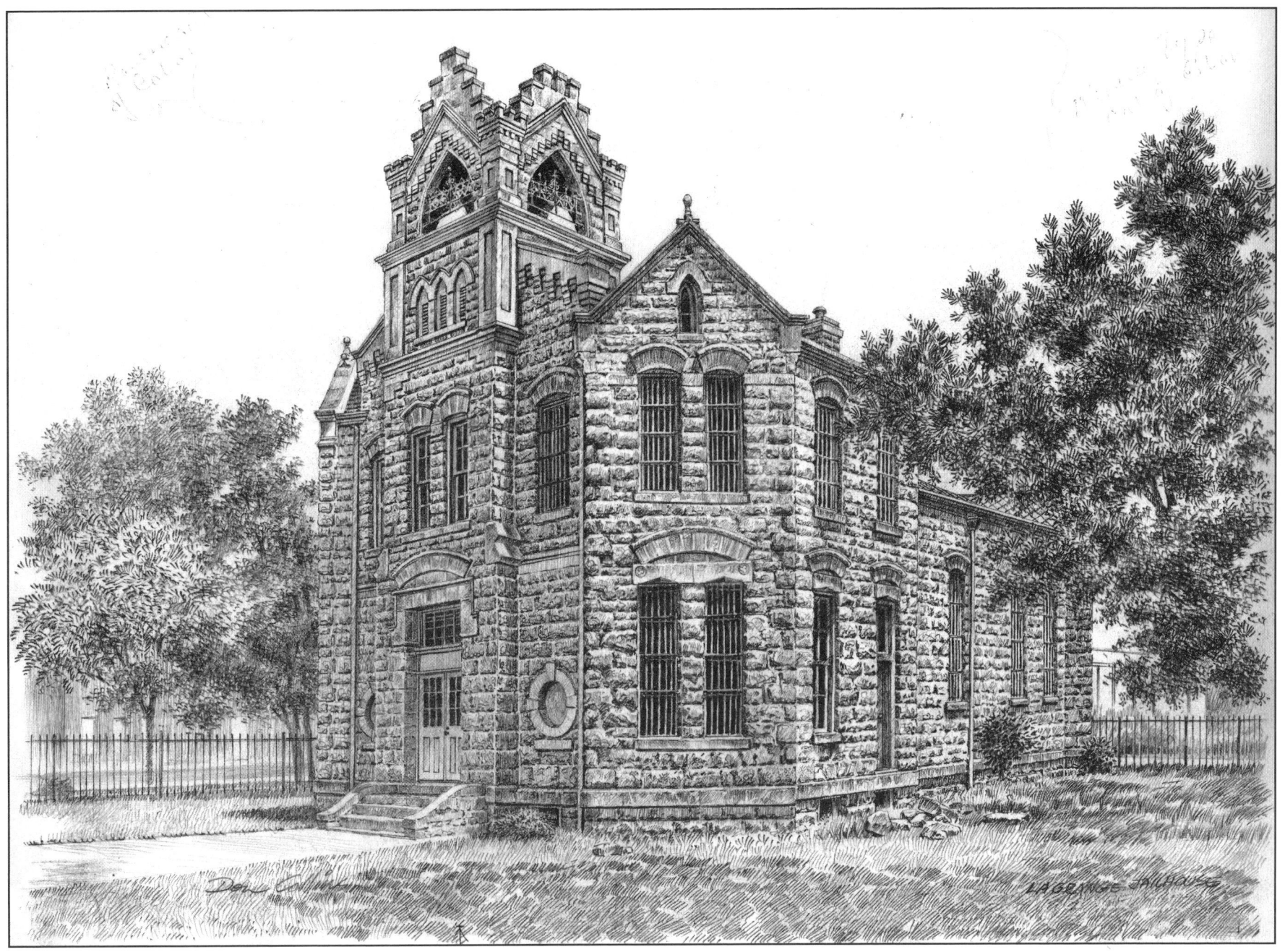

LA GRANGE JAILHOUSE

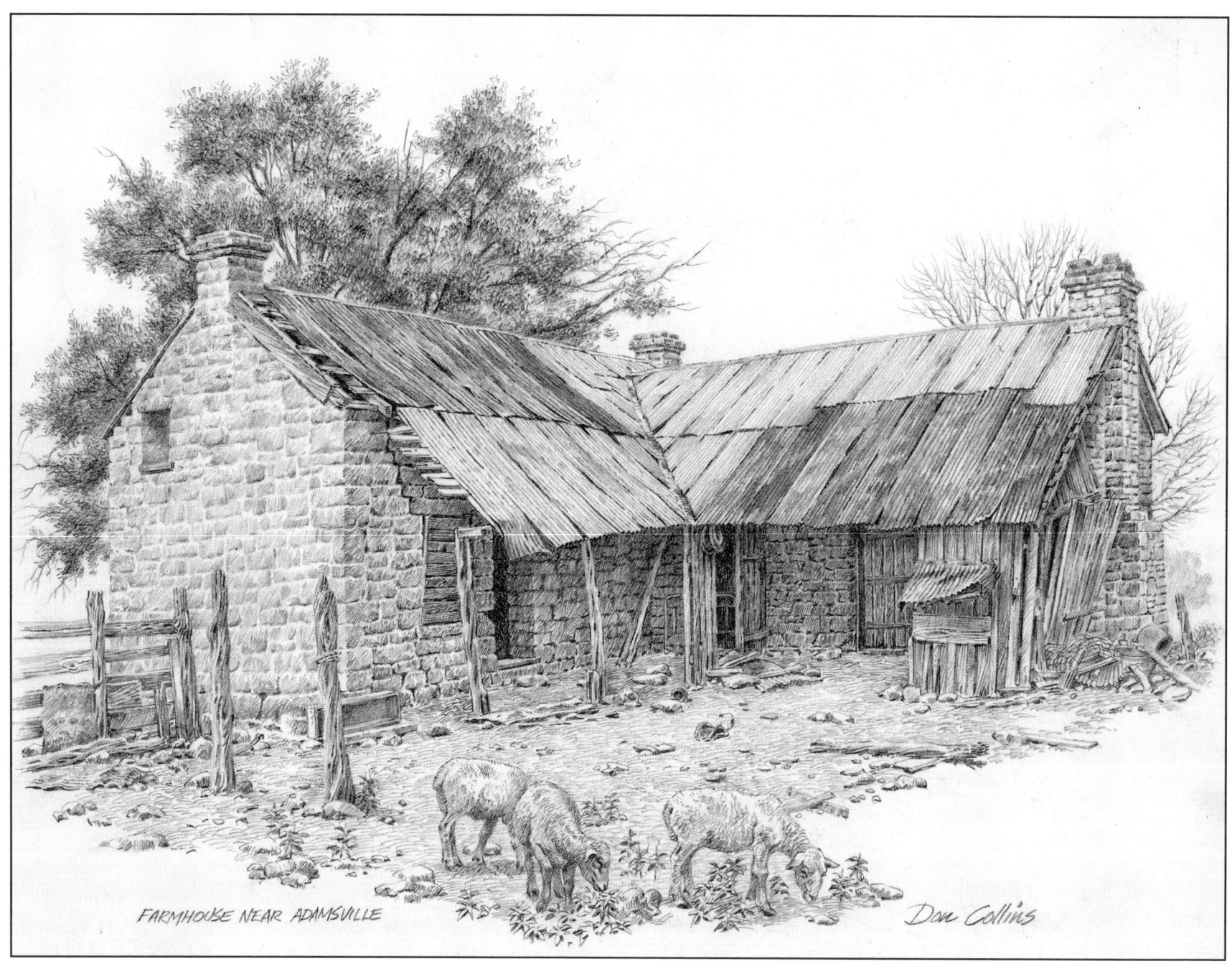

FARMHOUSE NEAR ADAMSVILLE

Don Collins

32

Adamsville is on U.S. Highway 281 north of Lampasas. It is an old town with several attractive buildings in it. This was a few miles north of it. This old cut-stone house with three chimneys really appealed to me. I found it totally abandoned probably a hundred, two hundred yards off the road. I kind of invaded their territory there and drove up and walked around to the back. It was interesting to me that a flock of sheep was grazing back there. It's very typical of the kind of things you see more over in the Fredericksburg area, and I was a little surprised to find it at Adamsville. This house is still partially preserved. An artist lives there in a small adjacent house, and she seems to be struggling to keep it together. It's an interesting building and worth preserving. There was a junk pile out in back that I wish I'd had a day to explore.

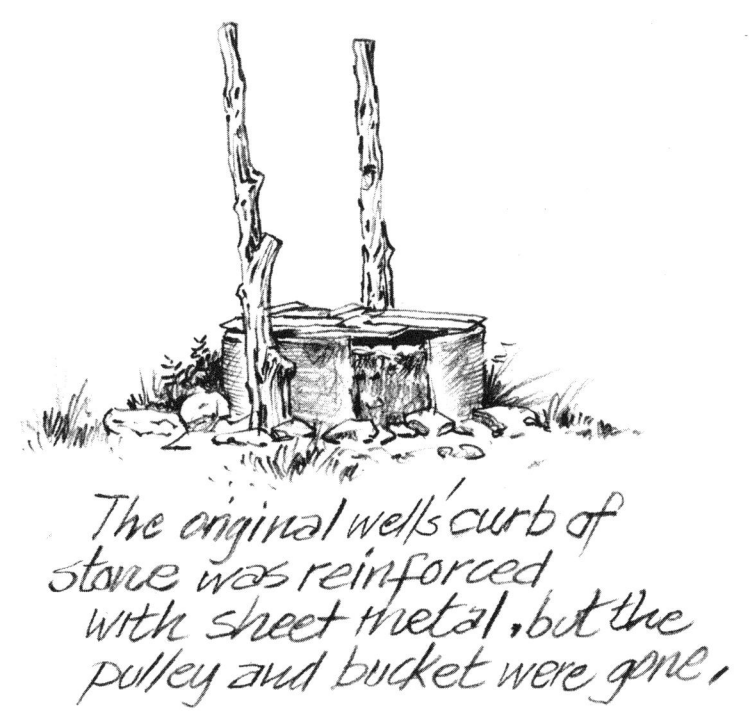

The original well's curb of stone was reinforced with sheet metal, but the pulley and bucket were gone.

14. Two Tired Trucks.

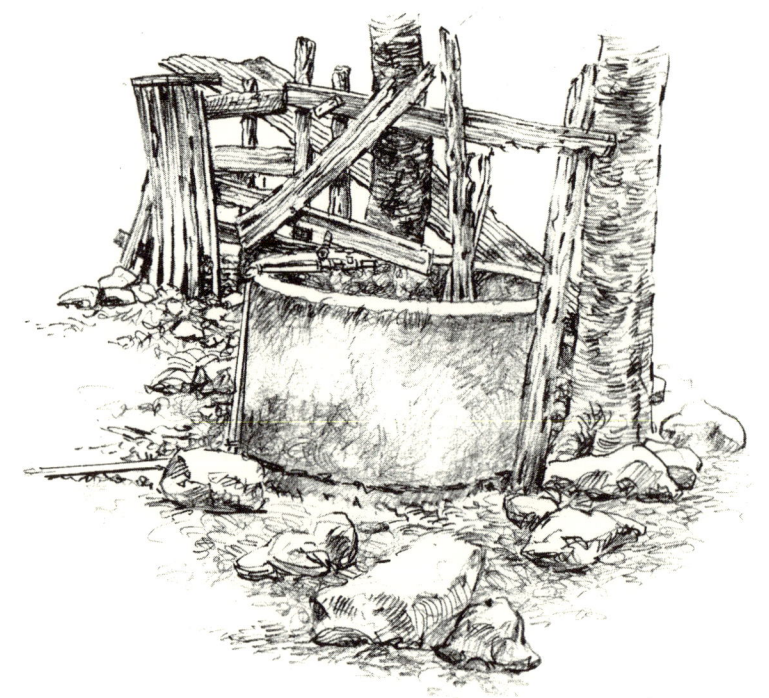

A dry tank and a tangle of litter and decaying boards, evidence that this is no longer a working farm.

The farm buildings in the background are actually on the property that belonged to my deceased brother, George. It's a beautiful two- or three-hundred-acre place on the bluff on the south side of the Colorado River overlooking the town of LaGrange. It has some rolling hills south of the house, and the barns sat atop one of these hills. Some years later an heir with a strong sense of order erased the old barns.

Here again I improvised. The trucks came from somewhere else. As a matter of fact, I believe the trucks are from Oklahoma. I took a little sashay up to Oklahoma many years ago and went through the Panhandle. That's where these trucks were resting together in a field at the side of the road. I have always been intrigued by old vehicles of one kind or another. These were sitting in the position you see them, but they were not anywhere close to the barn outside of LaGrange. That's the whole story on it—it's bringing together two elements that I am fond of and combining them.

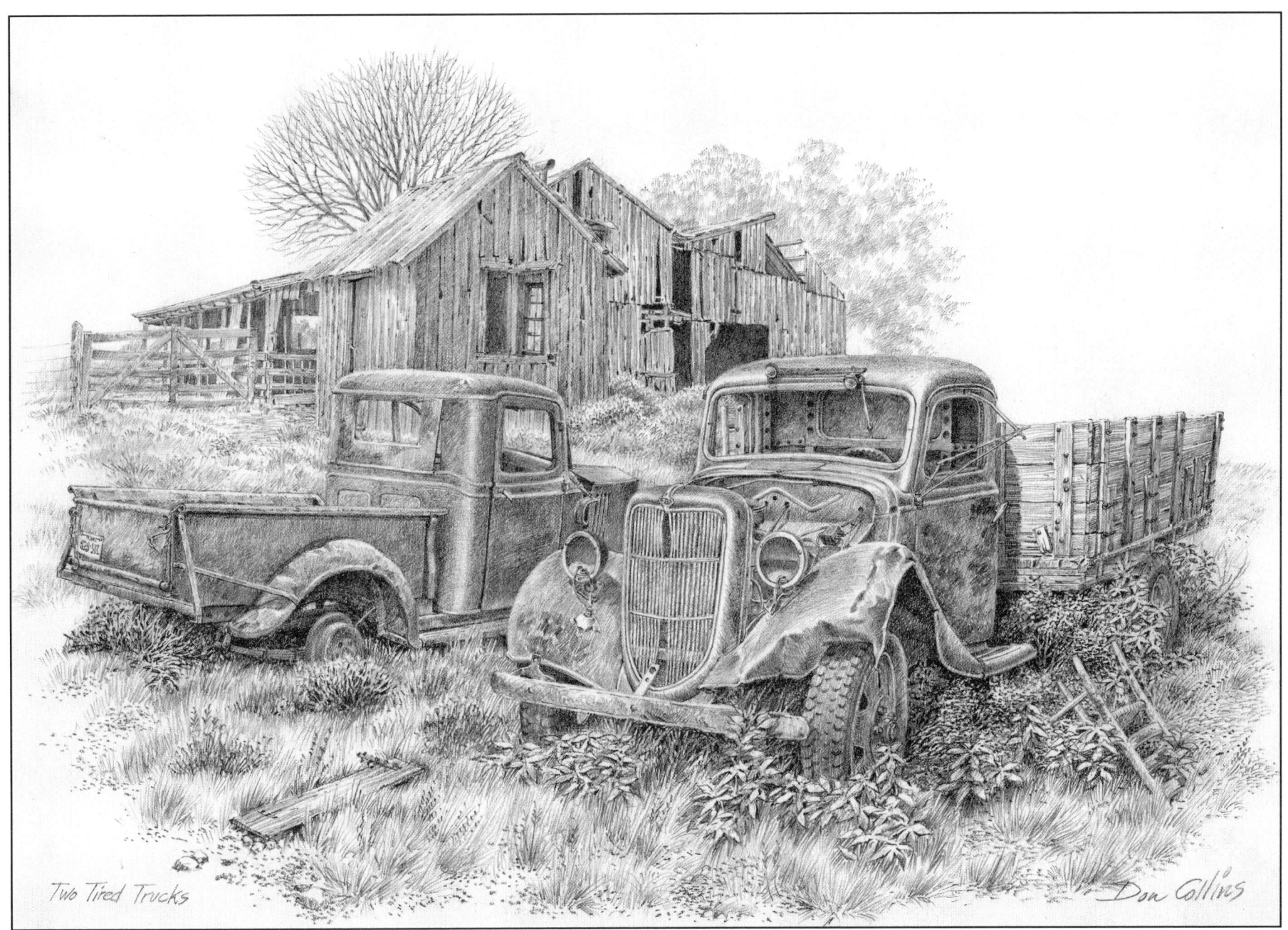

Two Tired Trucks

Don Collins

35

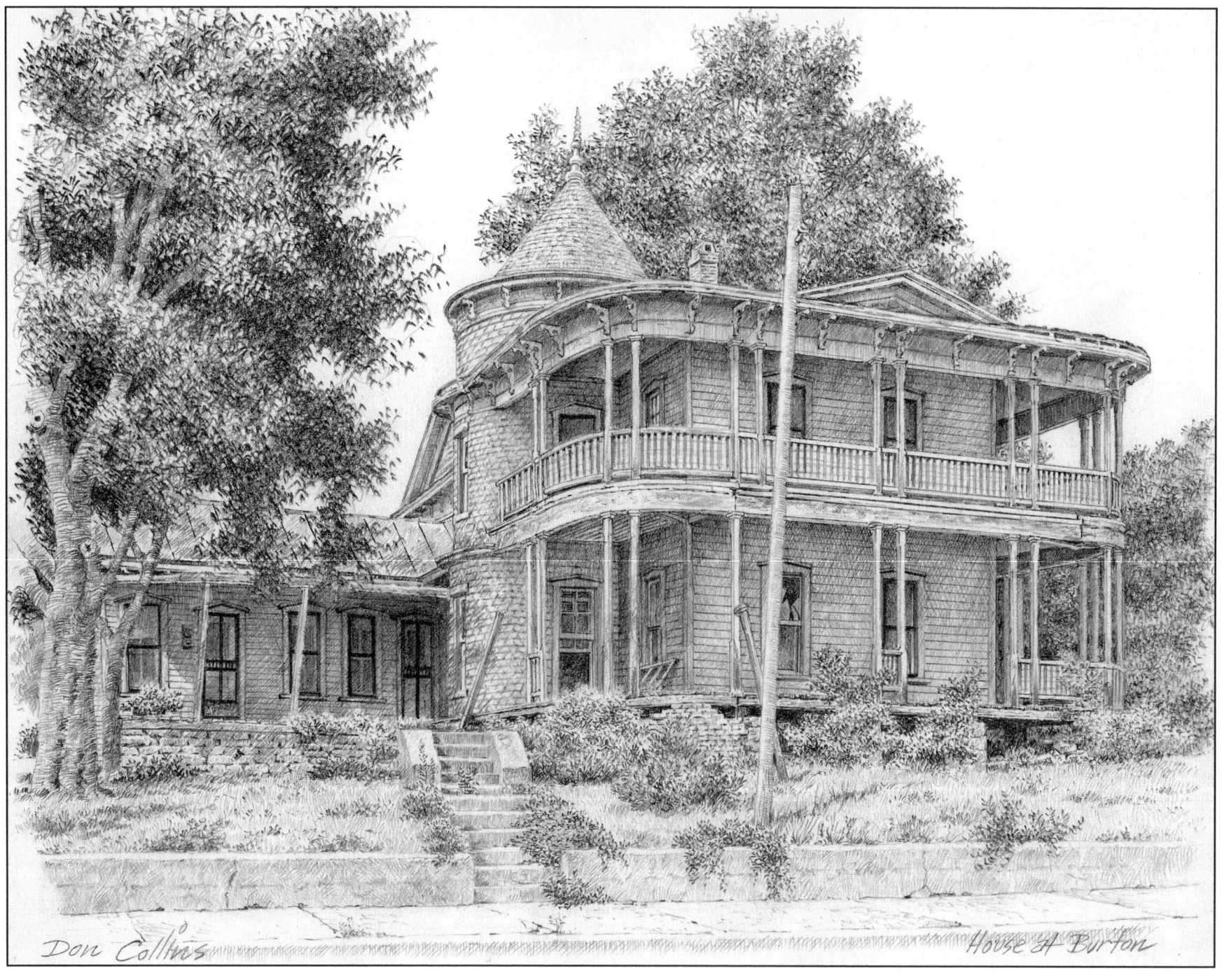

Don Collins   House A Burton

This is a magnificent old house. It has a lot of things to intrigue the artist: an impossible-to-build curve on the upper and lower porches, a shingle-covered tower, and then a cone-shaped roof on top of that. What a fascinating combination of geometric shapes!

After I made this drawing, some entrepreneur came along and totally restored the place, put it back together and turned it into a bed and breakfast, and was very faithful to the original. I don't know whether that owner is still in place or not. I think it is still occupied and stands right in the center of Burton as one of the more prominent features. It is only a couple of blocks away from the old Burton cotton gin.

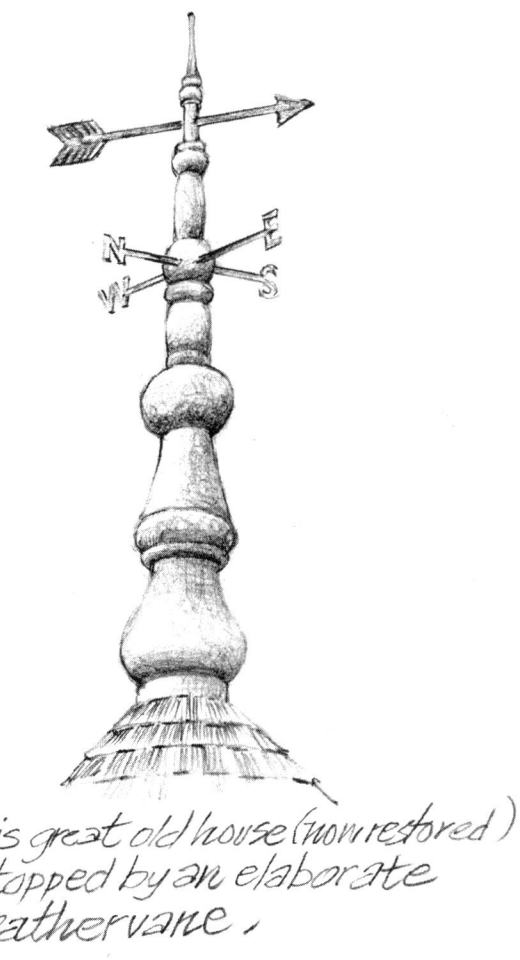

This great old house (now restored) is topped by an elaborate weathervane.

16. Barn at Shelby.

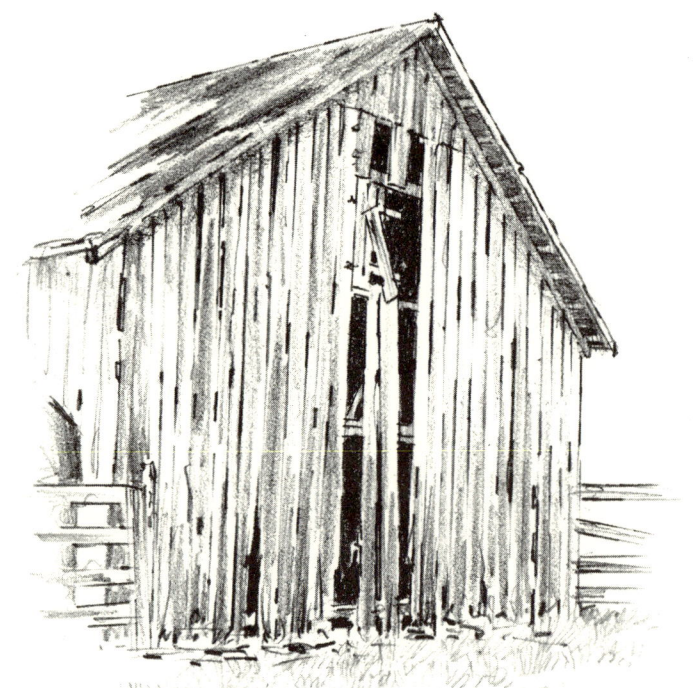

The structure and roof of the barn
at Shelby were sound, but the
siding was not doing as well.

Shelby in Austin County is an interesting little place. This barn that I found there has several things that attract the artist's eye. It is a big wooden building, to start with, and it has a typical rusty roof. The barn stands at the end of a long lane of trees, a tree-shaded lane off the main road in the little town. I'm attracted to any building that you can see through. I spend quite a bit of time painting and drawing those things. This barn has symmetrical bays on either side and a big gable covering the entrance.

Shelby is a very small place. No commerce there to speak of, maybe a gas station or convenience store … just the kind of thing that an artist likes to stumble across.

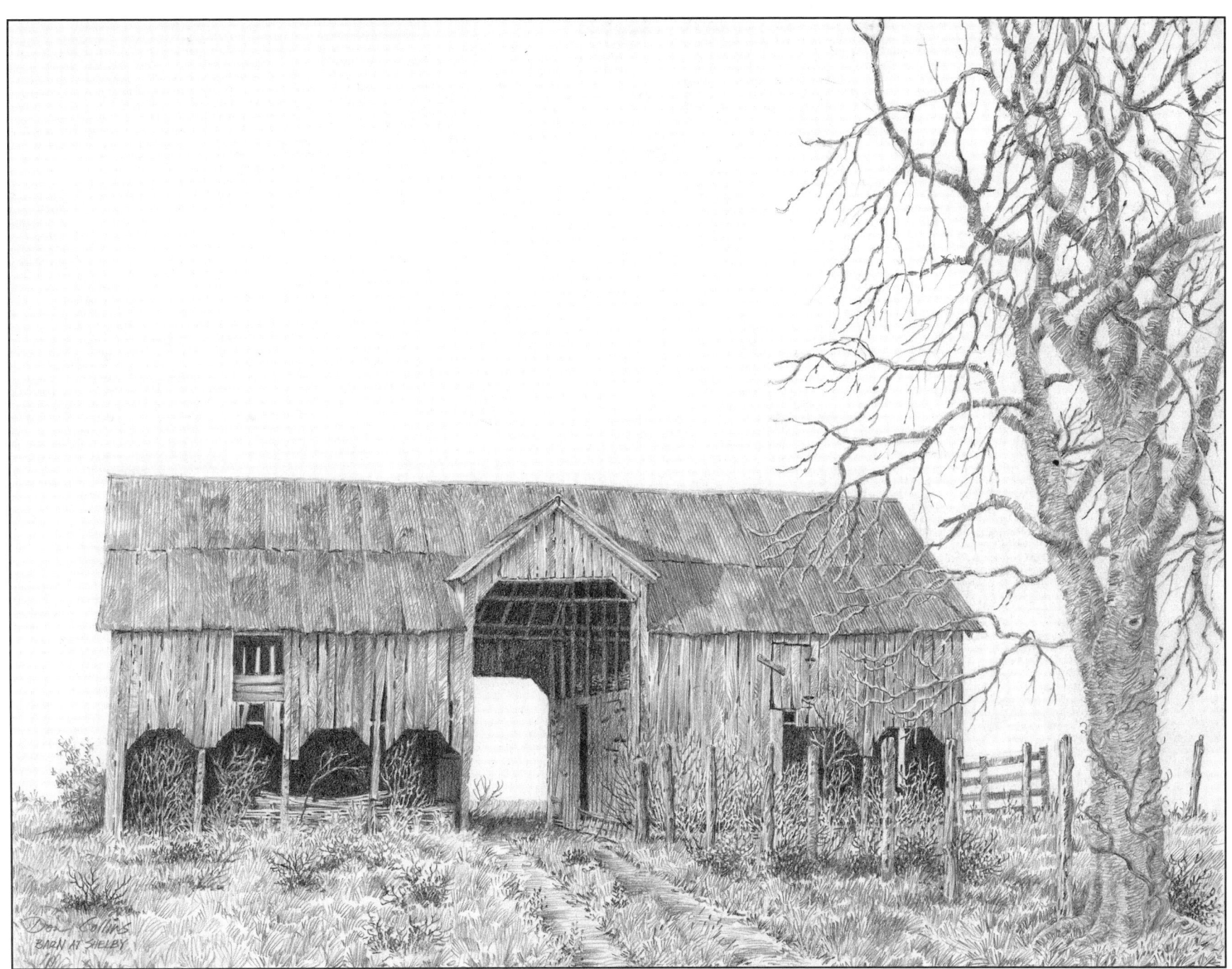

BARN AT SHELBY

PART TWO

South Texas

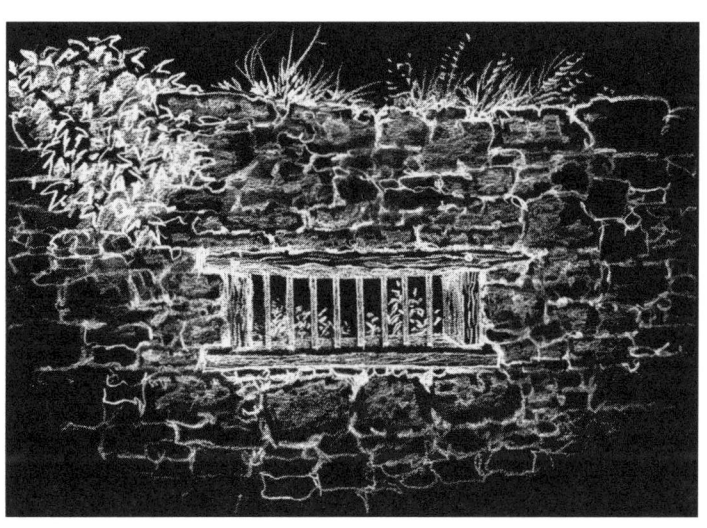

17. School at the John Ruckman House, Old Helena.

The story of this drawing goes back quite a way. I probably found Helena about '81 or '82. It's in an area I'd never been in before, and I was attracted by the name. I knew there was a Helena in Montana, but I never heard of one in Texas. So I went down to the Karnes County part of the world.

At the south end of Helena stands this enormous mansion, a two-story house, with porches and a walk all around. It was totally abandoned; there was nobody anywhere near. As I walked around I discovered what looks like a schoolhouse attached to the south end of the building. It has the place up there to hang the bell. As you peer inside it looks as though it might have been a schoolroom. After all these many years, the cypress lumber is still in good condition. After I was there, there was a fire set. I don't know who set it or what happened, but there was scarring on the front of the building, but somehow it survived. The building has fallen on even harder times since I did the drawing, which is depressing. It is really an interesting old place.

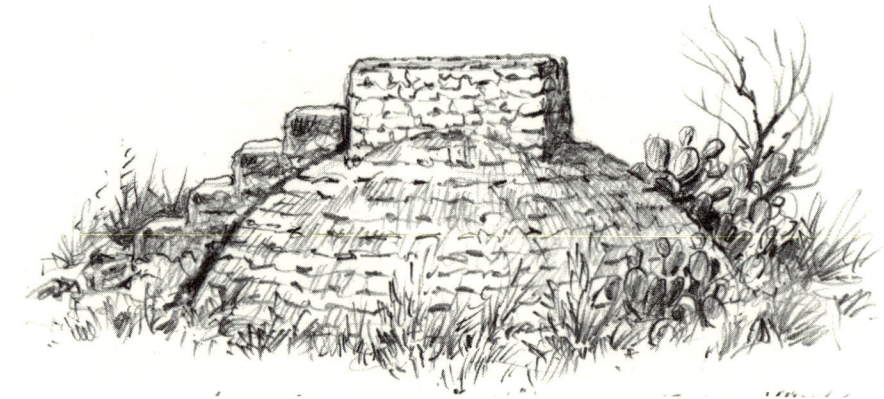

Behind the Ruckman house is a large domed cistern, with a set of steps leading to the squared-off top.

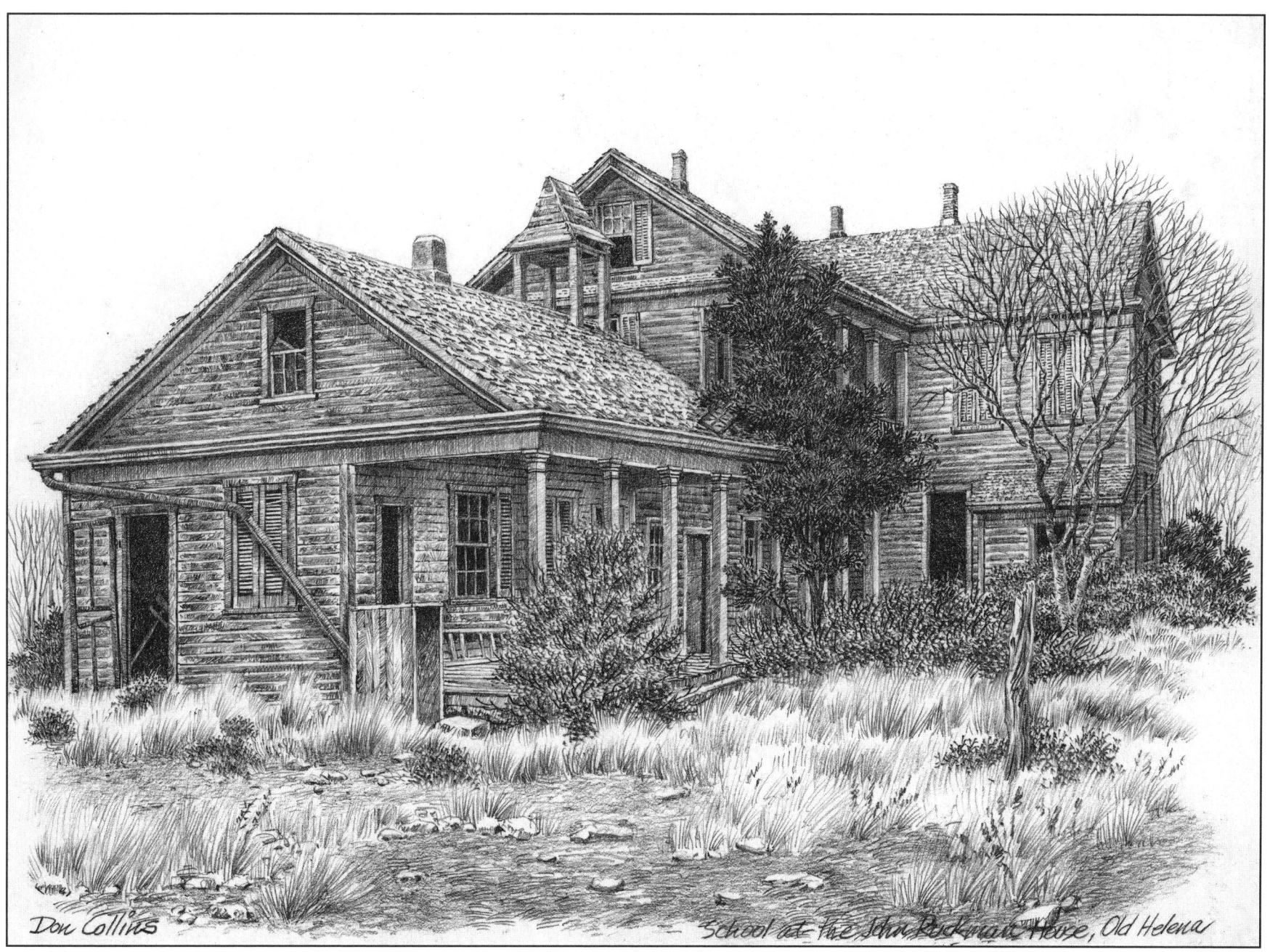

Don Collins

School at the John Rockman House, Old Helena

18. Mid-Nineteenth-Century House of Sillar
(*Limestone Particulate*), Guerra, Texas.

Guerra in Jim Hogg County is deep in the brush country southwest of Hebronville. I went down there to visit a long-time rancher, Bill Hellen. I went with my buddy, Dwain Kelley, and we had a grand time being shown around the brush country and getting access to things that we would have otherwise never seen. Bill speaks fluent Spanish and was raised on the ranch next door. His family has been there for many years, and he is totally conversant on everything down there.

Bill is the one who showed us this house at Guerra. The "town" is just a wide spot in the road. It's typical of that country. It is surrounded by cactus and things that bite you. Bill pointed out this house and others constructed from a substance called sillar, which is a limestone particulate we call caliche in English. It's much lighter and softer than Hill Country limestone. They quarry it in blocks and plaster over it. A great many structures, the older buildings down there, are built from that stuff.

This little house is of no architectural significance. It is a very straightforward symmetrical little thing with a nice fireplace and mantle inside. I was intrigued by the cactus growing on the roof. All in all, I was very excited about it. It's typical of the architecture in that part of the world. You have to get off the main road to find it.

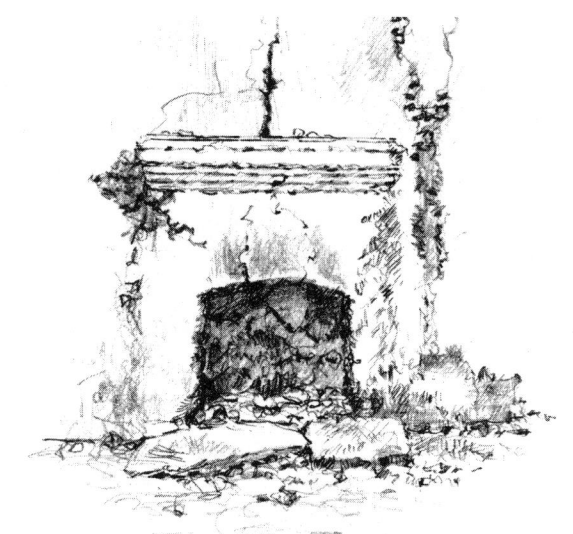

The small fireplace opening is flush with the north wall, with a modest mantel sculpted of adobe above.

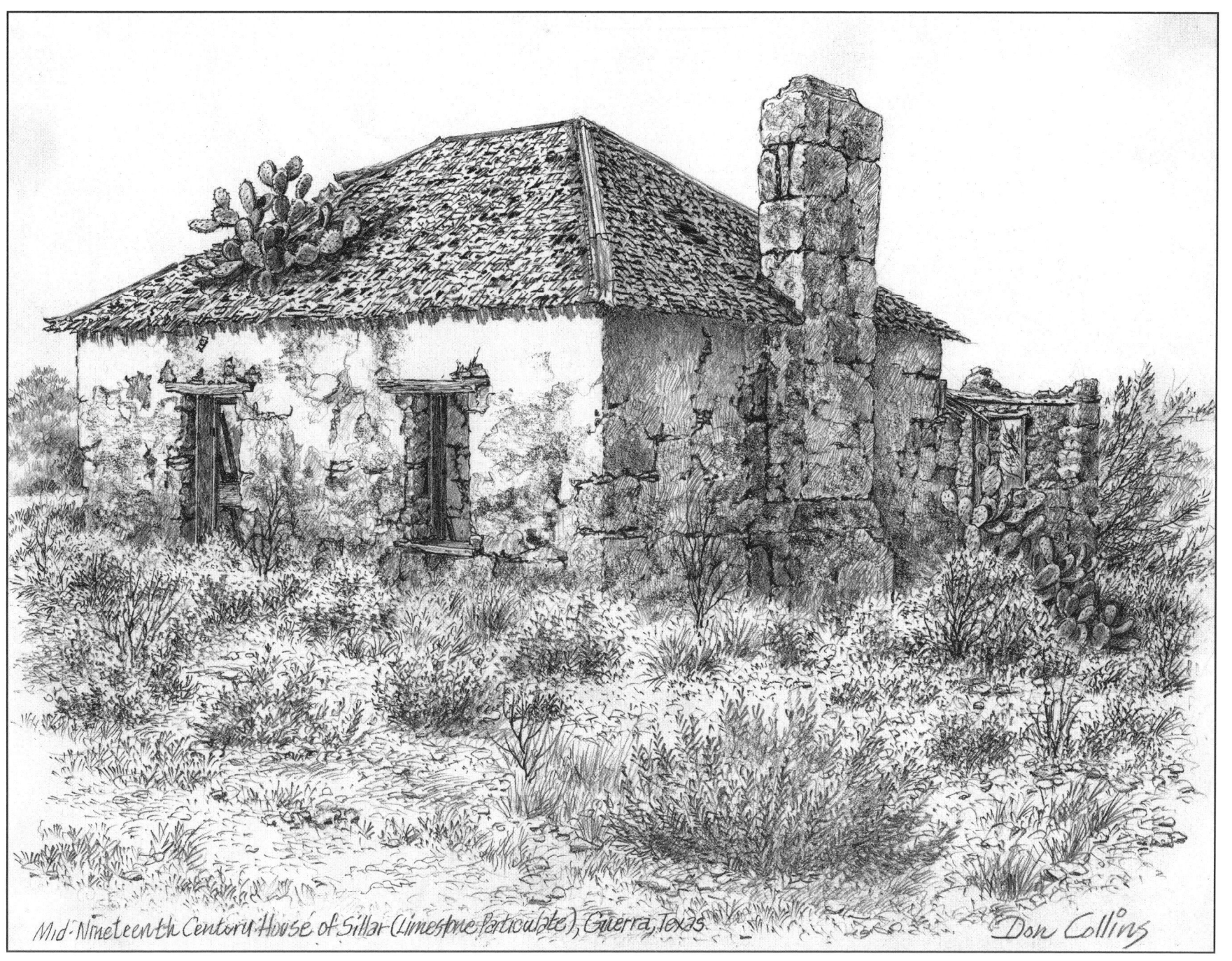

Mid-Nineteenth Century House of Sillar (Limestone Particulate), Guerra, Texas.

Don Collins

This beautiful old courthouse tells the story of local politics. Frio City lies right on the banks of the Frio River, and it used to be the county seat. It's in the brush country surrounded by ranches. I had heard about this old building, but I couldn't figure out how to find it or get into it. I knew that it was on private property. So I contacted the historical society in Pearsall, which is now the county seat. A lady there made some connections with the rancher who owns the property. I made an appointment and they allowed me in.

I had to wade through chest-high blood weeds to get through to this thing. It was in a sea of weeds on the banks of the dry river. Made out of beautiful caramel-colored stone blocks, it exhibits fantastic masonry workmanship. It has interesting matching capped chimneys in the front and back. The whole thing is symmetrical; everything you see in this view is repeated on the backside.

There are various stories about what happened, but basically Pearsall thrived, I suppose got a railroad, and Frio City didn't, so voters moved the seat of government to Pearsall and left this building as it stands. In the middle of a ranch, today nobody gets in there. It is very much private land.

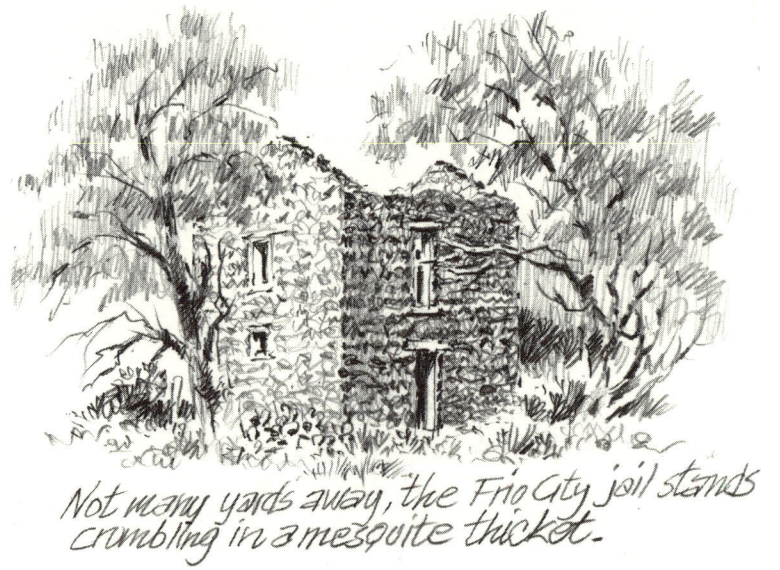

Not many yards away, the Frio City jail stands crumbling in a mesquite thicket.

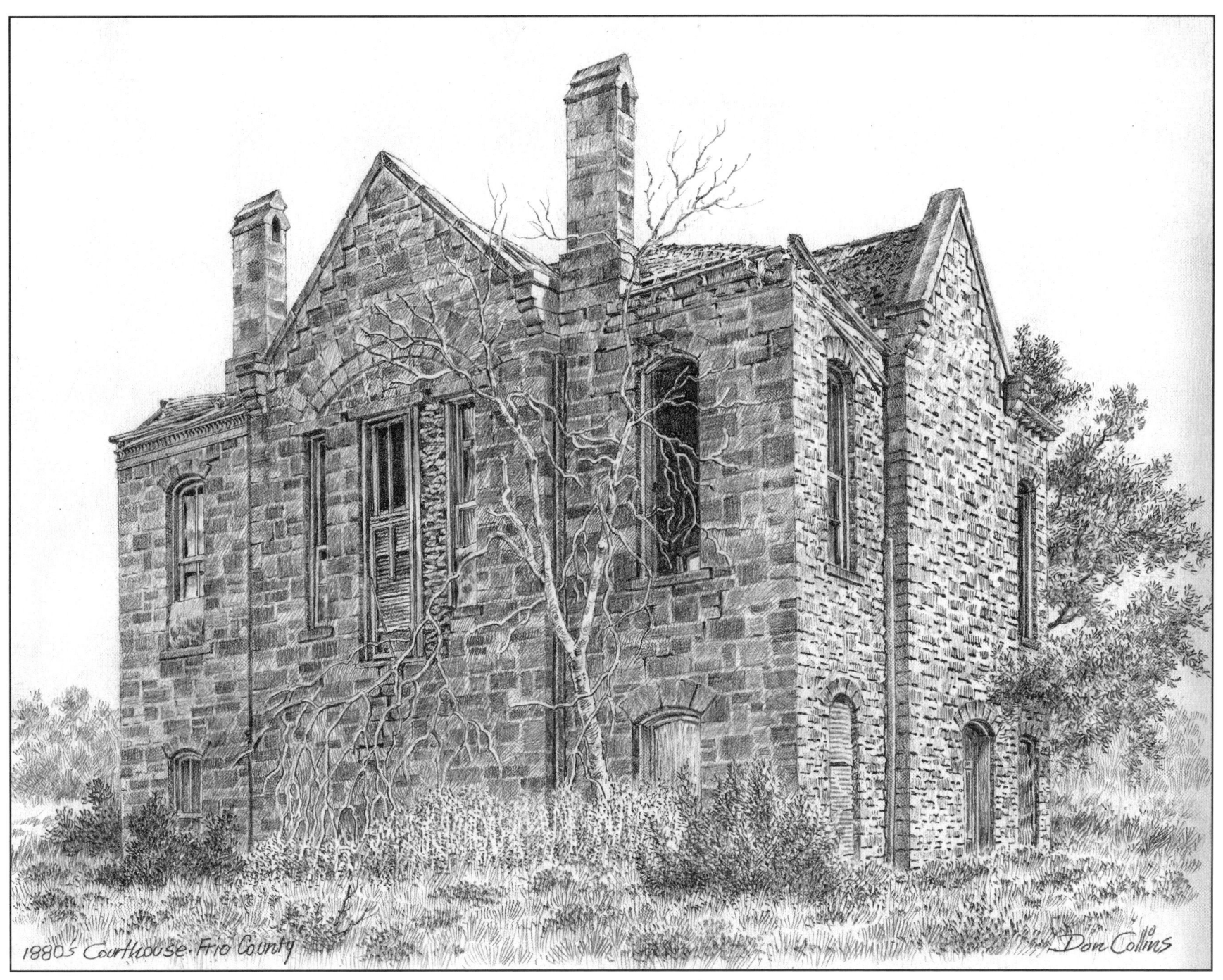

1880's Courthouse, Frio County

Don Collins

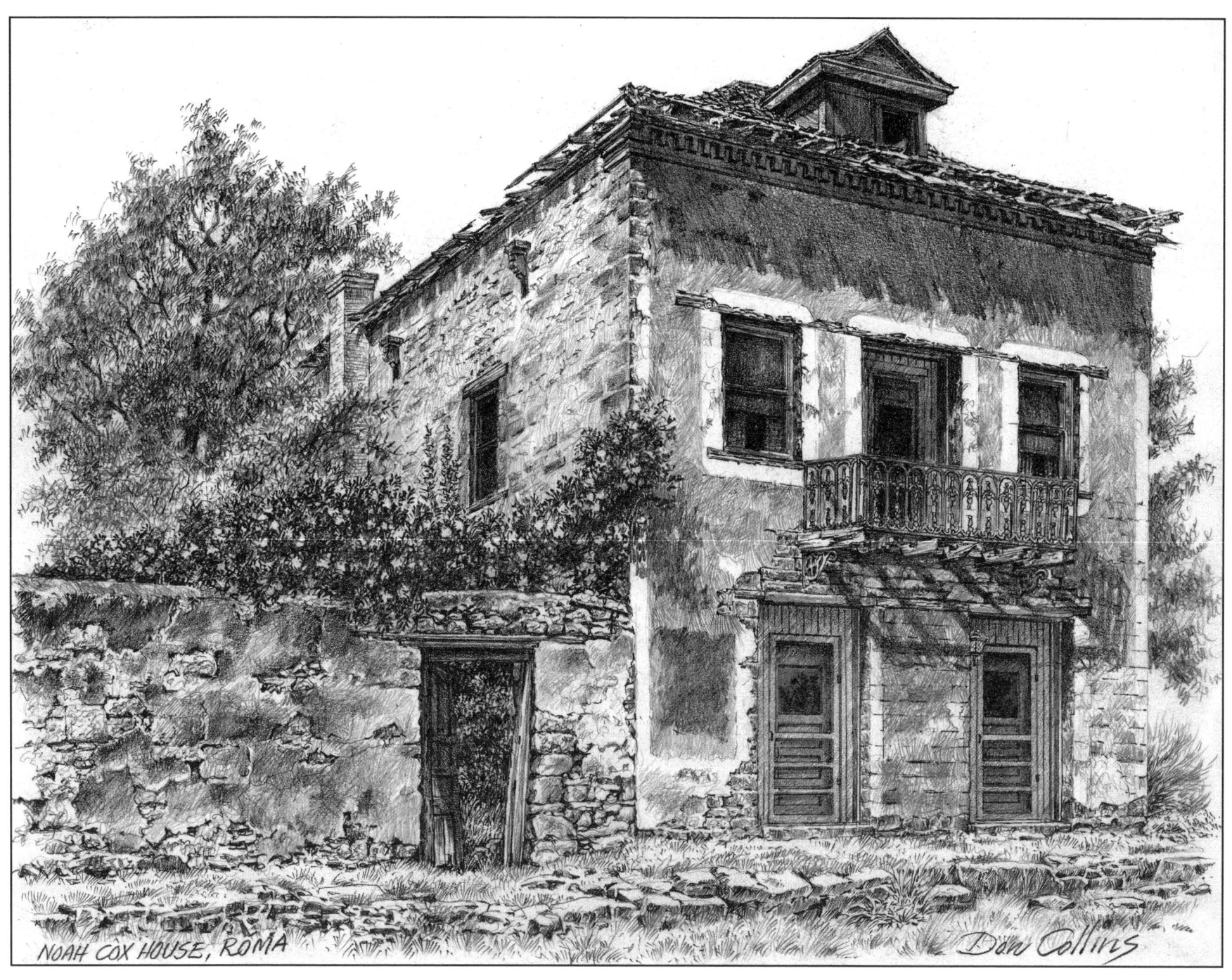

NOAH COX HOUSE, ROMA

Don Collins

20. Noah Cox House, Roma.

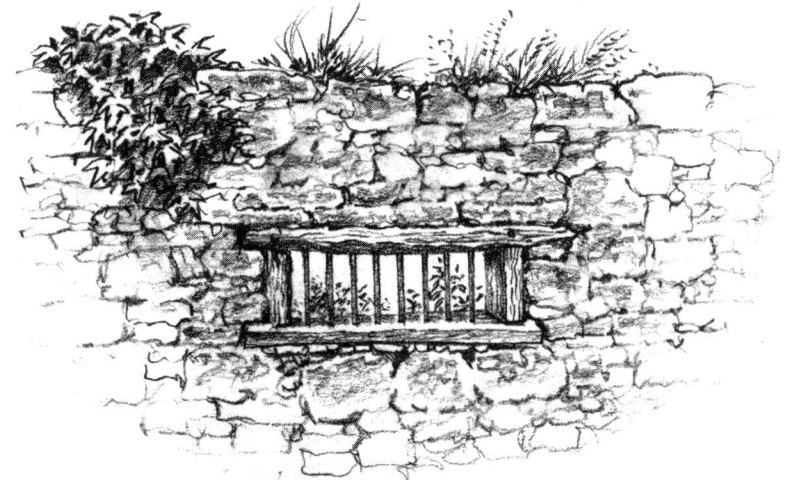

The massive wall surrounding the Cox house gardens is pierced by a number of these roughly-made barred openings

I saw this house the first time that I ever went to the border, and I photographed it then. Unlike many of the places in this book, the Noah Cox house at Roma is often photographed and publicized. It is a great piece of architecture. The thing sits just a few yards from the Rio Grande across from Ciudad Aleman.

Time has done wonderful things for the entire surface of the building. It has various shades of earth colors. They hint of its being painted several different times, but it's not painted now. Everything has combined to make it a fantastic, warm, great old building.

21. San Rafael Chapel, Randado Ranch, Randado, Texas.

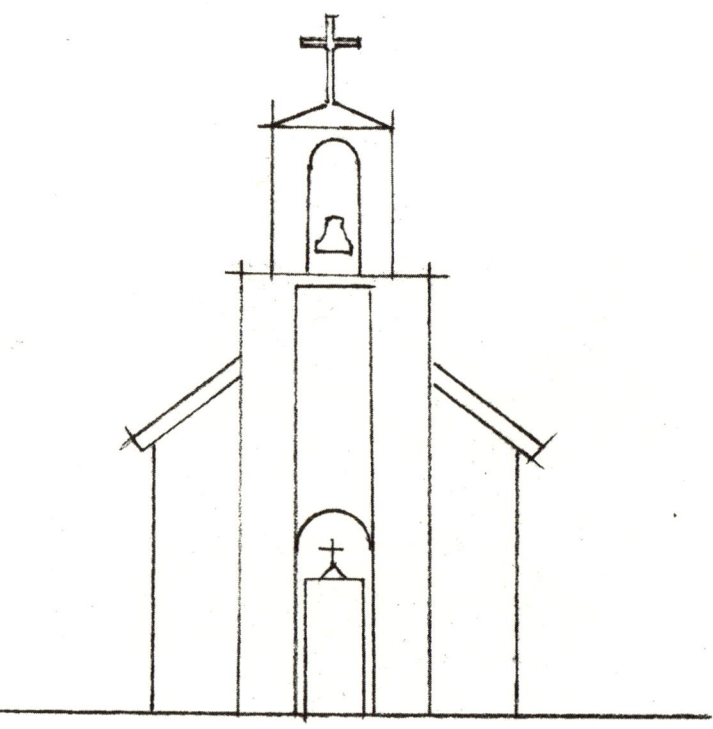

This little church lies south of Hebronville on the Randado Ranch. The Randado Ranch is an old family-owned property that goes way back. At one time where the chapel and ranch headquarters stand there used to be a town. There is evidence of small houses, just foundations, all up and down. They formed a sizable little village.

I was led to this on this trip to South Texas by Bill Hellen, the Jim Hogg County rancher. He took me to the adobe chapel, where there are still occasional services conducted by a visiting priest. Inside it's very quiet and cool. We were there I guess in the heat of August, and it was probably twenty degrees cooler in there. The chapel has a very mellow interior, a lot of old wood, and a lot of the old appurtenances that go with a church like that. Of course, you can tell an architect didn't have anything to do with it. The congregation built it. The people on the site did the best they could.

Beautiful little San Rafael chapel represents architecture refined to the barest essentials, giving it almost a modern look, in spite of its great age.

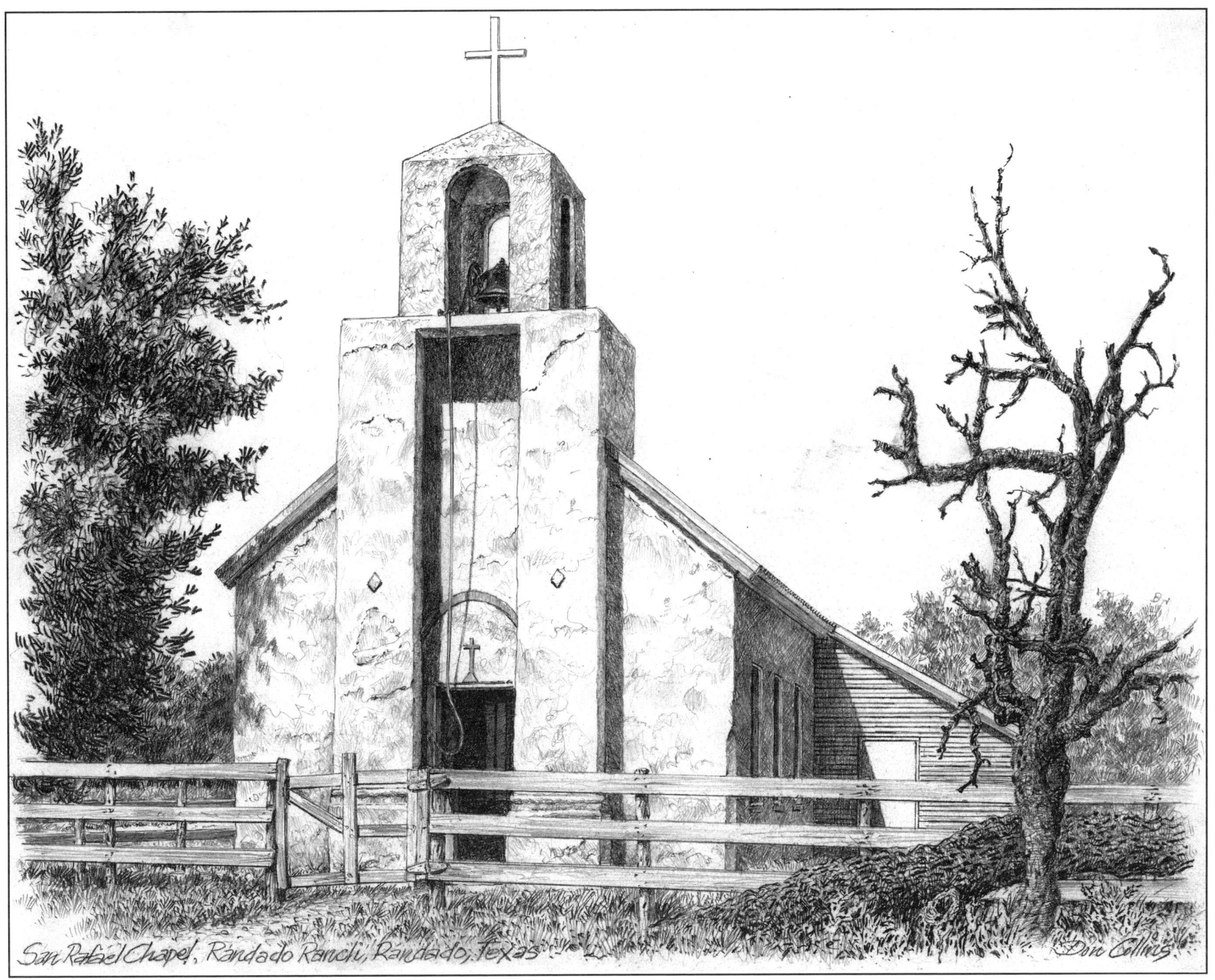

San Rafael Chapel, Randado Ranch, Randado, Texas Don Collins

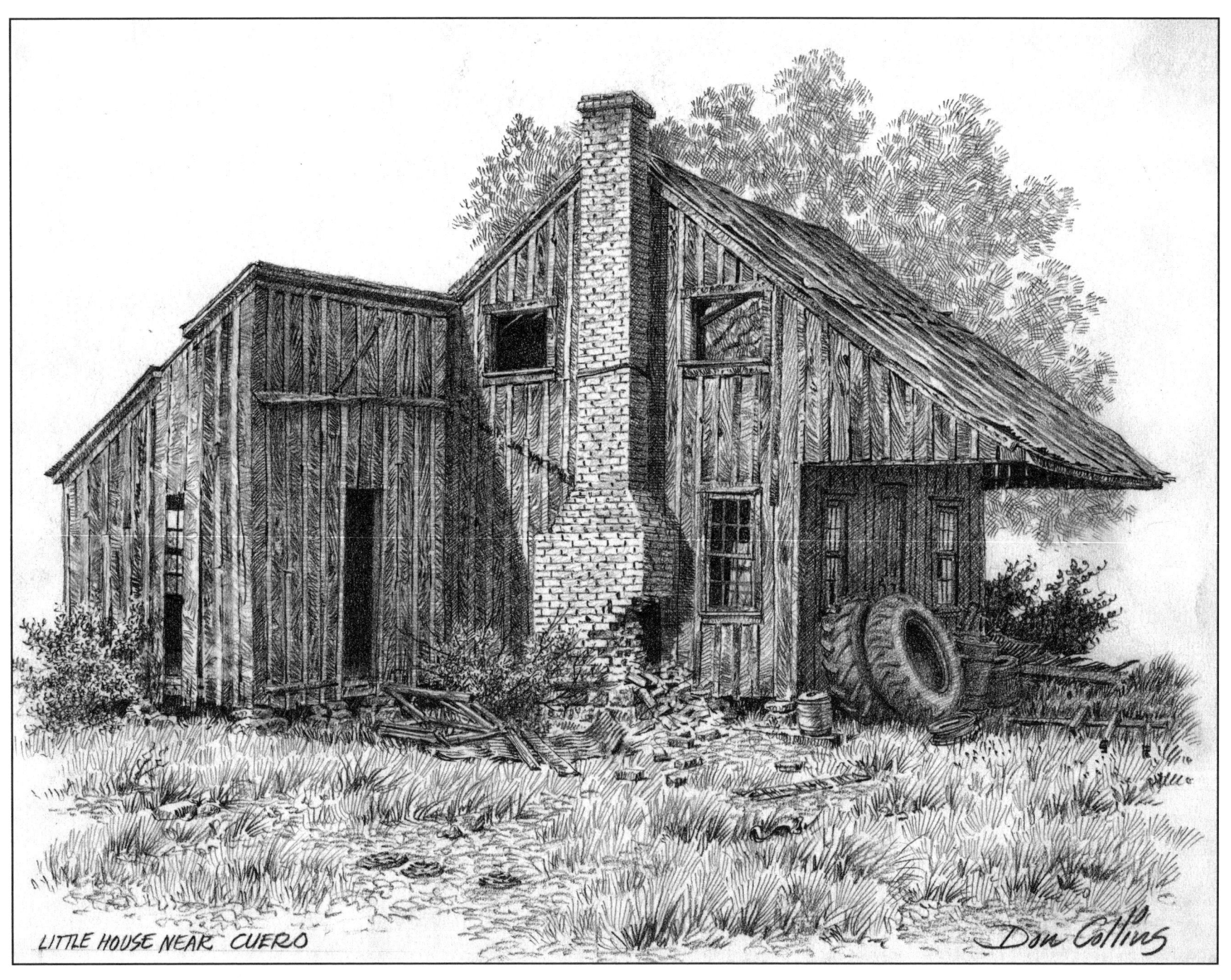

LITTLE HOUSE NEAR CUERO

Don Collins

22. Little House near Cuero.

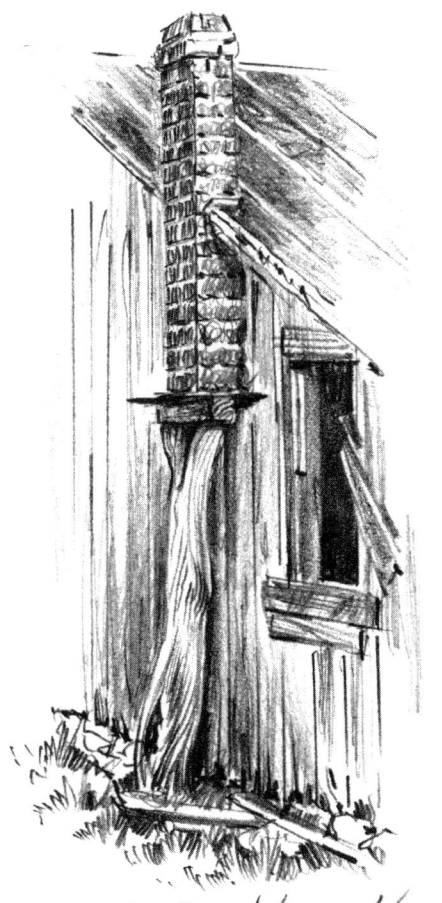

*On the far side, a chimney
perched atop a forked log!*

This is a house of absolutely no architectural significance. I drew it because of its interesting geometric shapes, its steep roof, its two stories, and its board-and-batten construction. I suppose at one time there were posts holding the porch up, but it is all cantilevered out and still holding on. It had a white brick chimney, which was kind of a fancy touch for a building like this.

This probably was a tenant house. It was never prominent enough to be the main structure on a big farm. I thought it was an interesting combination of shapes and textures. And . . . it's a good place to lean your tractor tires.

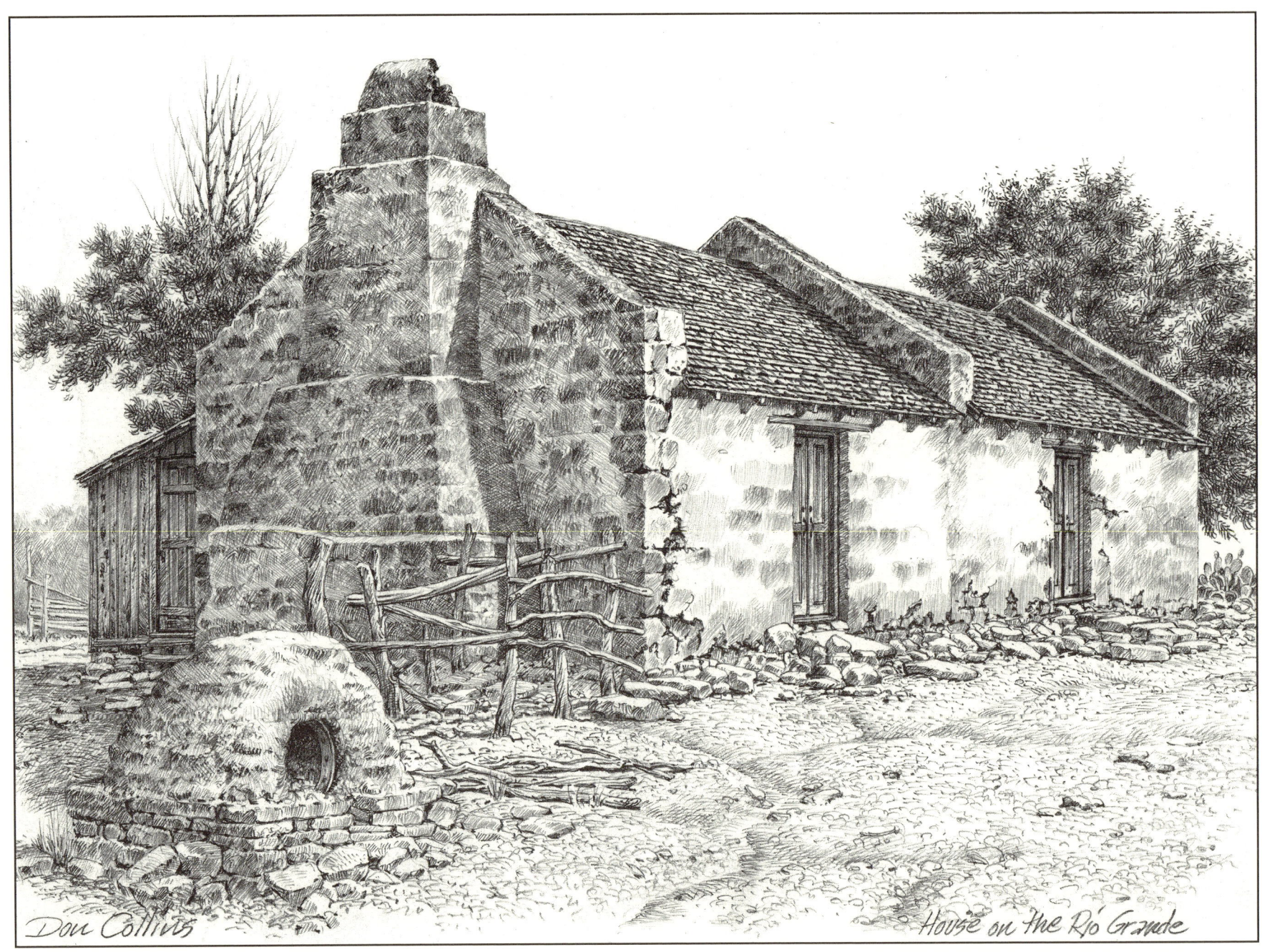

Don Collins

House on the Río Grande

This drawing comes from the very first trip I took to the Rio Grande, which had to be in the '50s. At the time they were building the big Falcon Dam down there, and this house was on the Texas side. I am sure it was later covered with water. It was right across the river from the town of Guerrero, Mexico, that I know was inundated. Several of us got caught up in looking at the areas that were to be flooded by the reservoir and we encountered this. I had never seen anything like it. When I drew the house, I moved the horno or outdoor oven from around back; I wanted to include it in the picture. It's a feature found at a lot of Mexican residences. We didn't try to get into the house. It wasn't occupied, but it was locked up. I was intrigued by the fact that the chimney takes up almost the entire end of the house. It's huge. In addition to heating, it was probably where most of the cooking took place. It's a shame to think that it is submerged now.

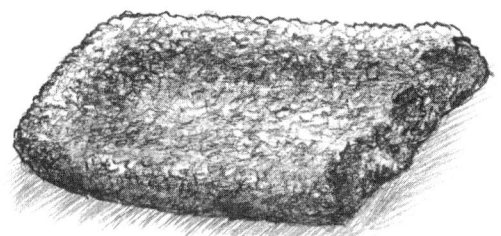

This house on the North bank was probably submerged when Falcon Lake was filled. The horno was around back (I took some artistic liberties.) The very large broken metate was nearby.

The Hill Country

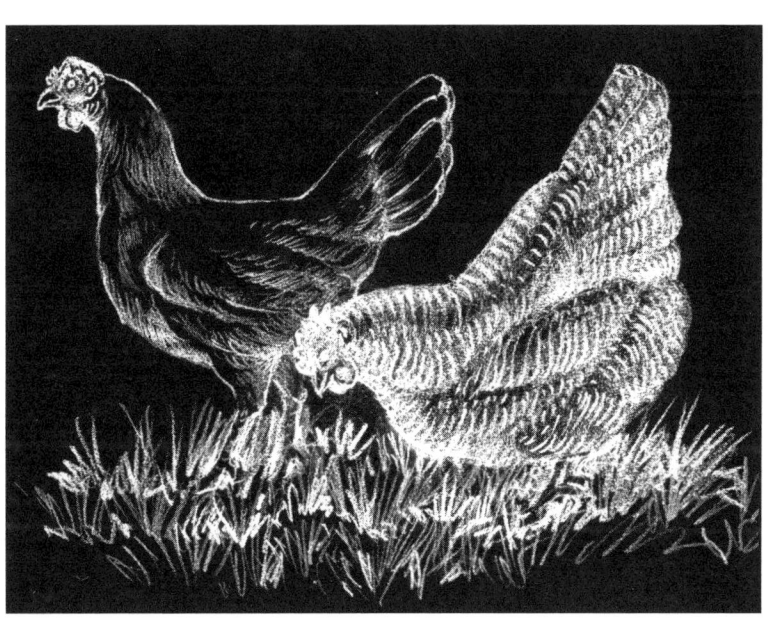

24. Central Texas Barnyard.

This place is in the Luckenbach area. It is on a road back there south and west from Stonewall in Gillespie County. It's just a collection of simple German-style structures, but I was intrigued by having them all grouped together the way they were. You have the main house with the typical double-sloped German roof on it, plus an American-style porch on the front. It has a nice old hand pump on the well out in the back. The house has a number of chimneys, as they always did, and stuccoed stone walls—a very neat and sturdy home. I presume they have grandmother's house out in the back, or maybe the mother-in-law's. It's a tiny little structure, oddly built. I was intrigued by the way they put together the set of three steps off the porch up to the door. I suppose the structure on the left is a utility building of some description. It has little ventilation windows in it. The same applies to the one in the foreground. The whole thing is just a pleasant typical Hill Country farmyard. It had all the things that attract an artist.

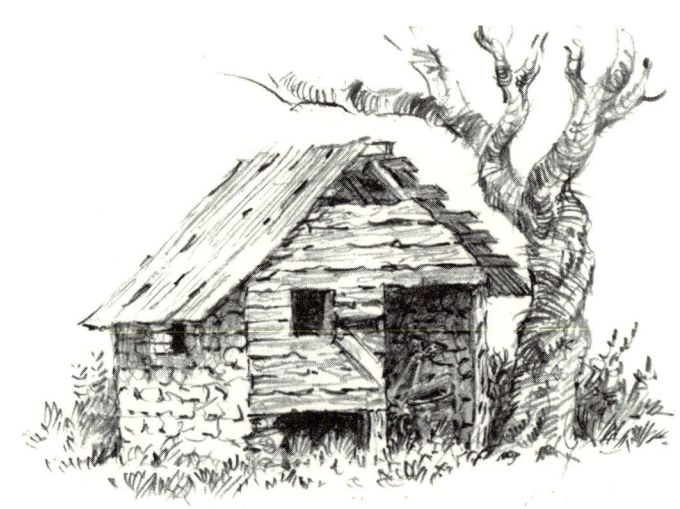

This small, rather makeshift building was in odd contrast to the solidly built stone structures around it.

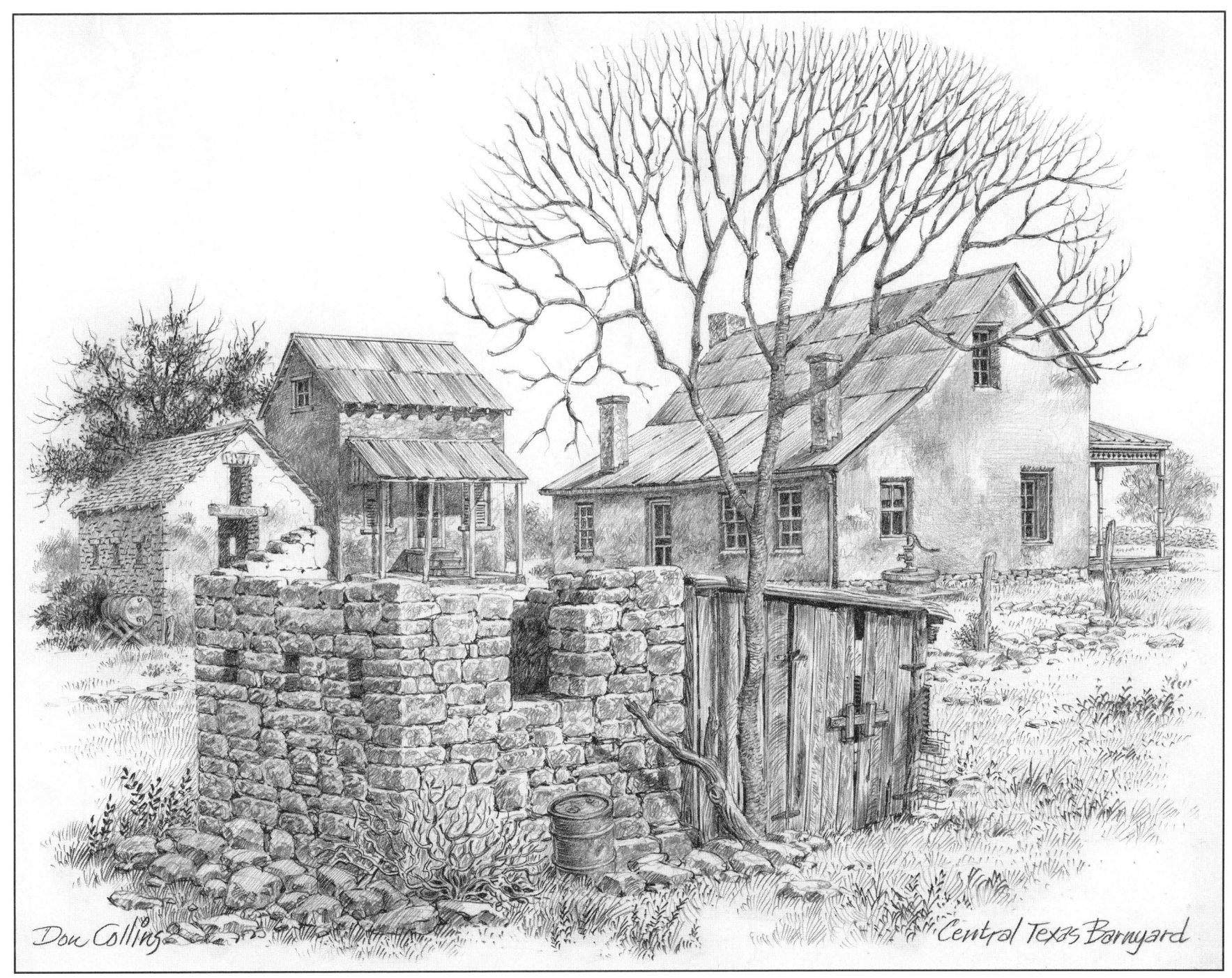

Don Collins   Central Texas Barnyard

25. Barn on the Little Blanco River.

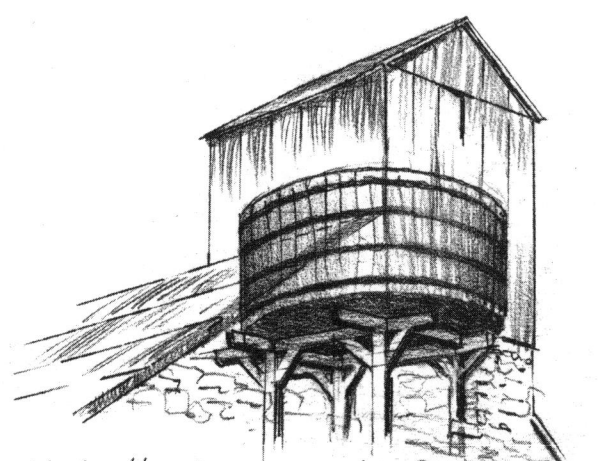

Up in the tower is a large cypress-lined water reservoir, intended for use in a brewery (some say a tannery). Supplied by an oversize windmill, it gave the farm great water pressure.

The Little Blanco is in Blanco County. The barn is off U.S. Highway 281 about a mile east of the road on the north bank of the river. I was actually directed to this place by my friend, Arlon Bindseil. When I visited here twenty-five years ago, he had relatives living in the house next door.

Arlon's great-grandfather erected this building. He put the odd structure on top because he wanted to start a brewery, and that covered his elevated water tank. The brewery never came off, so Grandpa never got to make his beer. The erstwhile brewery building found other use for hay, feed, and animals, and a massive, beautiful old barn it is. It's been there for a very long time, and it is going to stay there for a long time yet.

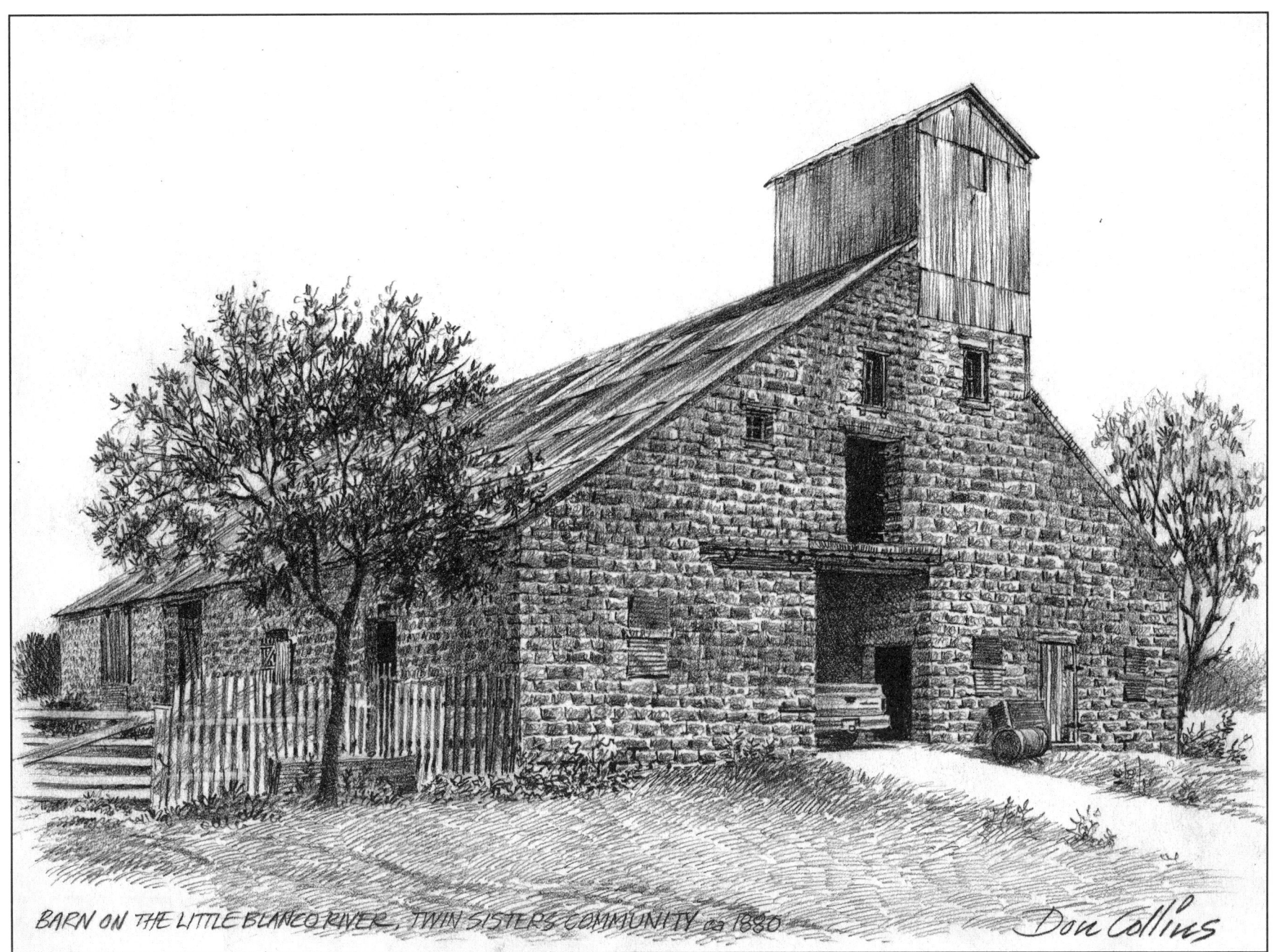

BARN ON THE LITTLE BLANCO RIVER, TWIN SISTERS COMMUNITY ca 1880   Don Collins

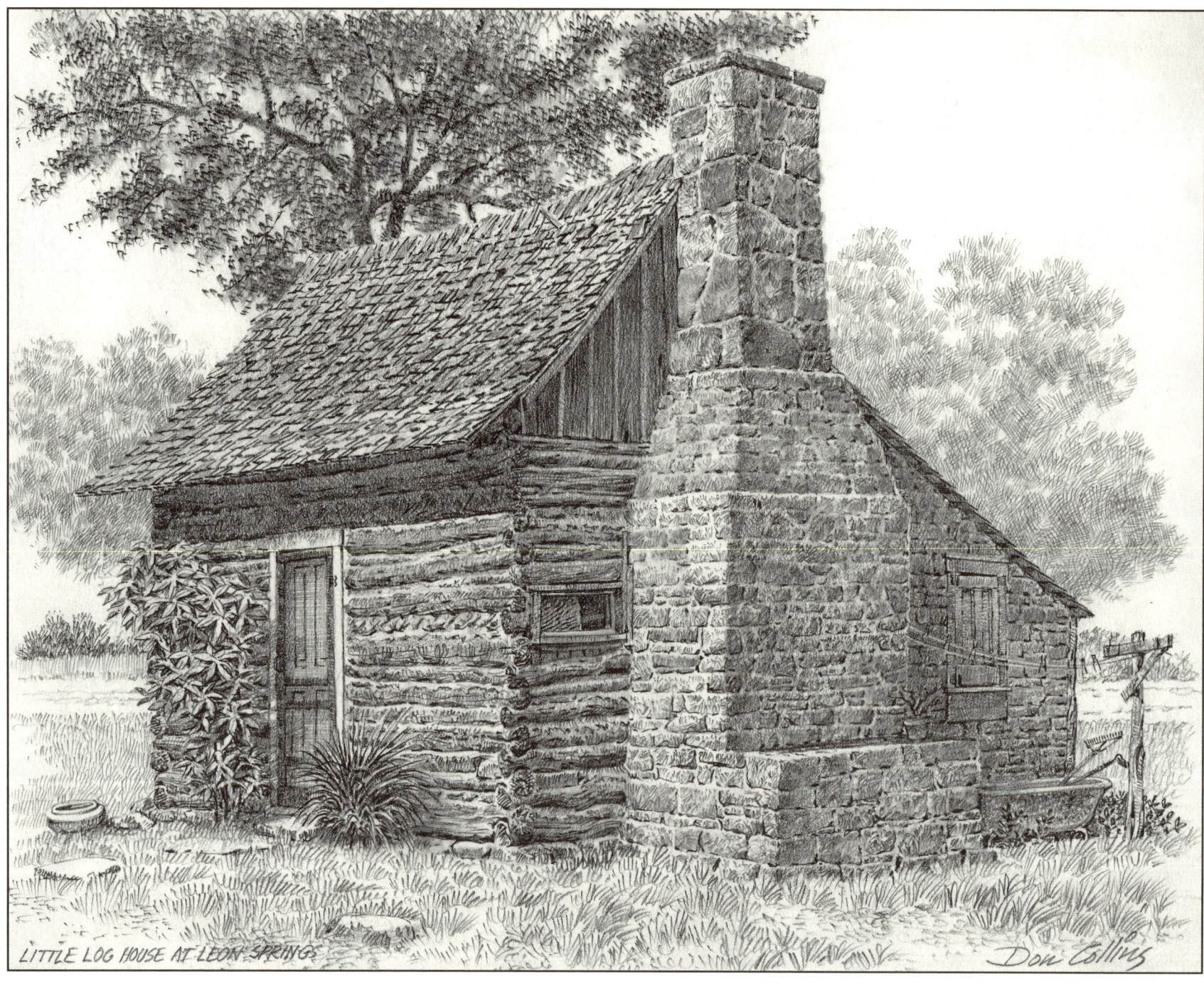

LITTLE LOG HOUSE AT LEON SPRINGS

Don Collins

26. Little Log House at Leon Springs.

Leon Springs has turned into a bedroom community for San Antonio, and now it's hard to find the things that interested me thirty, thirty-five years ago. Even so there are a number of buildings like this in the town. Almost all of them are German-influenced. They have the typical shape of a Teutonic house.

I was intrigued by this one because the fireplace at one end is almost as large as the cabin itself. Of course, as an artist I liked the fact that they had a little bathtub full of garden tools.

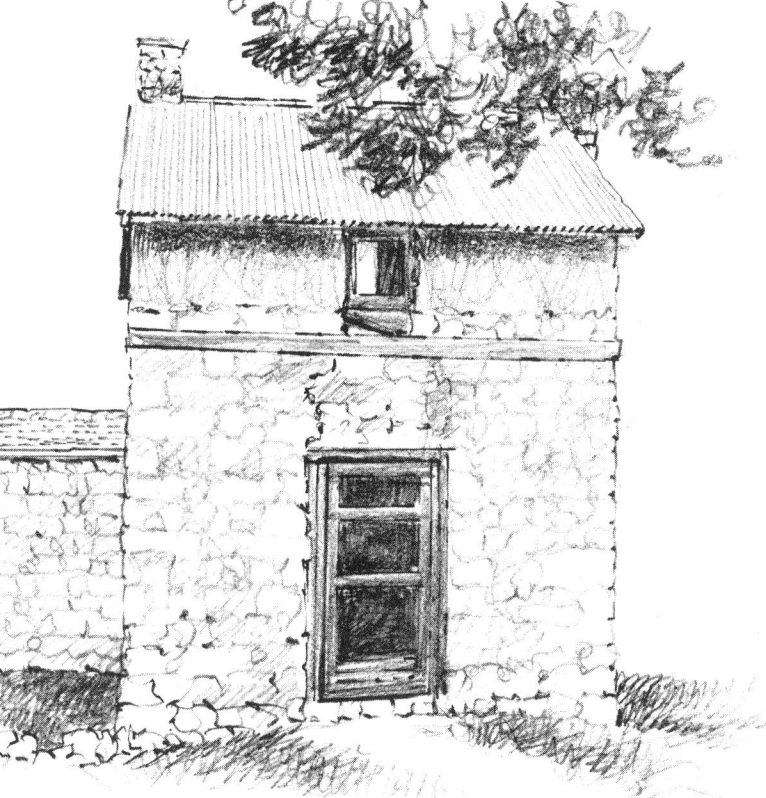

Just a few steps away is another small, well preserved pioneer house.

27. Palisado House near Quihi.

This little dwelling near Quihi in Medina County is one of my all-time favorite houses. For some reason I felt a really strong personal reaction when I found it on the road west of the town. It's very unusual in that it's a palisado house. This construction consists of posts stuck in the ground and chinked and mortared and stuccoed. It is very unusual in that part of the world to find this style. The Alsatian immigrants who built it probably wanted to save rock and mortar.

Also there's some evidence that the house was a certain size and they expanded it, because it has a rock wall right in the middle that I don't think you would normally see. The fireplaces on the inside are fantastic; both of them are cooking fireplaces, very large. A full-grown person can just almost stand inside the one on the far end. The building is in pretty sad condition, obviously not cared for. Since making the drawing, I made another visit and found that it's declined yet further. It is a very old house. I'm sure it dates no later than the '50s, pre-Civil War. It's a very nice old house.

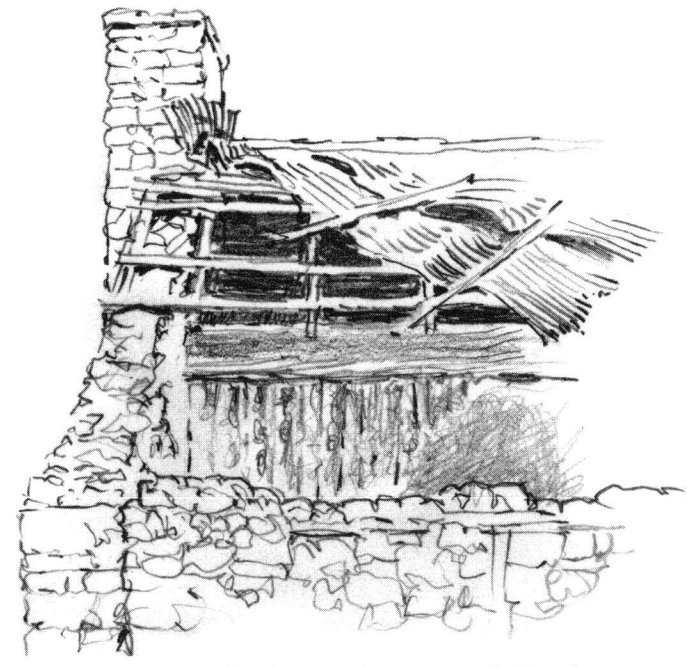

A look at the inside of the house shows the unusual palisado type construction on the interior walls as well.

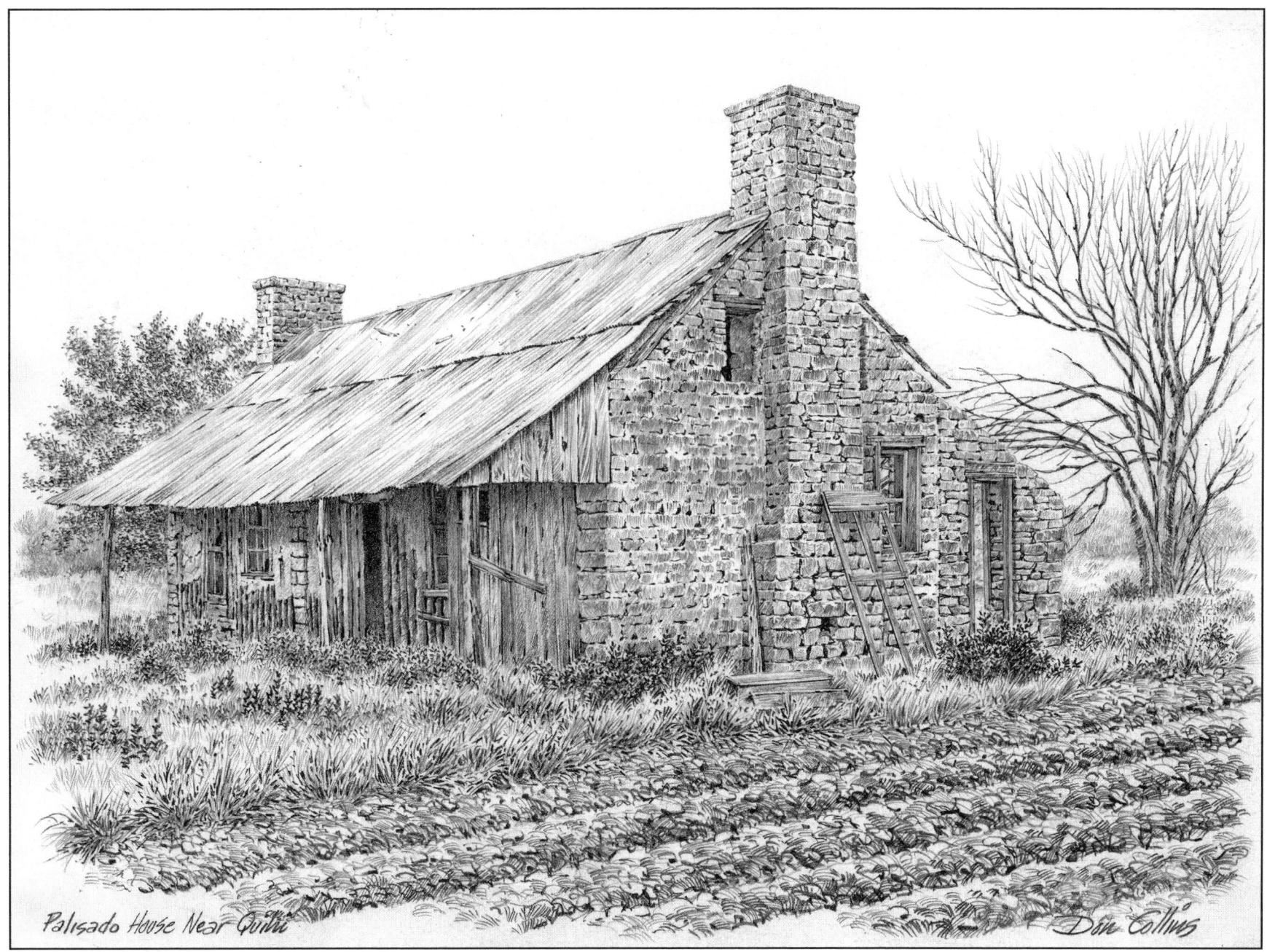

Palisado House Near Quihi

Dan Collins

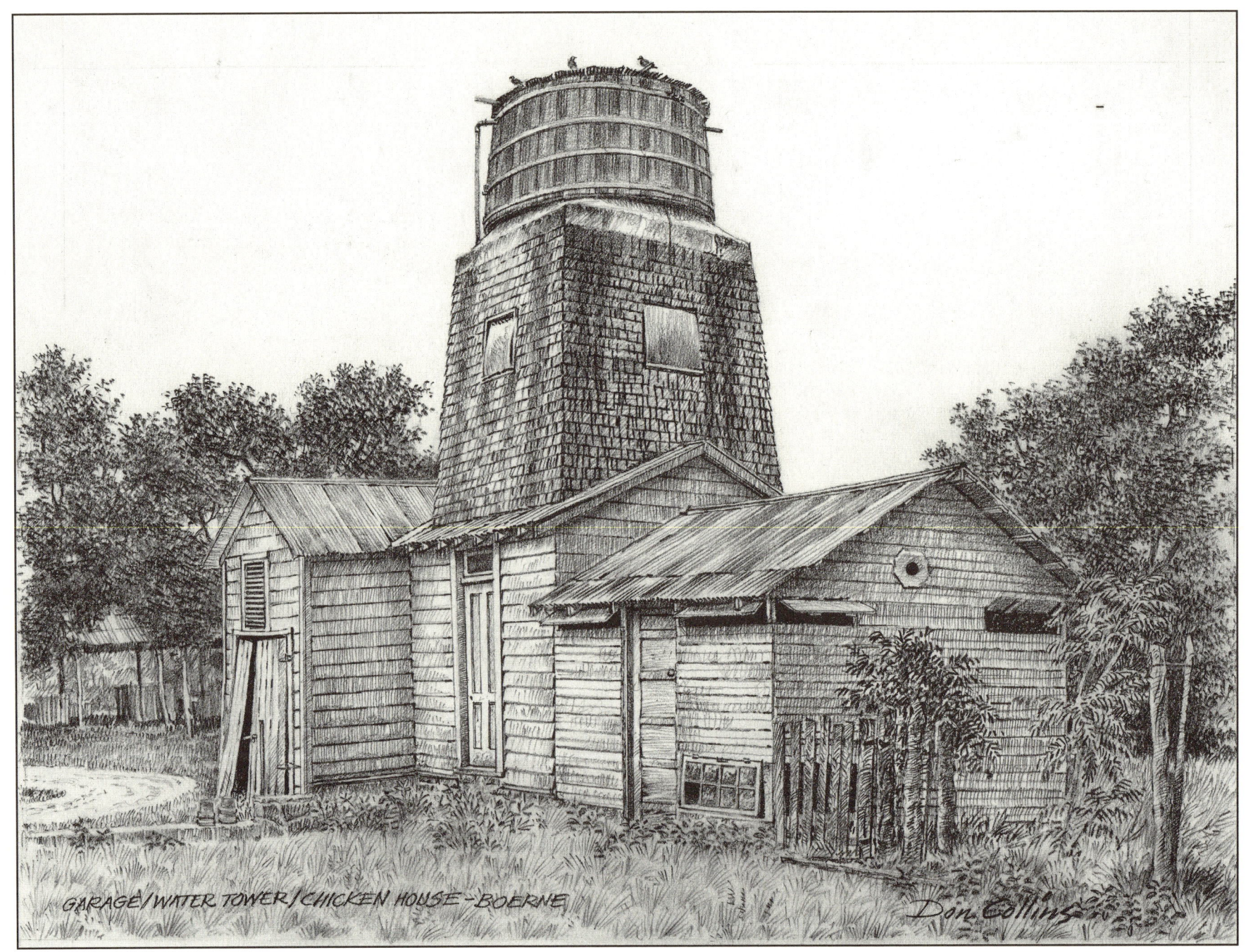

GARAGE/WATER TOWER/CHICKEN HOUSE-BOERNE

Don Collins

28. Garage/Water Tower/Chicken House, Boerne.

This construction is in the book because I thought it was interesting that they decided to have so many things going on in such a very limited space. They have a little one-car garage, suited to the Model T. It wouldn't accommodate a modern car. Then they have a nice water tower up high on a shingled tower. And then down below they have a bathroom, or at least a shower—an arrangement for bathing. Then on this end they decided to add a chicken house. It has proper ventilation, up under the eaves, and another opening, a hinged window down low so that the chickens can come and go during the day. What a very compact operation with a lot of things going on in a tiny, limited space. Thirty-five years ago it was right in the heart of Boerne, but I'm sure the building is gone now. I've been there a number of times since then and I can't find it, so others may have considered it an eyesore.

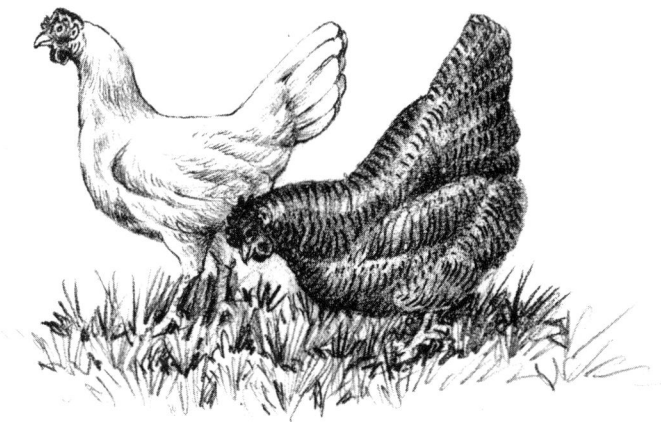

Behind the building I encountered a small flock of free-range urban chickens.

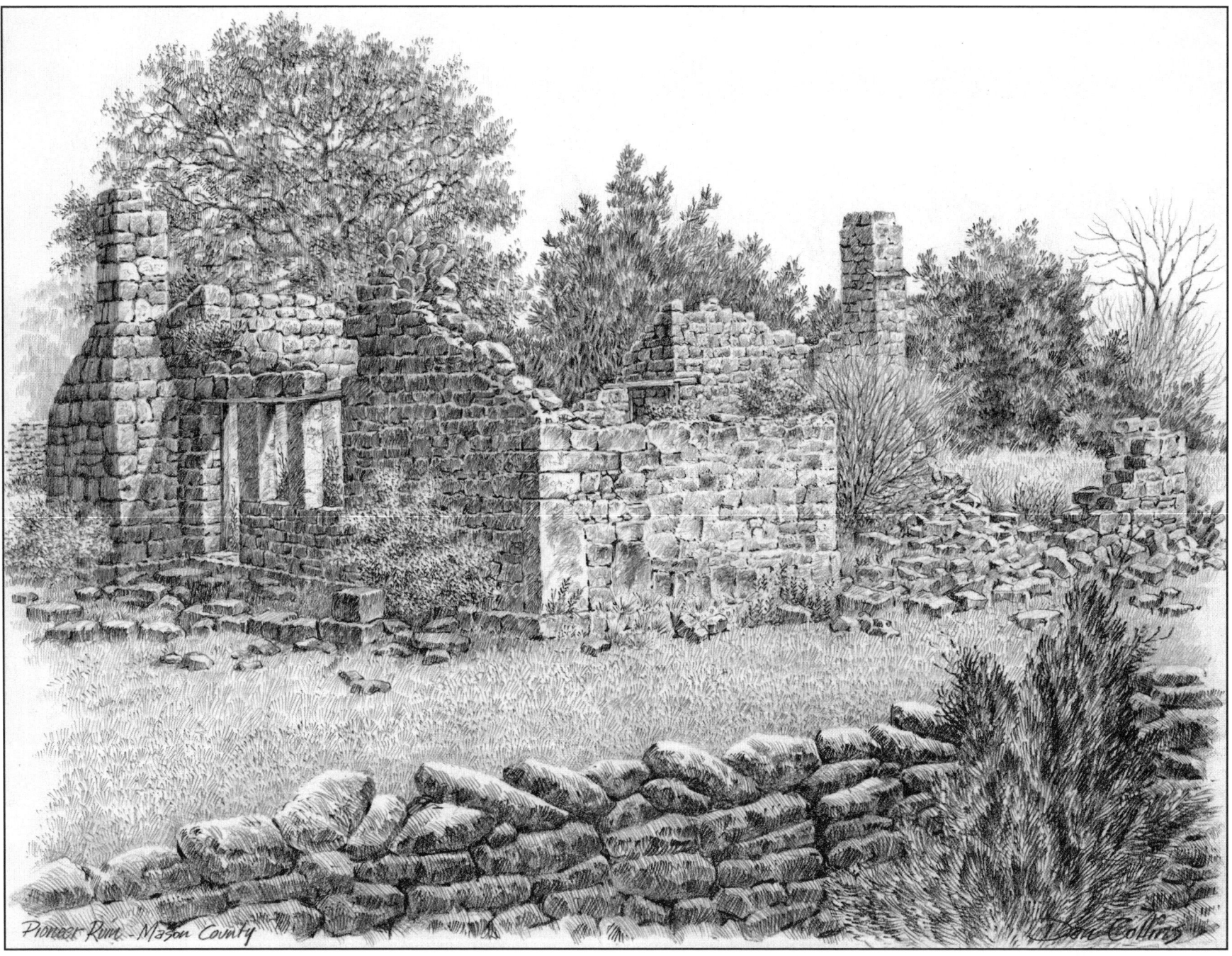

Pioneer Ruin - Mason County

Don Collins

29. Pioneer Ruin, Mason County.

This is a fantastic old piece of construction. I don't know much about the history of the place other than the fact that the builders were named Anderegg, but it intrigued me. It lies off to the right of Farm-to-Market Road 783 that leads from Doss to Mason. The ruins are surrounded by brush, and they are difficult to see. I spotted them one day and then got very excited. The house is made out of the reddish sandstone native to that area, but parts of it are huge slabs of white limestone that were obviously hauled in from somewhere else. You'll notice it in the lintels and in the corners.

In addition to a home, this place doubled as a defensive fort. There's a little angle that leads out this way. There's a flat piece of stone set in the wall with a hole drilled in it about three, four inches in diameter, so if a visitor standing at the entry on the far side was trying to get in, he'd be inches away from a rifle port. Assuming that you got inside and overcame somebody, facing into a wall there is yet another flat stone with a rifle port. They were prepared for anything. Addition-ally there was a chest-high stone wall of the same material all around the entire house with a very narrow gate and only one way to get in and out. The people who lived here were out there in the middle of the Indians and were ready for them.

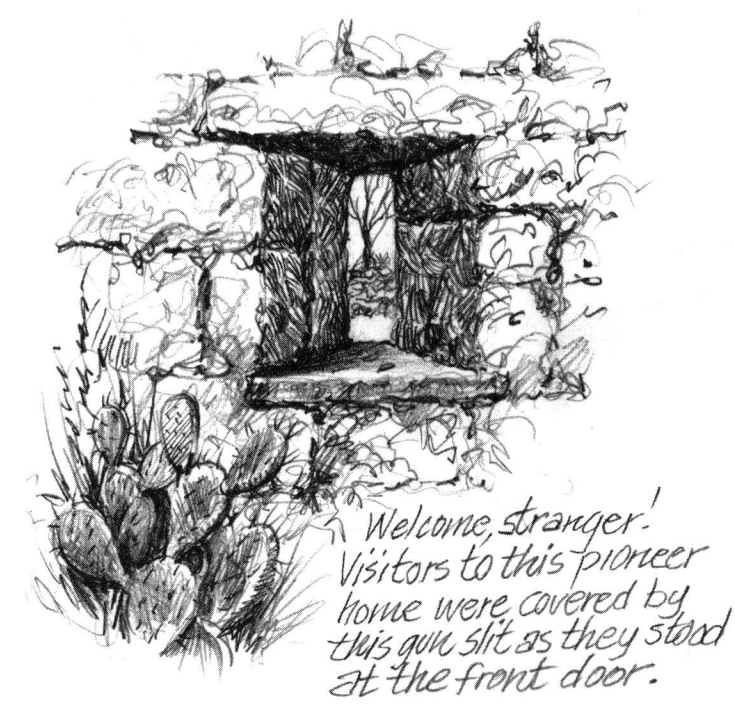

Welcome, stranger! Visitors to this pioneer home were covered by this gun slit as they stood at the front door.

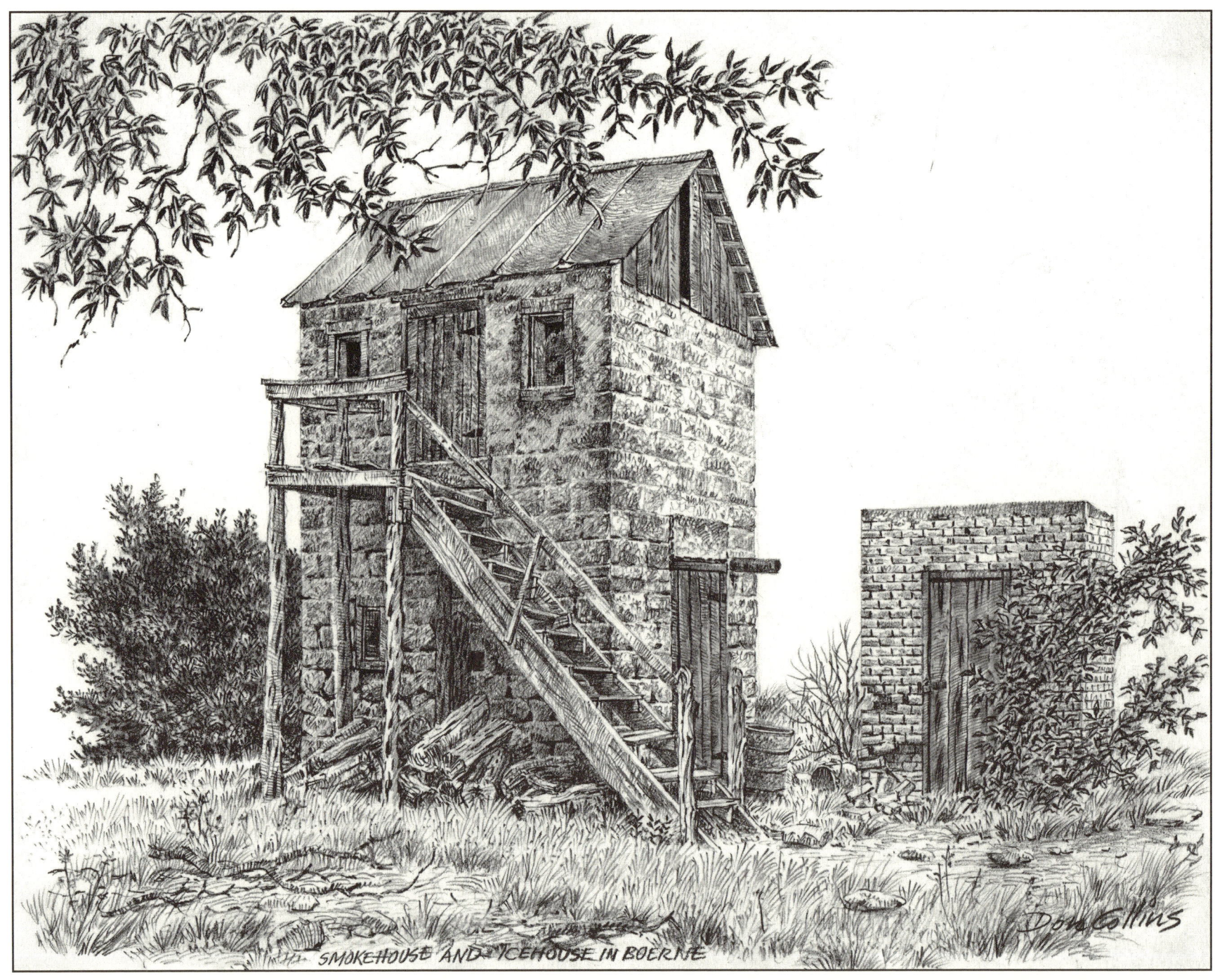

SMOKEHOUSE AND ICEHOUSE IN BOERNE

Don Collins

30. Smokehouse and Icehouse in Boerne.

This little smokehouse is a great curiosity. It was on the southern edge of Boerne about thirty-five years ago, and I never saw anything quite like it—a two-story smokehouse. I don't know why it was built like this, and there wasn't anybody to talk to. It stood next to a parking lot. The little structure next to it served as an icehouse. They stored block ice when the trucks made routine deliveries and dropped it off. Now it's gone. The parking lot's been expanded and the smokehouse and the icehouse were in the way. It's kind of a shame to see it go.

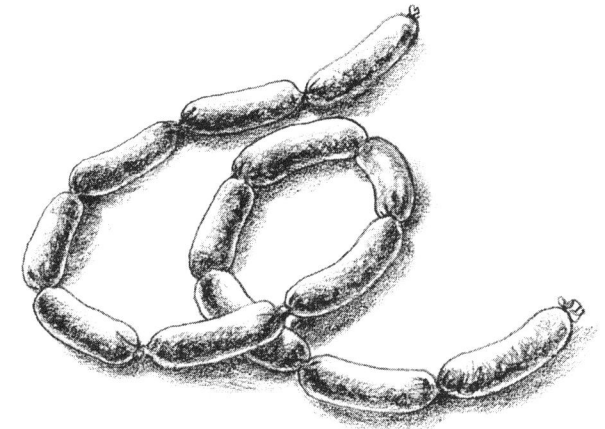

As I looked over this unusual old smokehouse, I wondered how many tons of delicious hill country venison sausage had passed through its doors.

31. Barn near Castroville.

This little barn used to lie, and maybe still lies, southeast of Castroville a mile or so out of town. It's just got great appeal to me. I like the way you drive through the opening there and the little storage room on the left-hand side. The old red wagon was moldering away out in front. Obviously the barn had not been used for a number of years, had no storage in it except for a few odds and ends that they had left behind. I like the way the pierced roof casts light and shadows on the wall; it's always interesting for an artist to try to capture that. A very quiet, remote part of the world there. Just a warm old barn. You can imagine all sorts of things, activities that had gone on there for many, many years, but not lately. I'm sure by now that the barn is gone. It was in a state of advanced decay at that time. I like the see-through feature. I love buildings where you can see the world on the other side. I don't know why; it has some kind of appeal to me.

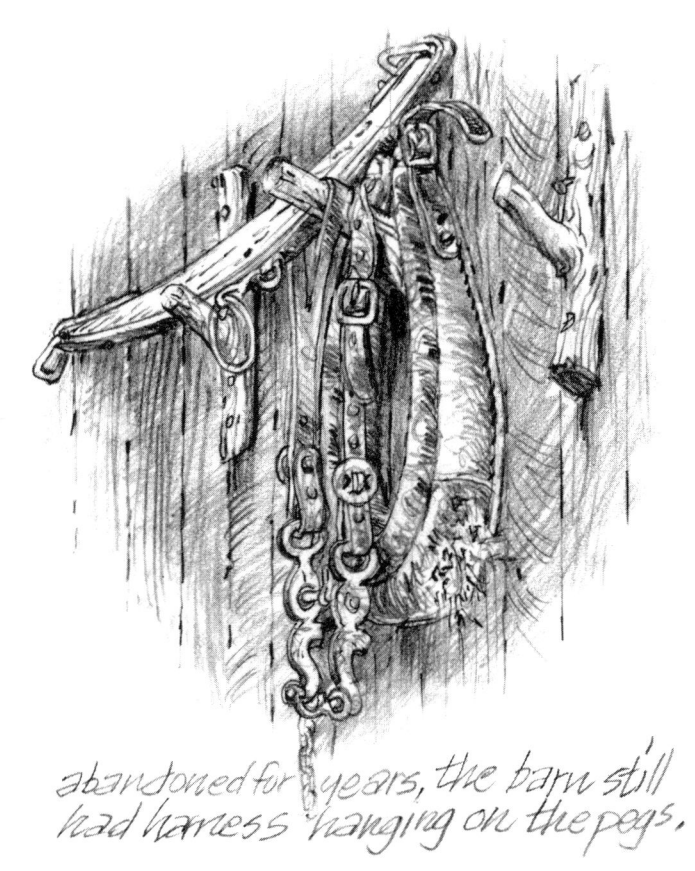

abandoned for years, the barn still had harness hanging on the pegs.

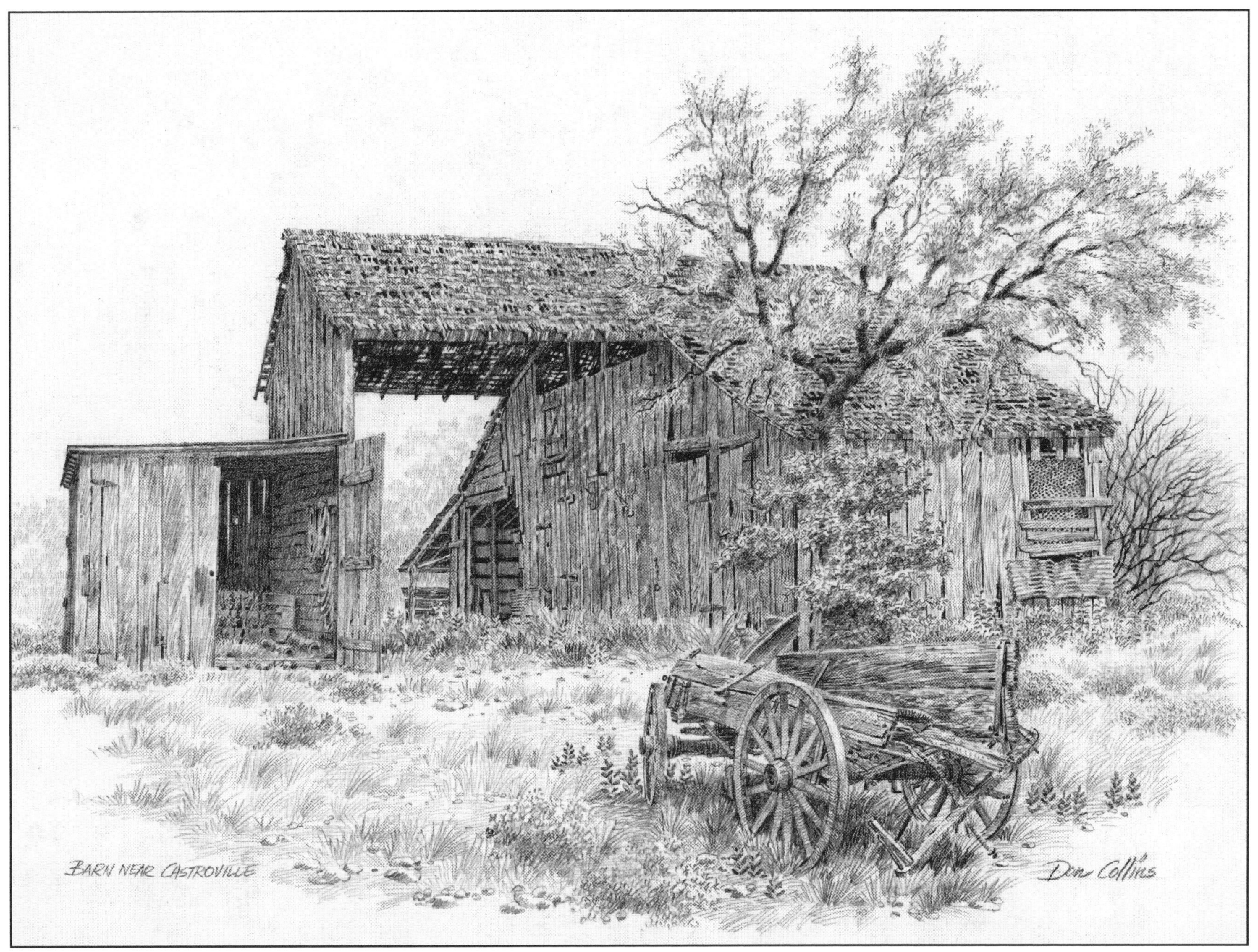

BARN NEAR CASTROVILLE

Don Collins

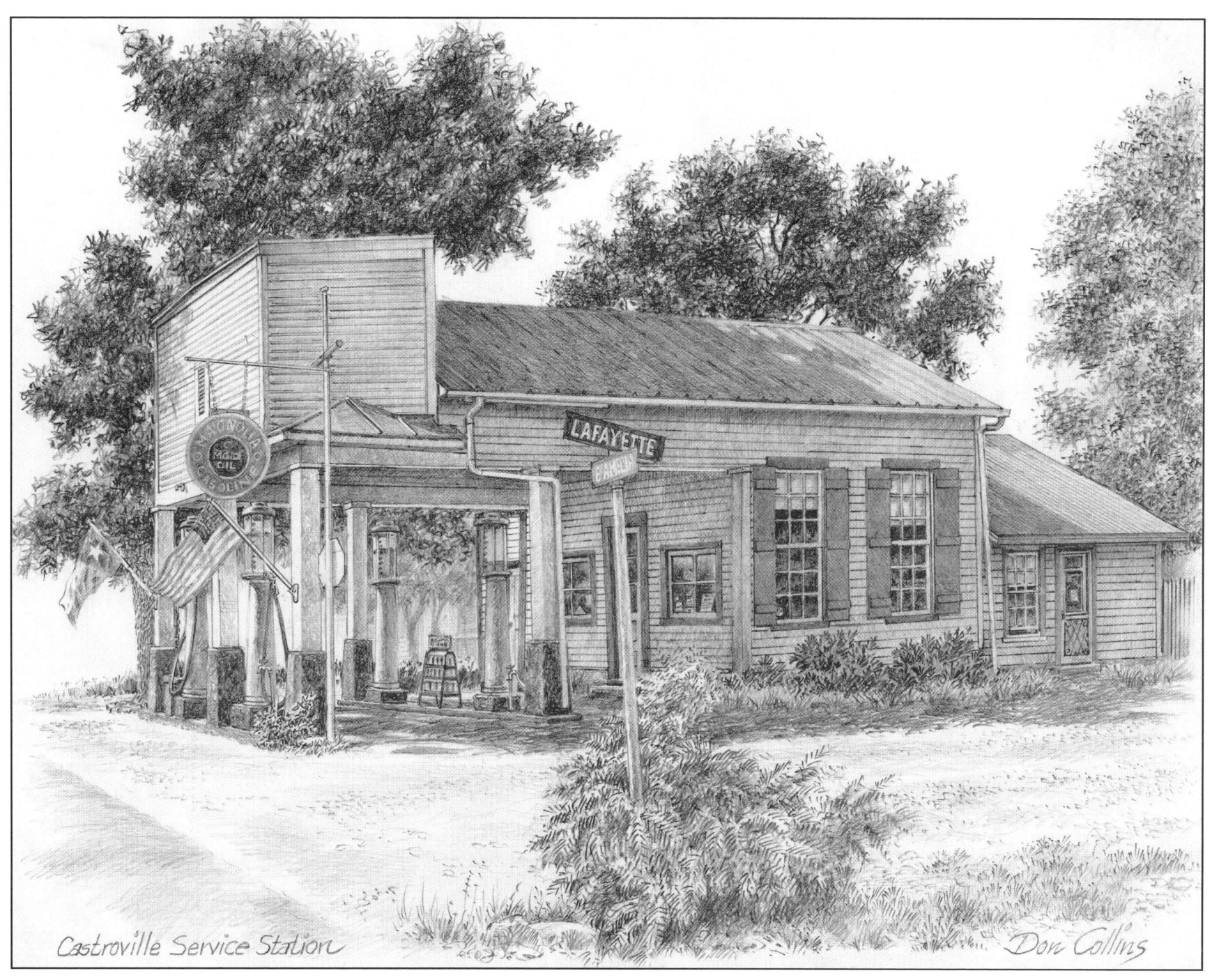

Castroville Service Station

Don Collins

32. Castroville Service Station.

This little building still exists in very good condition at Lafayette and East Amelia streets in Castroville. I had to fudge a little bit. It had been converted into an antique store, and the gas pumps did not exist any more. Instead there were a bunch of baby buggies and assorted junk in front. So I reinstalled some gas pumps just to lend a little authenticity to the drawing.

Fundamentally that's the way it's looked since the 1920s, built as a gas station with living quarters attached, which was commonplace in those days. It's been well maintained, and altogether is a very pleasant looking little wooden building. I like the little false front on top that must have lent importance. Or maybe it was just a place to put a sign.

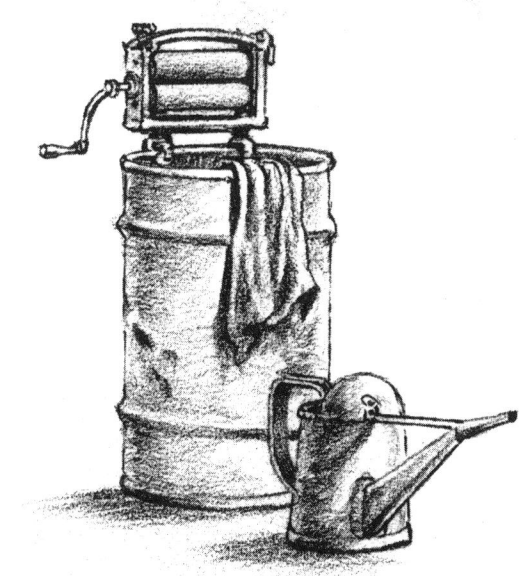

When this neat old station opened, you could expect to get your tires, radiator, and oil checked for free while the operators pumped the gas.

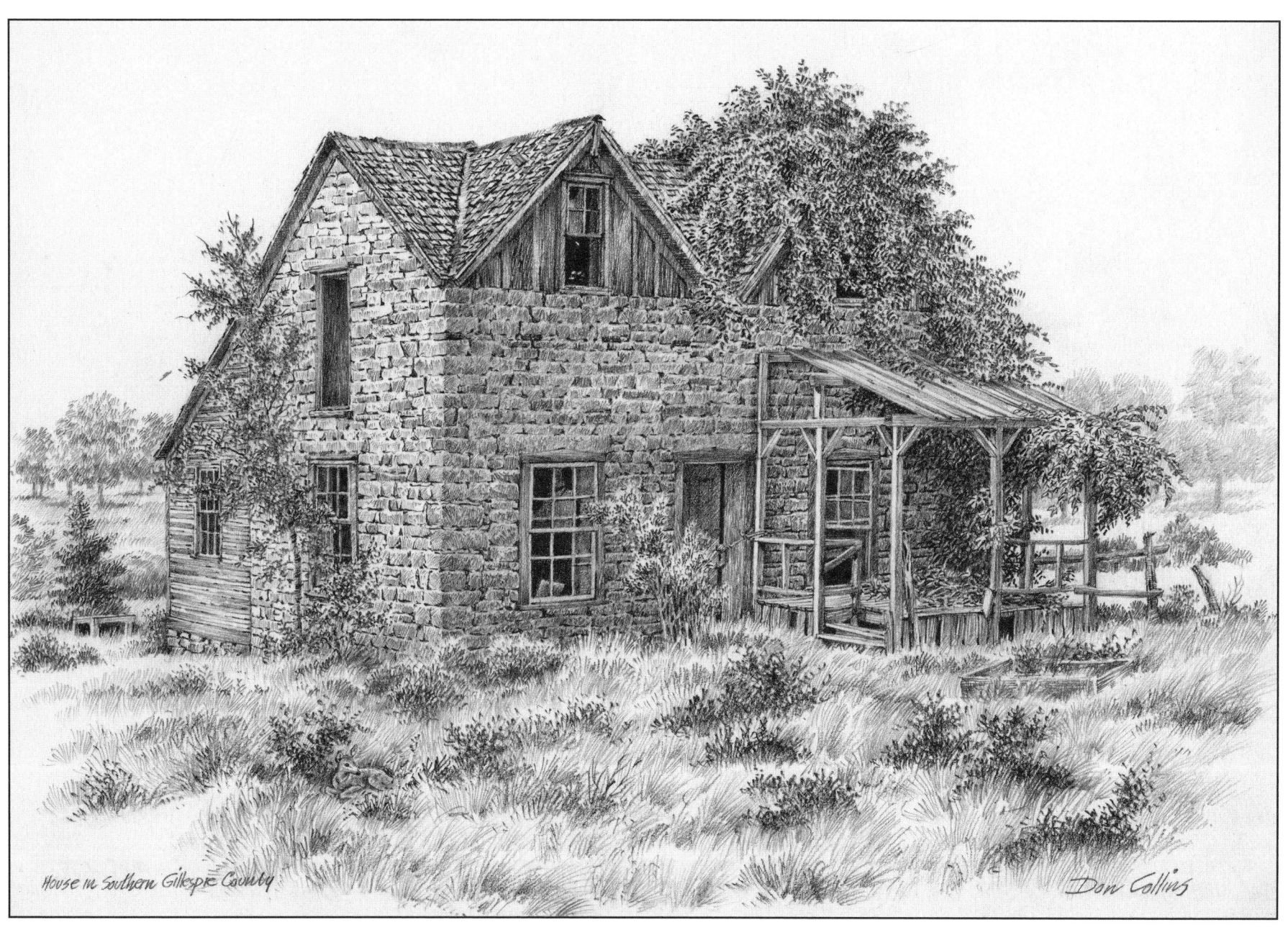

House in Southern Gillespie County

Don Collins

33. House in Southern Gillespie County.

It's not quite a typical Texas German house. This place has two unusual dormers that occupy virtually the entire front of the roof. It's got the typical German shape, the shed roof in the back, and an additional wooden shed built back there at a later date. Very sturdily built. The house shows a few little nods to quality like the gently arched lintels over the windows and doors.

An interesting thing occurred as I approached this house. I had walked a fair distance from the road, about a hundred yards. Then, all of a sudden, something jumped up and ran away, giving me a start. Immediately I thought, "jackrabbit," but then I looked and saw it was a fawn that had been hiding in the bushes. Its mother had placed it there just before I got there, and I had almost stepped on it. You can see it depicted in the foreground.

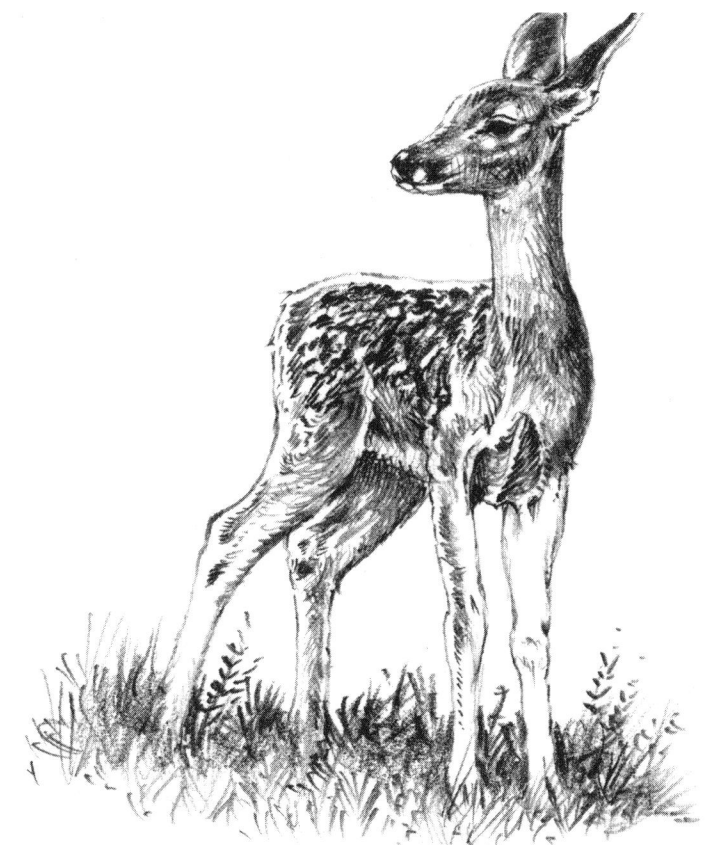

A fawn was hiding in the tall grass as I approached the house.

34. Pioneer Home at Quihi.

This house on the main street in Quihi has all the appeal that those German and Alsatian homes do. You know that they have been sitting there for a very, very long time and you wonder who they sheltered, who lived there, what they did. A very pleasant little dwelling, it had a low-lying, very large room on the upstairs. There wasn't a lot of headroom there except toward the center, but it was high enough to put your kids up there and give them a place to sleep.

It's pierced all the way through with a dogtrot. You can go all the way through to the back. They had an interesting old car parked in there that I couldn't get around to see very well, but it wasn't a Model T. The house has two fireplaces, one out of sight behind the roof.

The house now is in a lot of trouble, because you can see in this depiction the rocks under the dormer there are beginning to fall away as supports have weakened. I expect that it's going to go in a hurry when that happens. It's going to fall in two.

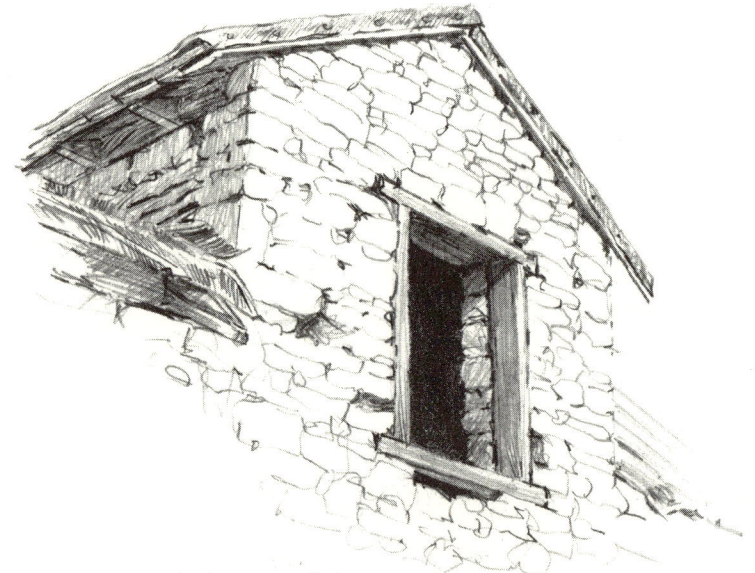

Quihi had a lot of Indian troubles in its early days... I wondered whether this window had ever seen any Lipans or Comanches passing by.

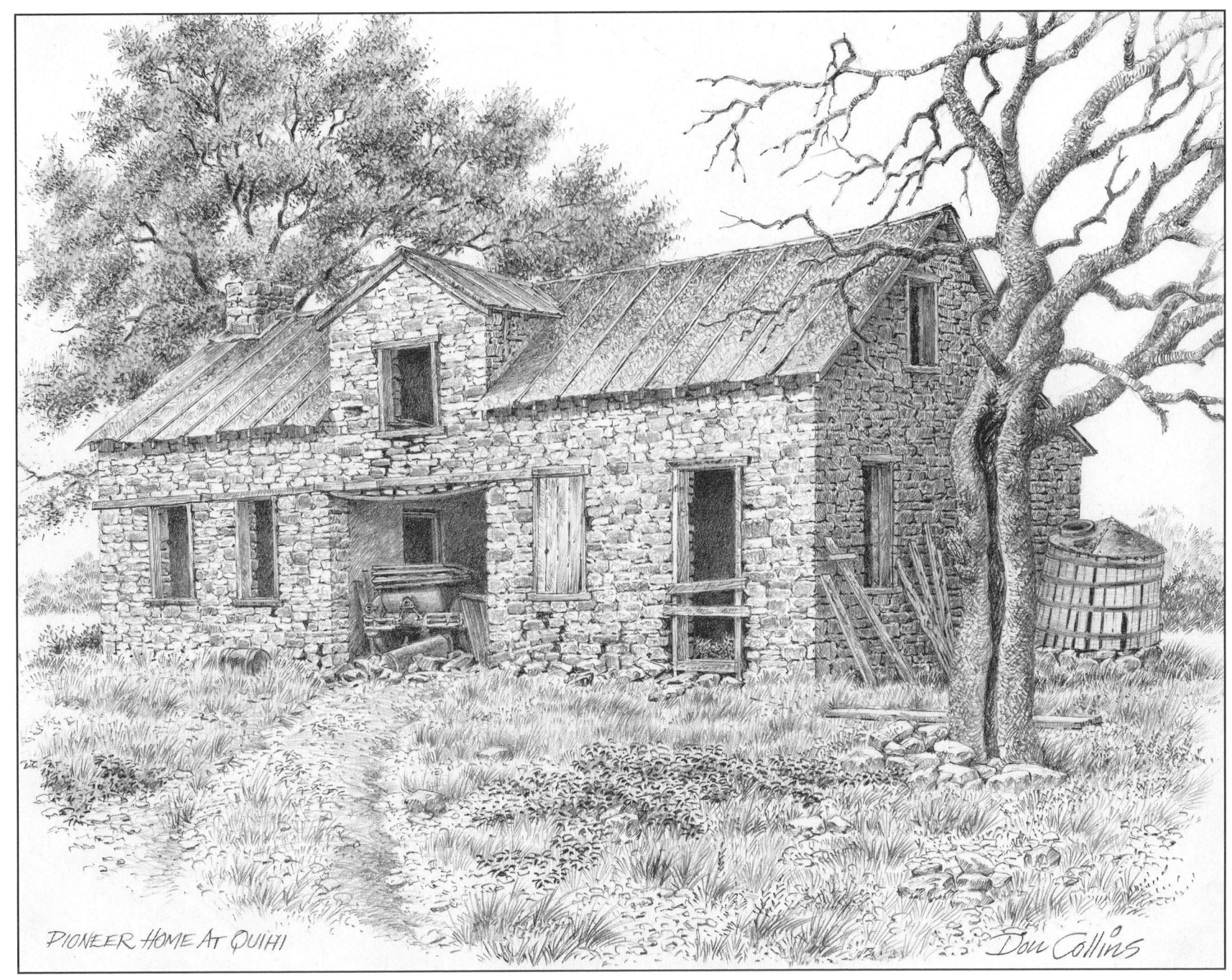

PIONEER HOME AT QUIHI

Don Collins

35. Morris Ranch School, Gillespie County.

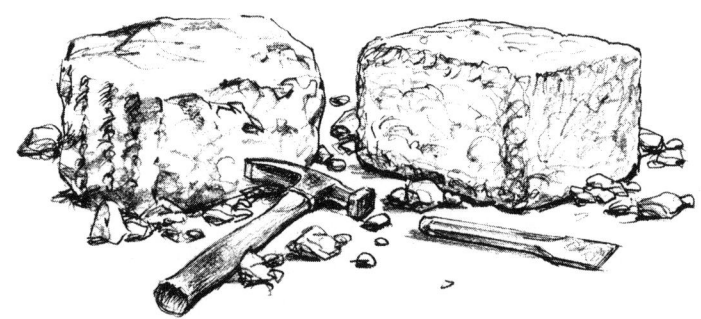

I am always amazed that the old-time artisans, using the most rudimentary tools, could transform raw stone into something as imposing and enduring as the Morris Ranch school.

When I walked up to this school, you can imagine how excited I was. I'd heard about the Morris Ranch School and sought it out. It's a startling sight out in that gentle Hill Country to be going down a country road and to come upon a structure of this size and magnificence. It's got as good a stonework as you're ever going to find in this part of the world. The work was so well done that in spite of its age, the building is standing tall. It is just magnificent. Every stone shows the mark of the mason. They are all shaped and fitted. It is just a tremendous piece of workmanship.

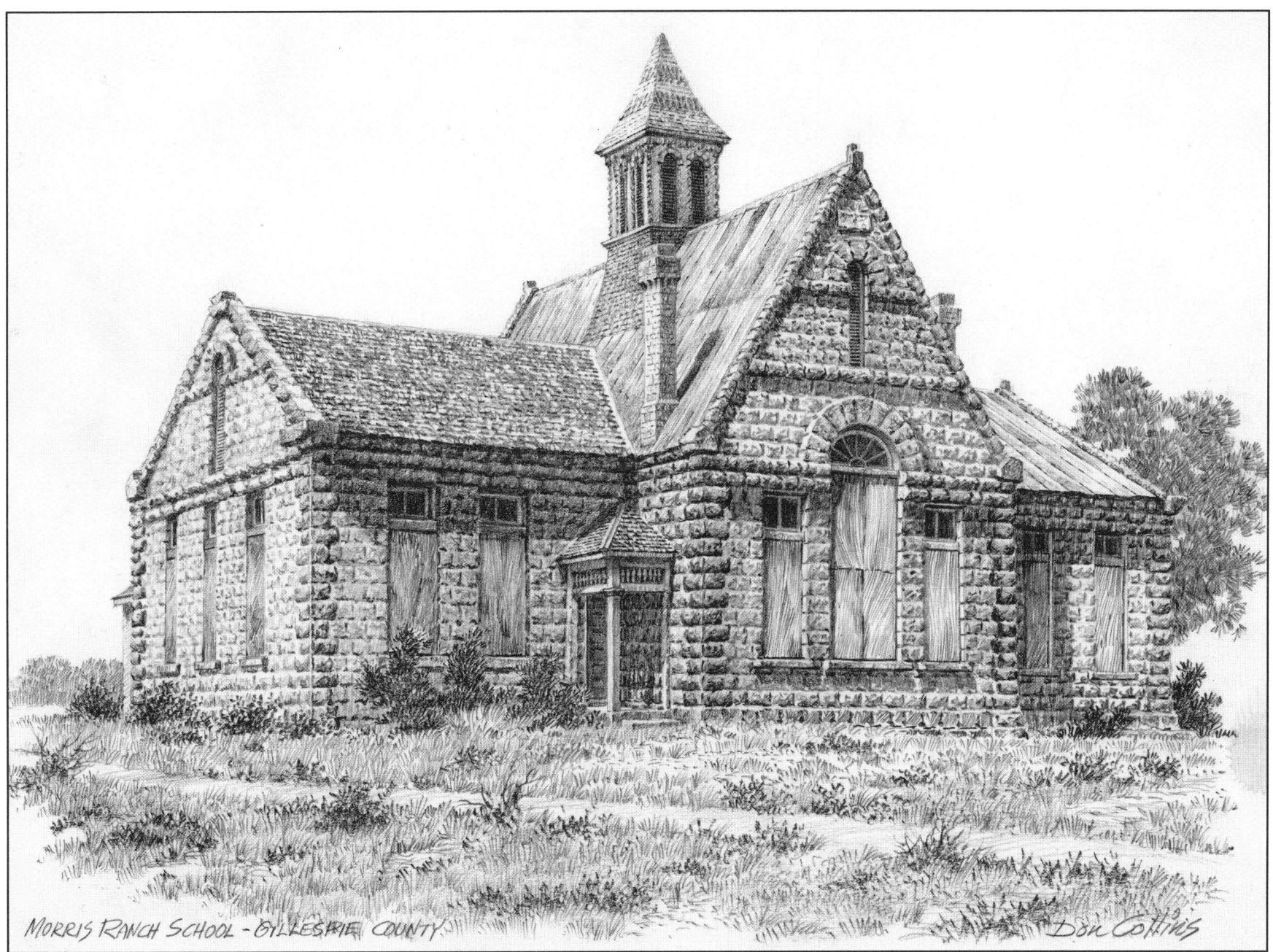

MORRIS RANCH SCHOOL - GILLESPIE COUNTY   Don Collins

36. Water Tower and Wash House, Mason.

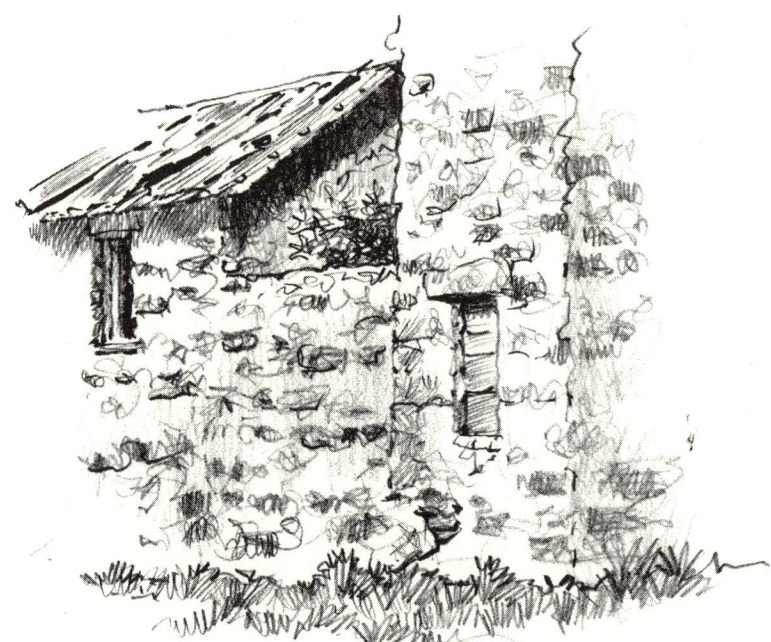

A small mystery ... a look at the other side reveals that the stairs between the tower and building lead to ... nowhere!

I know this is a water tower, but I'm not sure whether what's next door is a wash house. I just think it is. It was in the back yard of a house in Mason. All the elements are there. It's got water and all that. Somebody told me that there were trough-like fixtures inside, but I didn't go in there. The stone is russet, sienna, reddish sandstone, and it made up this very unusual little structure and combination of shapes. A very appealing little building.

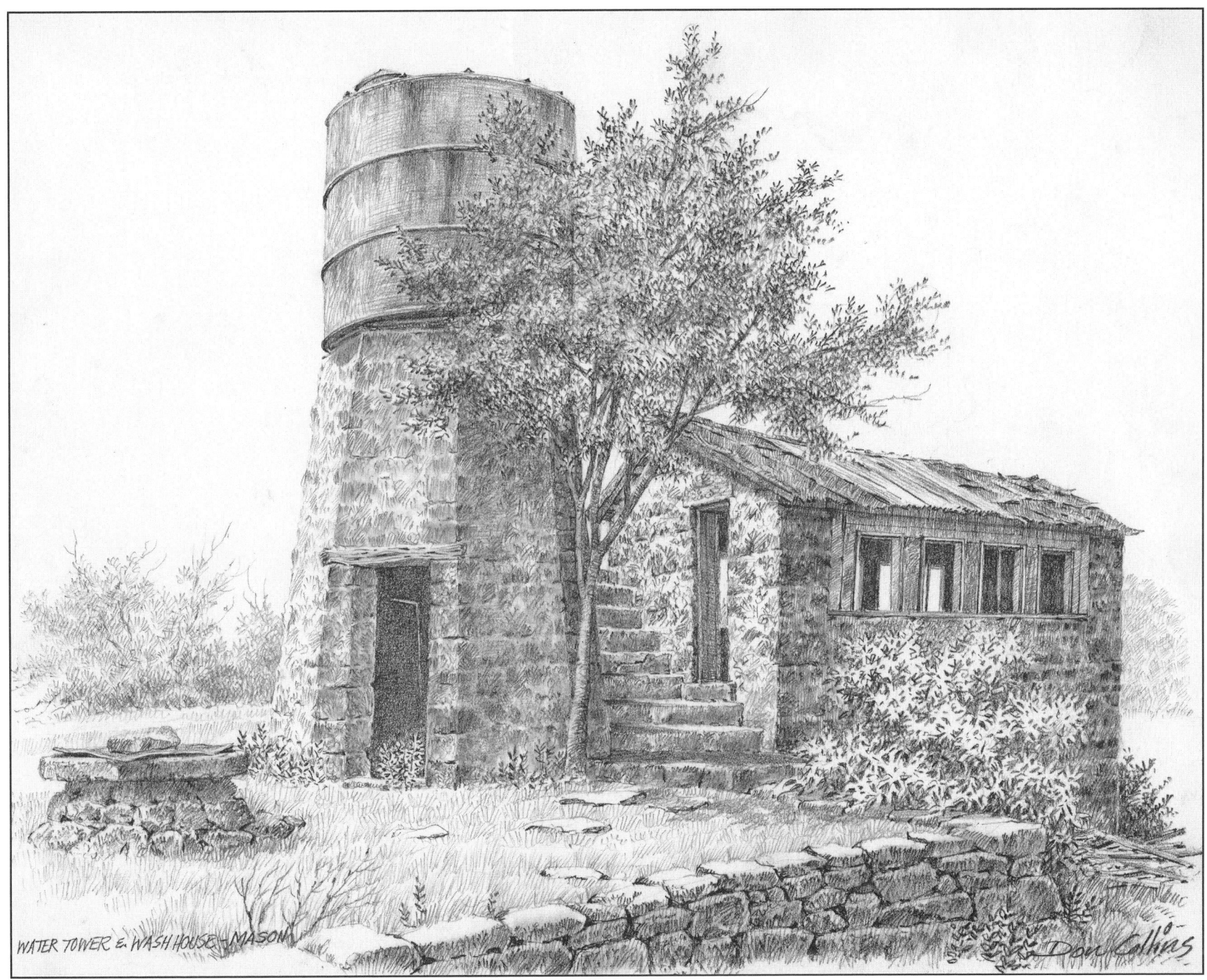

WATER TOWER & WASH HOUSE - MASON   Don Collins

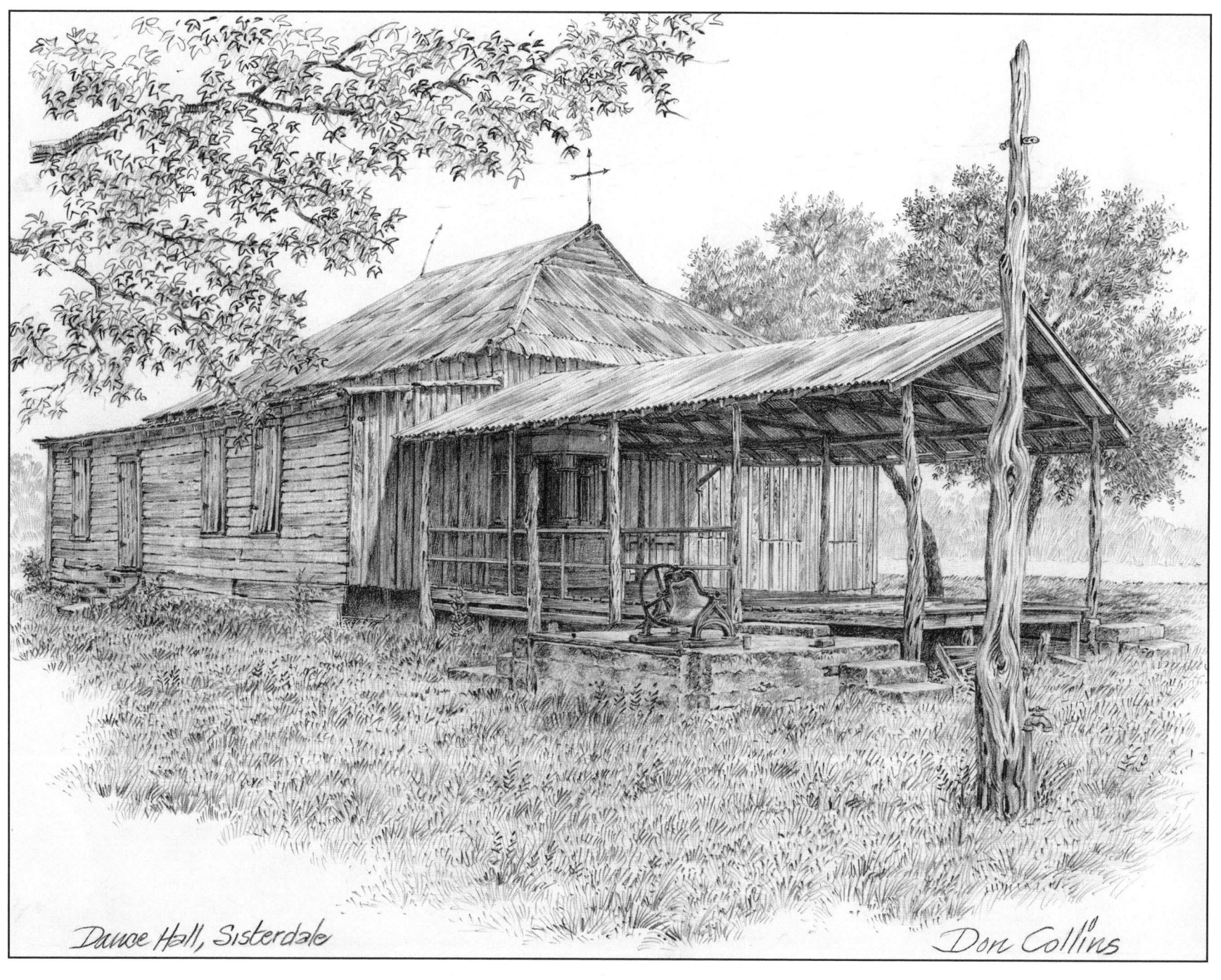

Dance Hall, Sisterdale

Don Collins

37. Dance Hall, Sisterdale.

This is one of my favorites. I can hear the Oom-Pah music right now. This is where all the good things happen at Sisterdale.

When you look at this building, you can see an intriguing element in the entryway. It has a formal ticket booth that they got from some place—a furniture-quality ticket booth made out of polished, varnished, shaped lumber. I suppose to get inside the big barn there you had to buy a ticket. The hall is equipped for summertime weather. It has hinged shutters all the way around so they could throw them open to get some fresh air inside.

The entire surroundings there are very serene. Sisterdale is way off of any beaten track. It's got a nice little saloon, bar, and grocery store across the road. A few inhabitants, a few very old houses, grand old trees, and a winery in the old cotton gin. I rang the bell one or two times, trying not to attract too much attention.

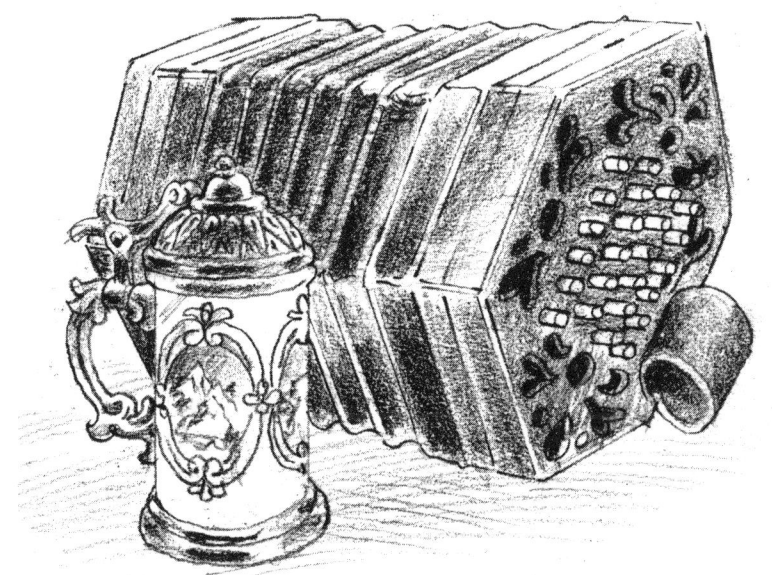

This great old indoor-outdoor dance hall was doubtless the fun center of remote Sisterdale.

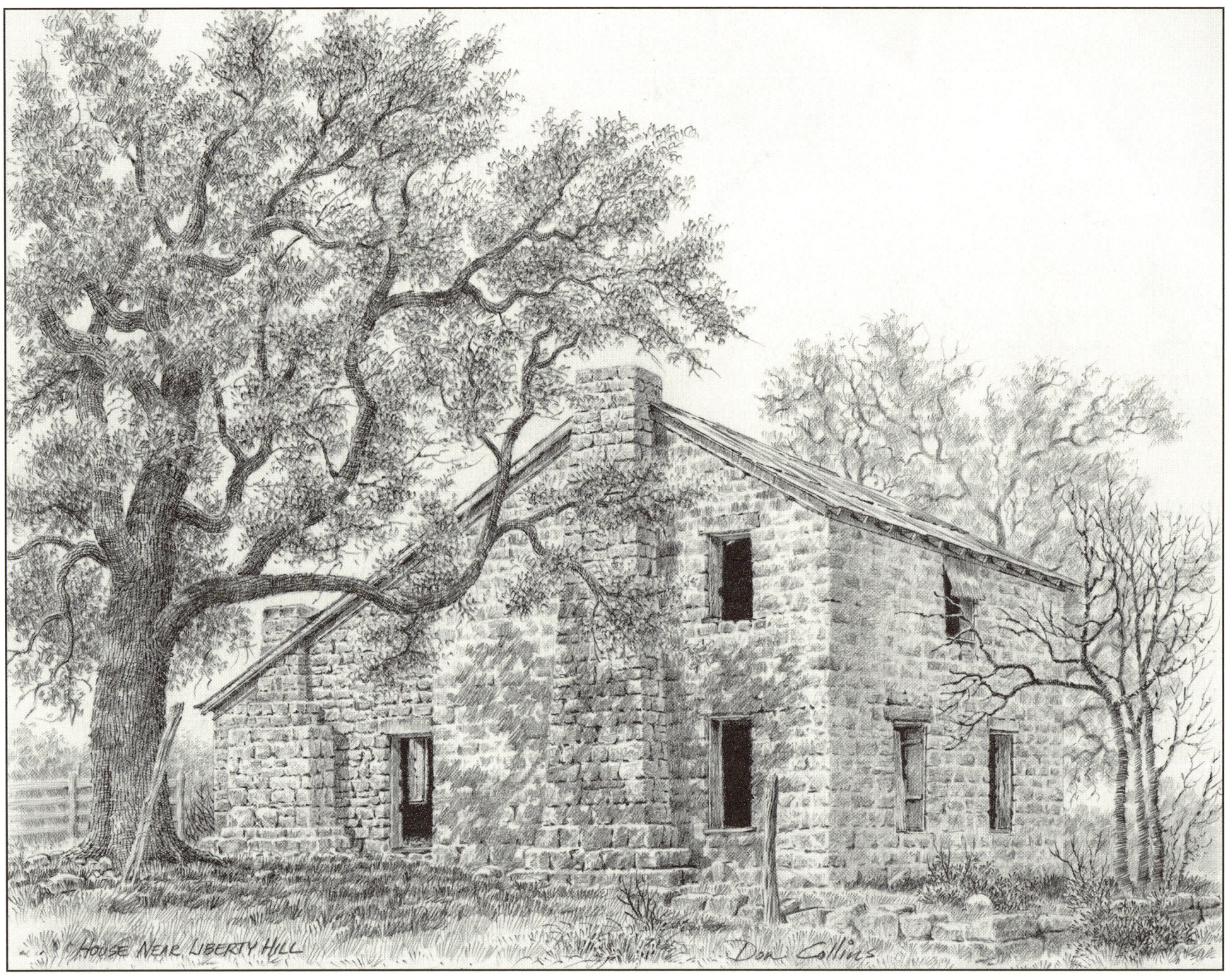

House Near Liberty Hill

Don Collins

38. House near Liberty Hill.

This house is near Liberty Hill, on State Highway 29 west from Georgetown on the road to Burnet. It used to be a little town, but it isn't any more. Instead it's becoming a bedroom community for Austin. When I made this drawing it was still small.

This big, beautiful house sits way up the hill on a winding road near Liberty Hill. I went through my usual process of excitement and headed up there to investigate. Of course, nobody was around; it was totally abandoned. It's a rather large house that shows to have been built in two stages. The stone on the back portion to the left is not cut and dressed by the same masons who built what's on the right, where it's more finished looking. The workman on the left put up a sturdy structure, but he was not nearly as skilled as the guy on the right, or maybe he was just in a hurry. He did, however, manage to put a tremendous cooking fireplace inside of his end. And inside that fireplace is plenty of headroom for a grown man to stand.

The good news on this is that a well-heeled couple looked me up several years after the calendar was made. Excitedly they said, "Somebody showed us this calendar and they thought it was our house and it is. We have gone in there and completely reconditioned and restored and remodeled the house and are living in it." And I looked at it later and it was a fine job of restoration. They saved the house and it's gorgeous. Of course, it has one of the better trees you'll ever see next to it.

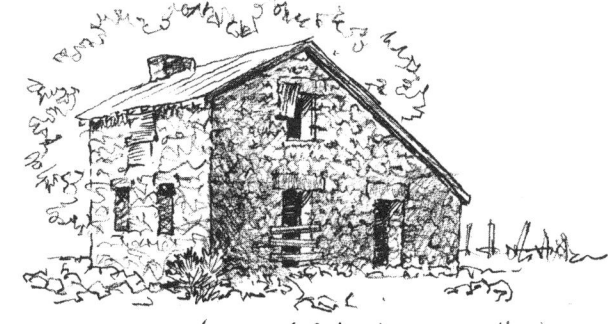

Eighteen-inch thick stone walls, huge lintel blocks and a decent roof allowed this old-timer to survive long enough to enjoy a complete restoration.

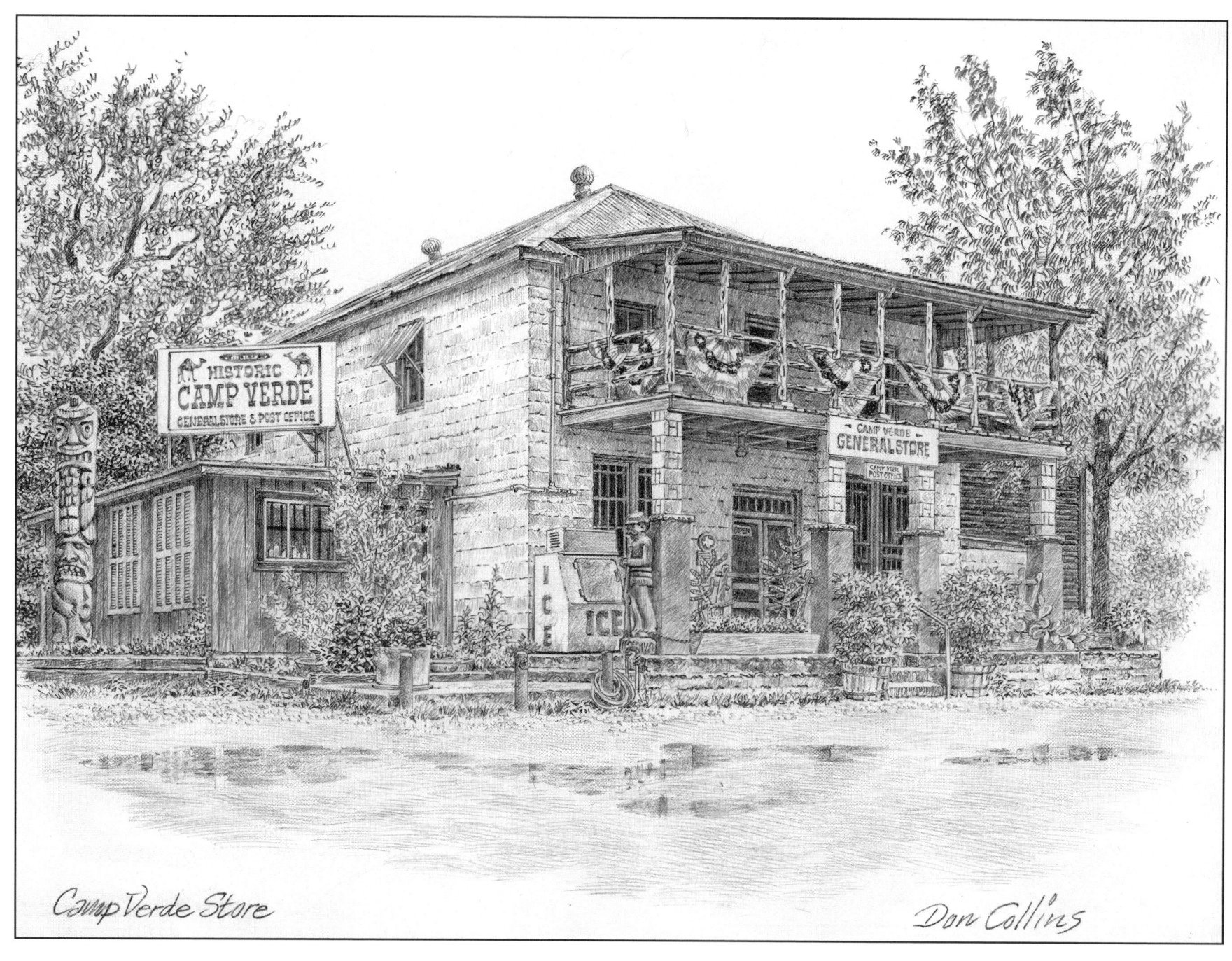

Camp Verde Store

Don Collins

39 . Camp Verde Store.

Camp Verde's primary place in history is that it was where the U.S. Army began its camel experiments in 1856. There's not a great deal to see at the old army post. There are some camel barns and officers' quarters on private property. The biggest visible presence is the great old two-story Camp Verde Store. It is a mellow old building out in a very pleasant part of Kerr County, still doing business. That's where the locals around there can get their necessities. The banners stay up there permanently; this is not the Fourth of July. The proprietor celebrates all year long. The place has some interesting touches. He's collected a wooden Confederate soldier. And then he's got a totem pole a long way from Alaska. An old country mercantile store, one of the few that is still actually in operation.

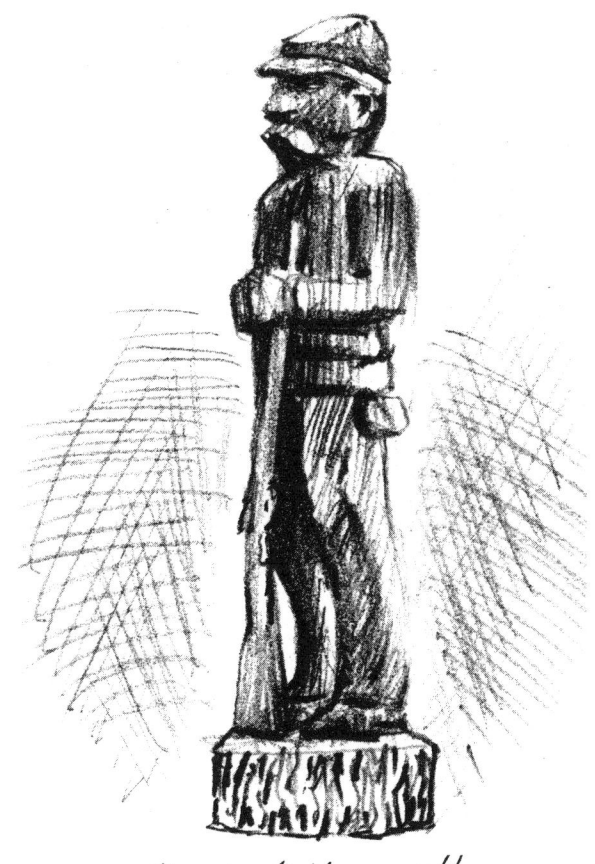

*Sturdy civil war soldier
stands guard outside
Camp Verde store.*

40. Barn at Burnet.

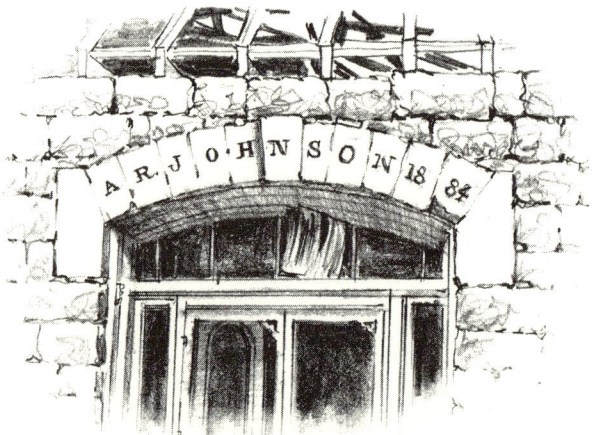

At the home near the barn, the construction date is carefully carved over the doorway.

What a barn! I found this back in the '70s just east of Burnet. Adjacent to the barn stood a rock ruin of the same quality, remains of a large house with a mansard roof, an unusual roof for that part of the world. The house was really in pretty terrible condition. Because the barn still had utility, the later generations had taken pretty good care of it. So I did the barn. I think I did a painting of the barn too.

Several years later I was at the Laguna Gloria Festival art show in Austin and President Johnson's old press secretary, George Christian, came in the booth and introduced himself. He expressed excitement because his grandfather had built the barn. Then he sat down with me and told me more about it. He said the barn was extremely unusual because his grandfather had been in the Civil War and had been blinded. He had been a very active surveyor prior to the Civil War. He had several sons, and they too had been in the business with him before. Christian told me that his grandfather took up surveying again. He had such a mathematical mind that the boys would run the lines and call out the numbers and the unsighted grandfather would make

the calculations in his head. The old man pursued that for another ten or twelve years with his sons, and he surveyed a large swath of West Texas. George said that his grandfather and one of his former slaves built the barn after the war. Now how they pulled this off, I don't know, but they wound up with an enormous, sturdy, good-looking barn that is still in use today.

The house has been totally restored. Somebody bought the house and put the whole thing back together in proper fashion. It's extremely well done, back to the original. I understand it was a bed and breakfast for a while and may yet be.

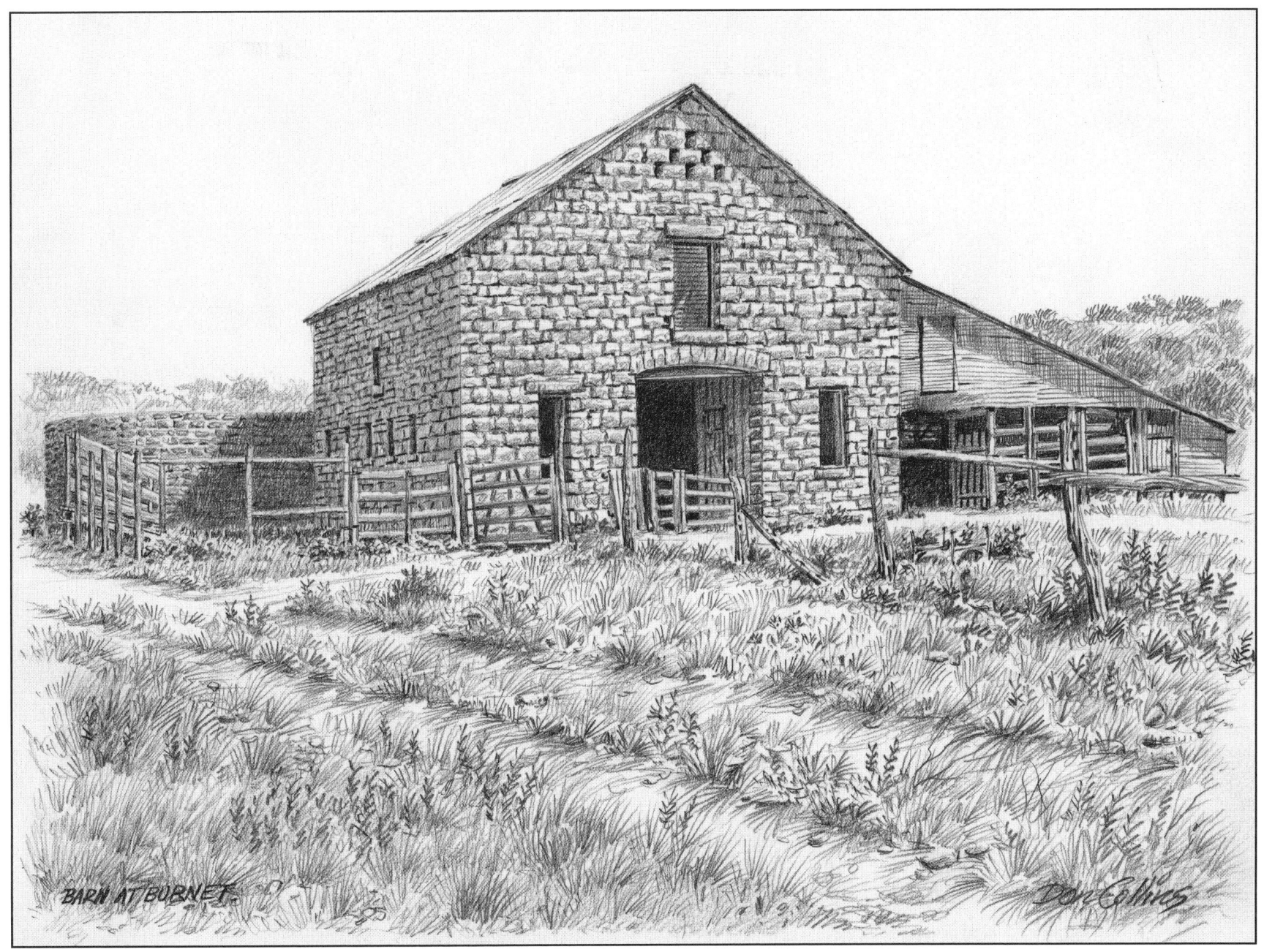

BARN AT BUBNET.

Don Collins

41. Old Bank at Comfort.

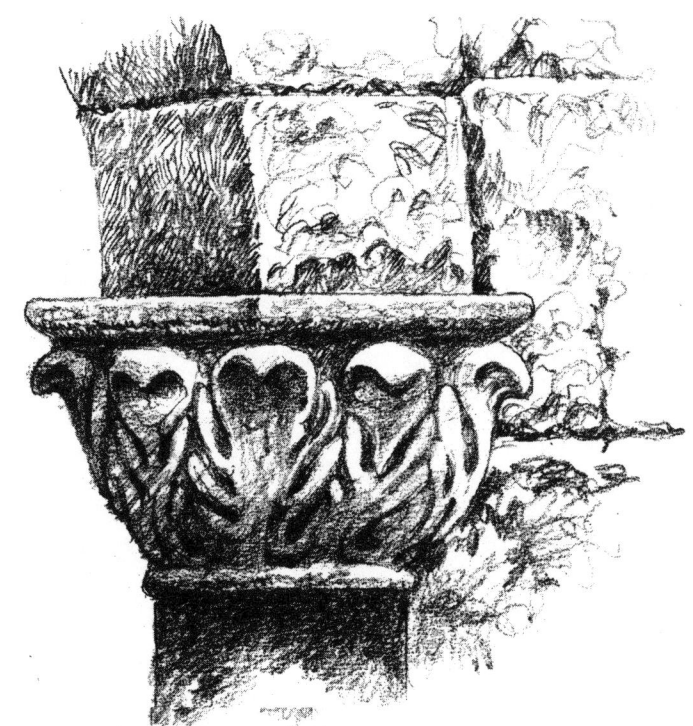

These delicately carved capitals were a nice touch in the midst of all the ruggedly chiseled limestone blocks.

The old bank at Comfort is small but imposing for its size. The builders were expressing wealth and security. It has a few really nice architectural touches. The interesting carved limestone capitals on top of polished granite columns are unusual. It has extremely well done masonry with all sorts of little elements and arches. All in all, a sturdy, imposing structure. It expresses exactly what it is. If you didn't know, you would still identify it as a bank. And it's in good condition.

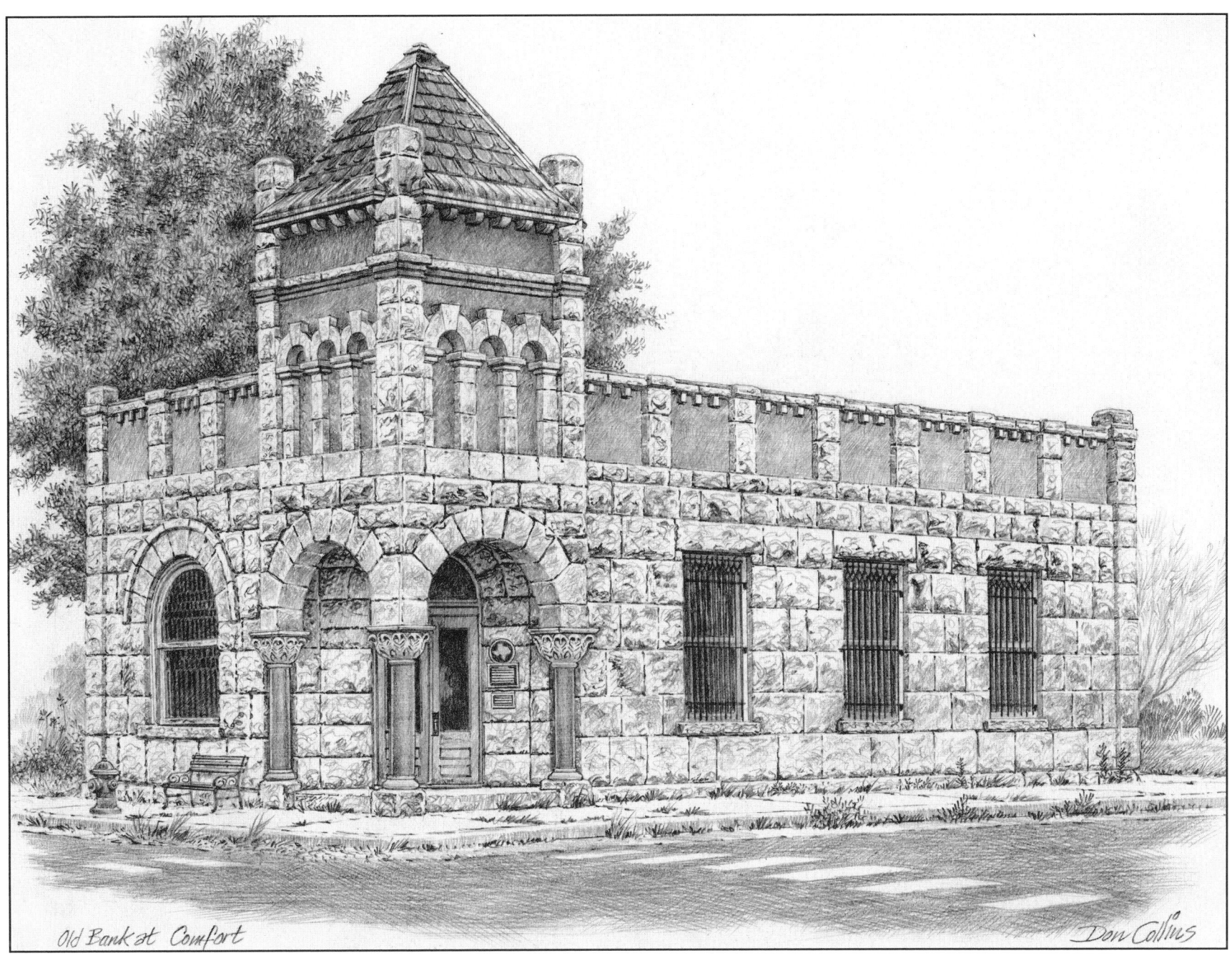

Old Bank at Comfort

Don Collins

42. Barn at Riomedina.

Again this is just a typical old wooden Texas barn. The little ventilation structure on top is something that I see often. A structure like this is exciting for an artist to run across, because it's alive with color, shape, and texture—a challenge in all directions. It has kind of molded itself to the ground. It's on a rise on a hill as you come west into Riomedina from San Antonio.

You can see that it's leaning in several different ways, but it doesn't appear to be falling down. It just kind of made itself comfortable on top of that hill. It's still there as far as I know and still in some use. Over the years you can see the efforts that have been made as things rotted away, slipped away, fell off, blew off. There's years of patching here and shoring up there—a lot of evidence of not enough care but effort to keep it going anyway.

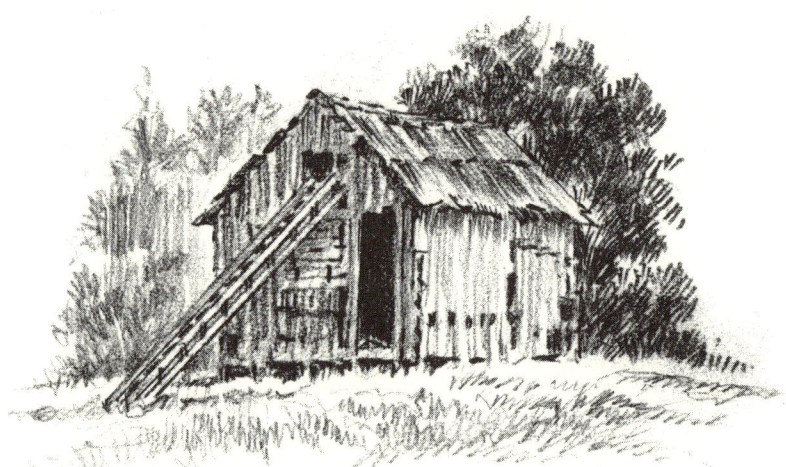

Just South of the barn is another, smaller one, patched up, propped up, and not in much better condition.

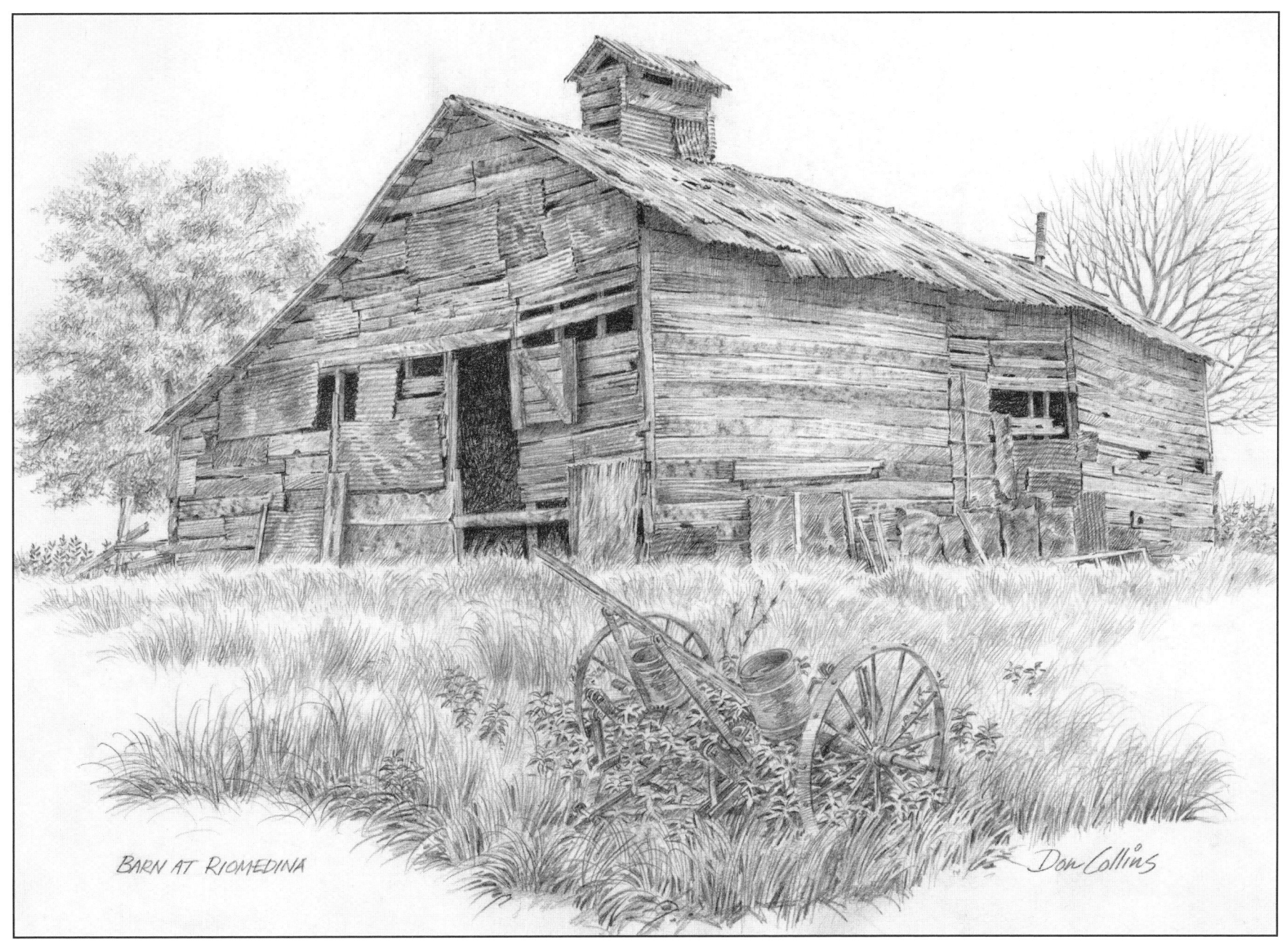

BARN AT RIOMEDINA

Don Collins

95

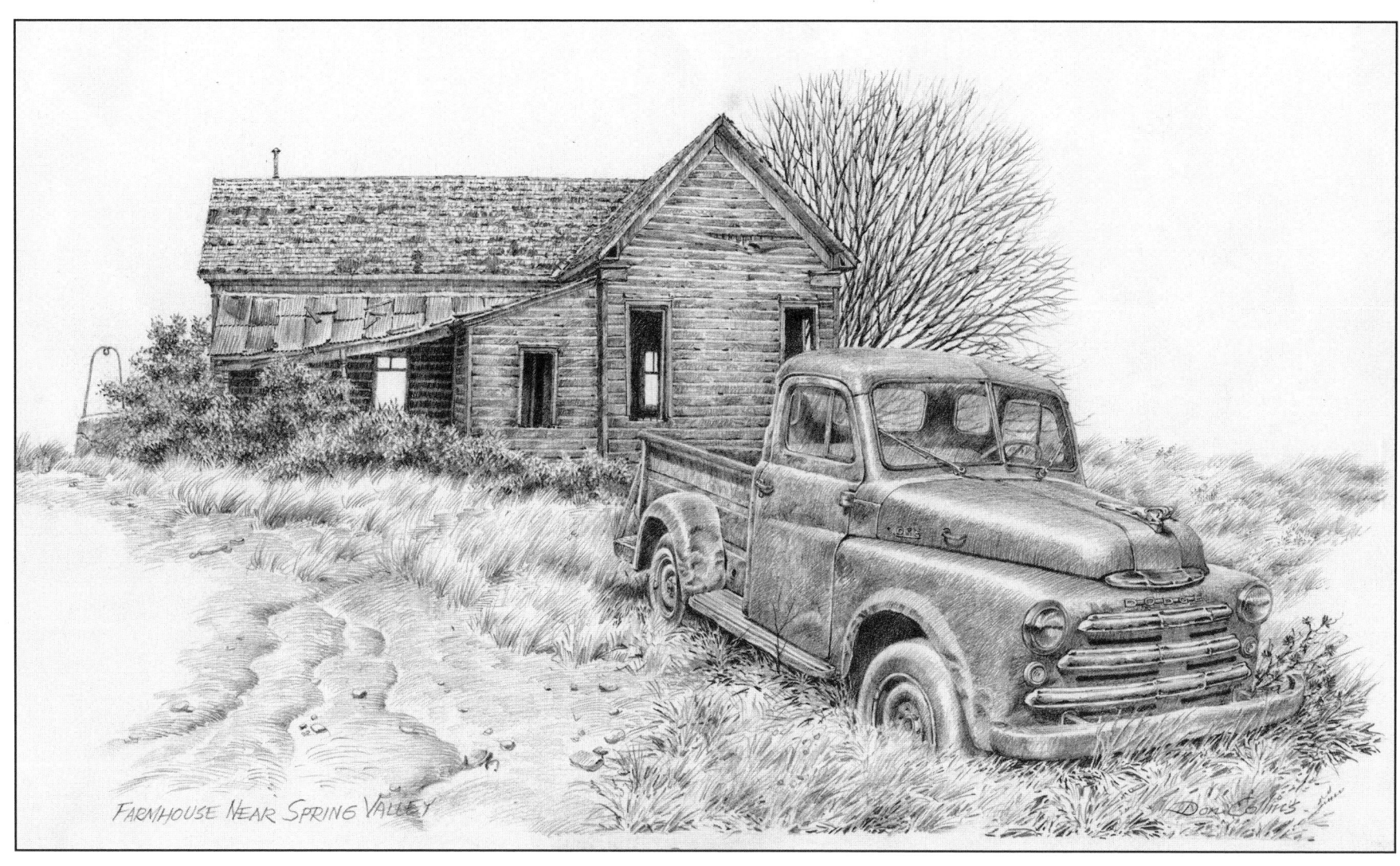

Farmhouse Near Spring Valley

43. Truck and House, Spring Valley.

The place doesn't show any notable architecture, but it evokes emotion because it's an old, tired farmhouse on the way out. It has a cistern with an iron hook over it to hold the bucket and all that. And you can imagine all the activity that once took place here. It was in a beautiful area on State Highway 71 in Llano County on the way toward Brady. On my last trek out that way, the house was gone.

Here's where a little selfishness comes in. That's my old '49 Dodge truck in the picture. I acquired this one-ton pickup in 1981. My daughter Amy was sixteen when she and I trekked up to Arkansas and got it from a retired farmer up there, and I've had it ever since. I still have it. I just had to have some excuse to put my truck in a picture, so that's what I did. I like the combination of elements there, an old farmhouse and an old truck, so I managed to get the two of them together.

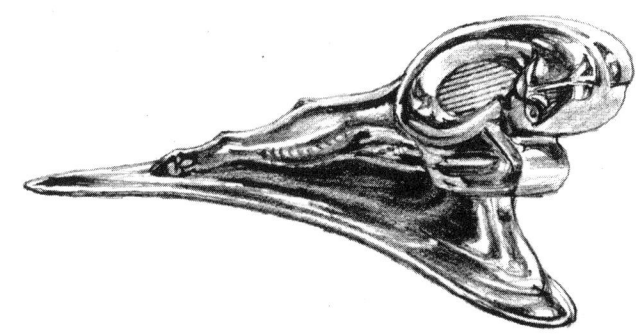

The hood of the clunky old '49 Dodge is graced by a startlingly modern 'ram' ornament.

PART FOUR

The Panhandle Plains

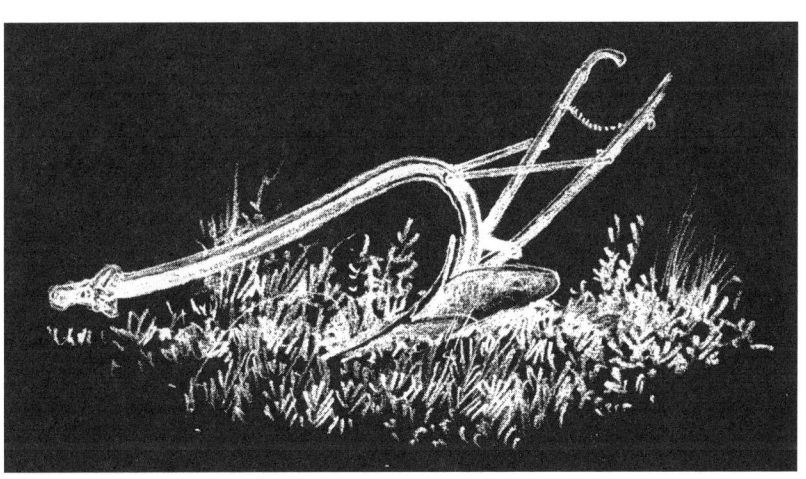

44. Former Courthouse, Rayner, Stonewall County.

I know very little about the courthouse in Rayner except that it was yet another case where a town lost the county seat. Here in Stonewall County, Aspermont, nearer the center of the county, became the seat of government in 1898, leaving Rayner to wither away. The courthouse didn't fall into disrepair as many did but instead was taken over as a ranch headquarters. At the time I saw it, it appeared to prosper. It looks like a courthouse misplaced out in the middle of nowhere. A lot of cows, not a lawyer in sight!

The Rayner courthouse looms up impressively out of the flat brush-covered West Texas terrain.

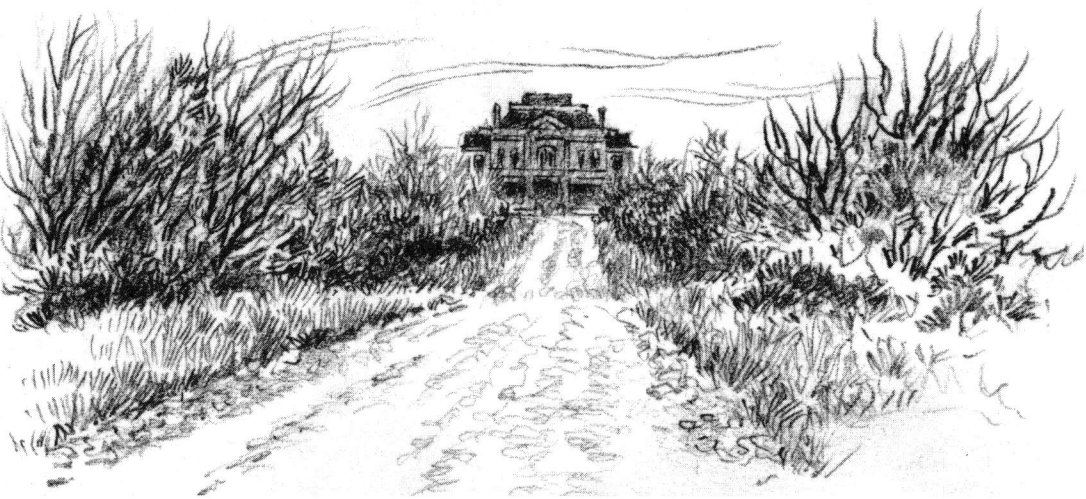

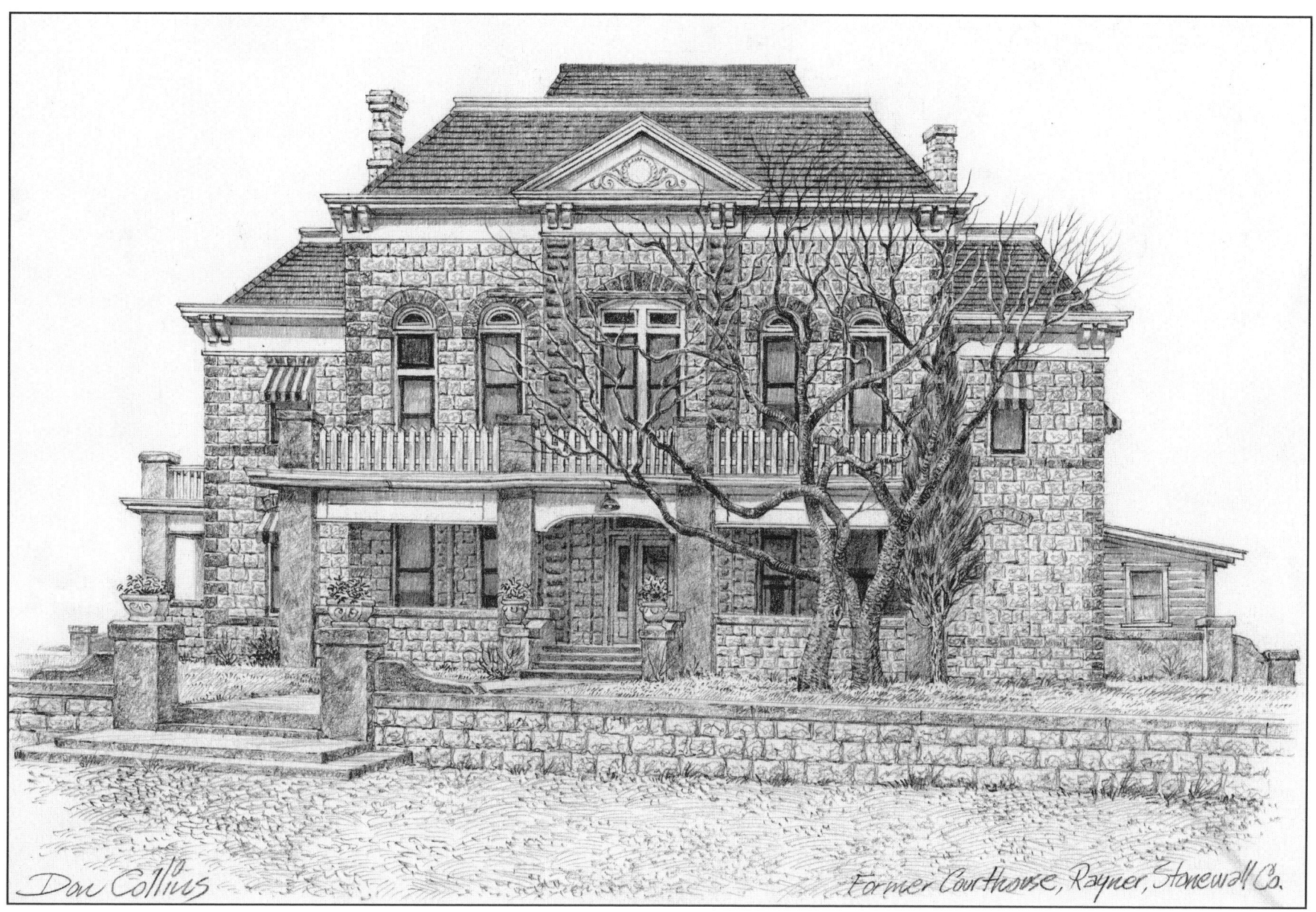

Don Collins

Former Courthouse, Rayner, Stonewall Co.

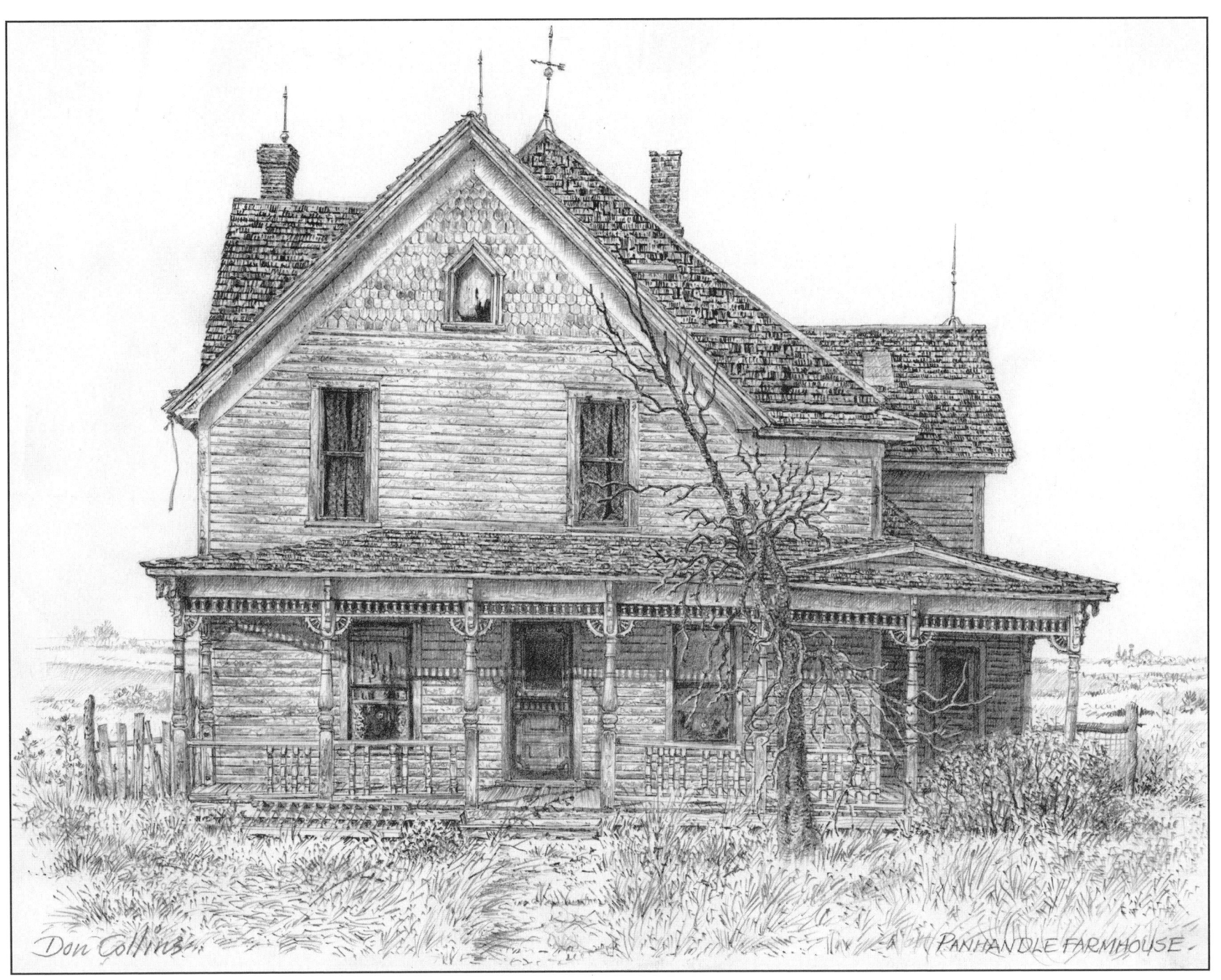

Don Collins. PANHANDLE FARMHOUSE.

45. Panhandle Farmhouse.

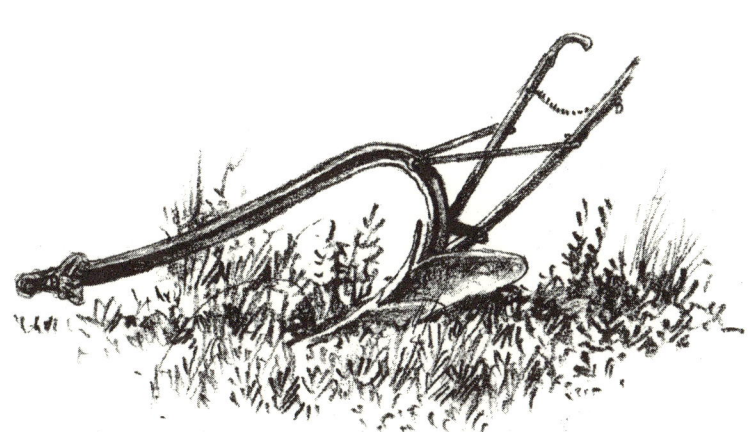

The plough that broke the plains?
Amid the usual agricultural
debris – this graceful old sod
breaking plow.

I could not retrace my steps to this house if I had to. It was somewhere up on the plains. I would say the nearest identifiable town would be Floydada, because I had relatives there. I always thought the region was kind of bare of anything that an artist would like to look at, and I still think so. But, during one foray out in that part of the world I was driving down a country road, part of that square grid of country roads that they have out there, and I came across this old house. Apparently it had been a very prosperous place at one time, and there were a bunch of abandoned farm buildings around it, all out in the middle of a cotton field. It didn't appear to me that it could have ever been a very inviting place to live, but that's from a guy who comes from where there are hills and trees. At one time it must have been fancy; there was a little shingled gable, decoration on top of the chimneys, and nice lightning rods. I'm sure it was a nice house when it was first built there, but that's long since gone.

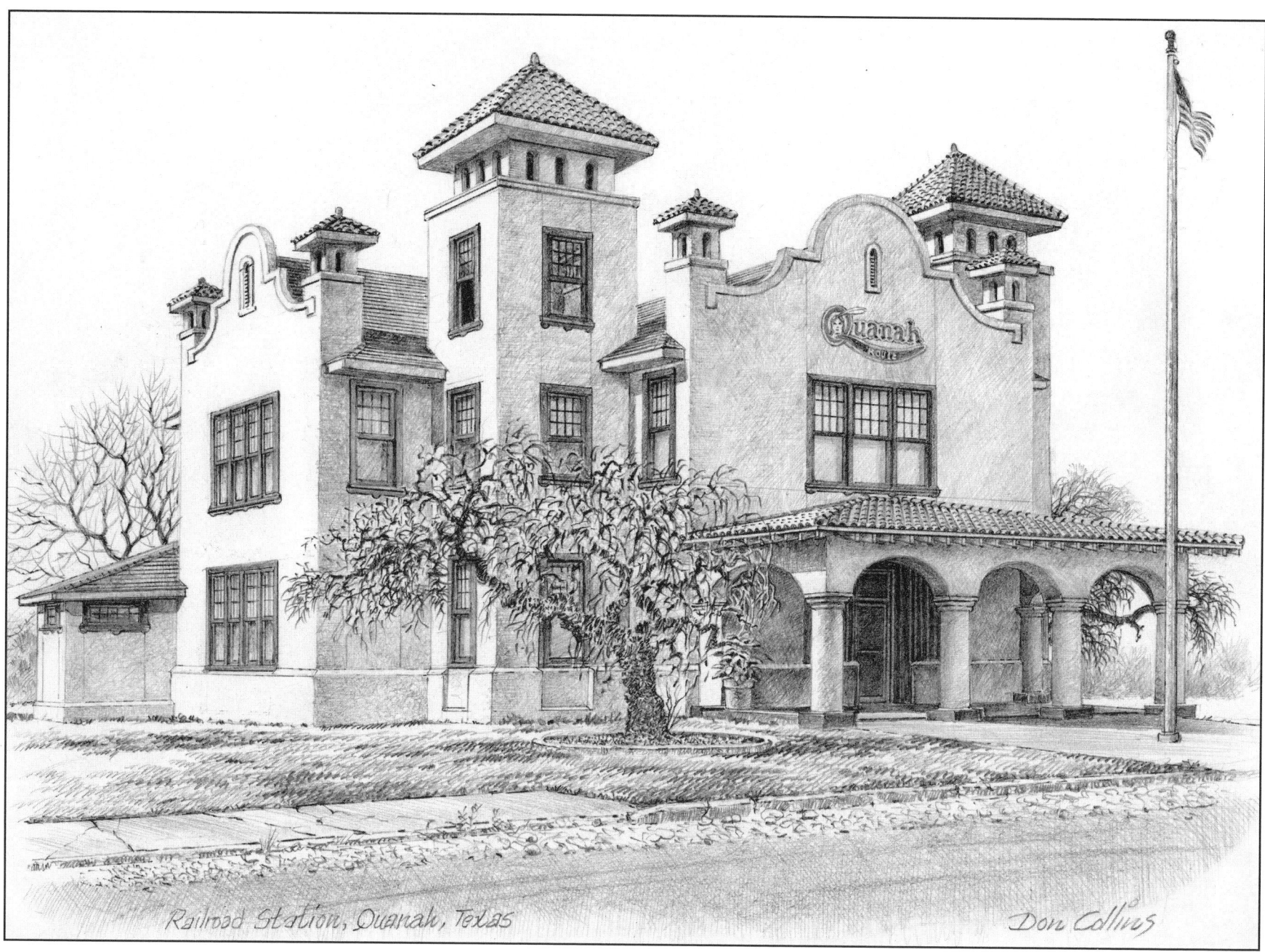

Railroad Station, Quanah, Texas

Don Collins

46. Railroad Station, Quanah, Texas.

You won't believe it, but I found this on the Internet. I was deliberately looking for railroad stations. This is the depot for the Quanah, Acme and Pacific in the town of Quanah. It is quite a handsome railroad station. I was surprised by the elegance of the thing. It's a very good looking little whitewashed building in good condition.

They used good architects, C.H. Page and Son of Austin. They were noted for high quality buildings. As a matter of fact, the firm is still in business. Today it's Page, Sutherland, Page. They're still going strong after like a hundred years or so.

I made a deliberate run up to Quanah to pick up that railroad station.

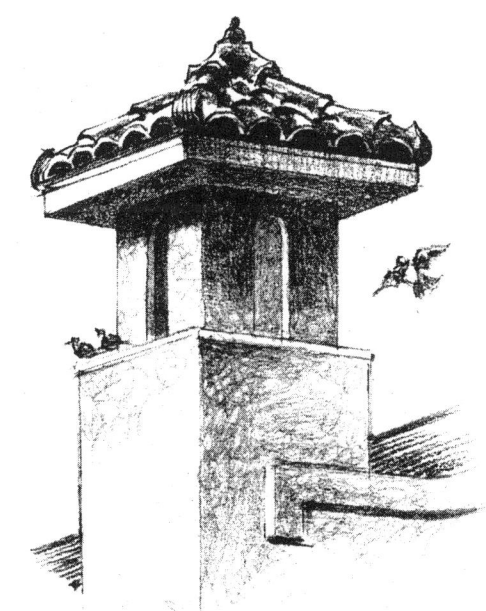

Wearing it's age well, the handsome Quanah, Acme, and Pacific station is remarkably well preserved.

47. Abandoned Panhandle Feed Mill.

Well, my memory fails me, because I went with my friend, Bill Barrick, on an art-seeking expedition. He is absolutely convinced this is in Albany and I am convinced it is in Dumas. We've been having an argument about it for two years. At one time I had it labeled Dumas and I erased it and put a generic name on there so I wouldn't have to get into a fight with anybody about it.

This mill provides wonderment to the artist. It's all metal, and it's corroded and rusted into a medley of colors. And then, of course, there are textures and shapes. It is just a myriad of spidery little tubes and pipes and things leading in all directions—a major challenge to draw and paint. I was happy to draw it, but I don't think I ever want to paint it.

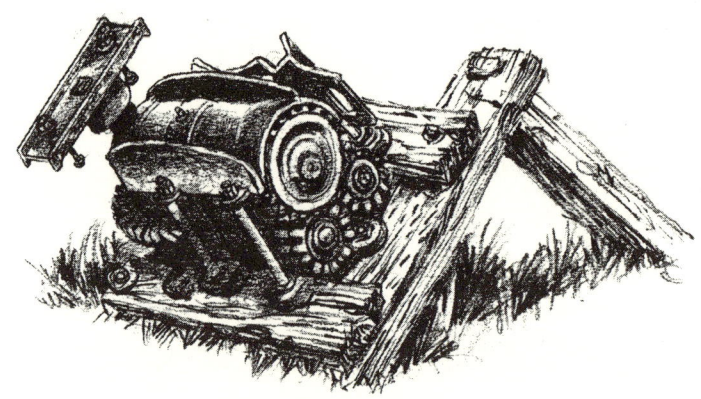

Whatever it's purpose, this interesting old piece of junk, like the rest of the mill, appears to have seen it's day.

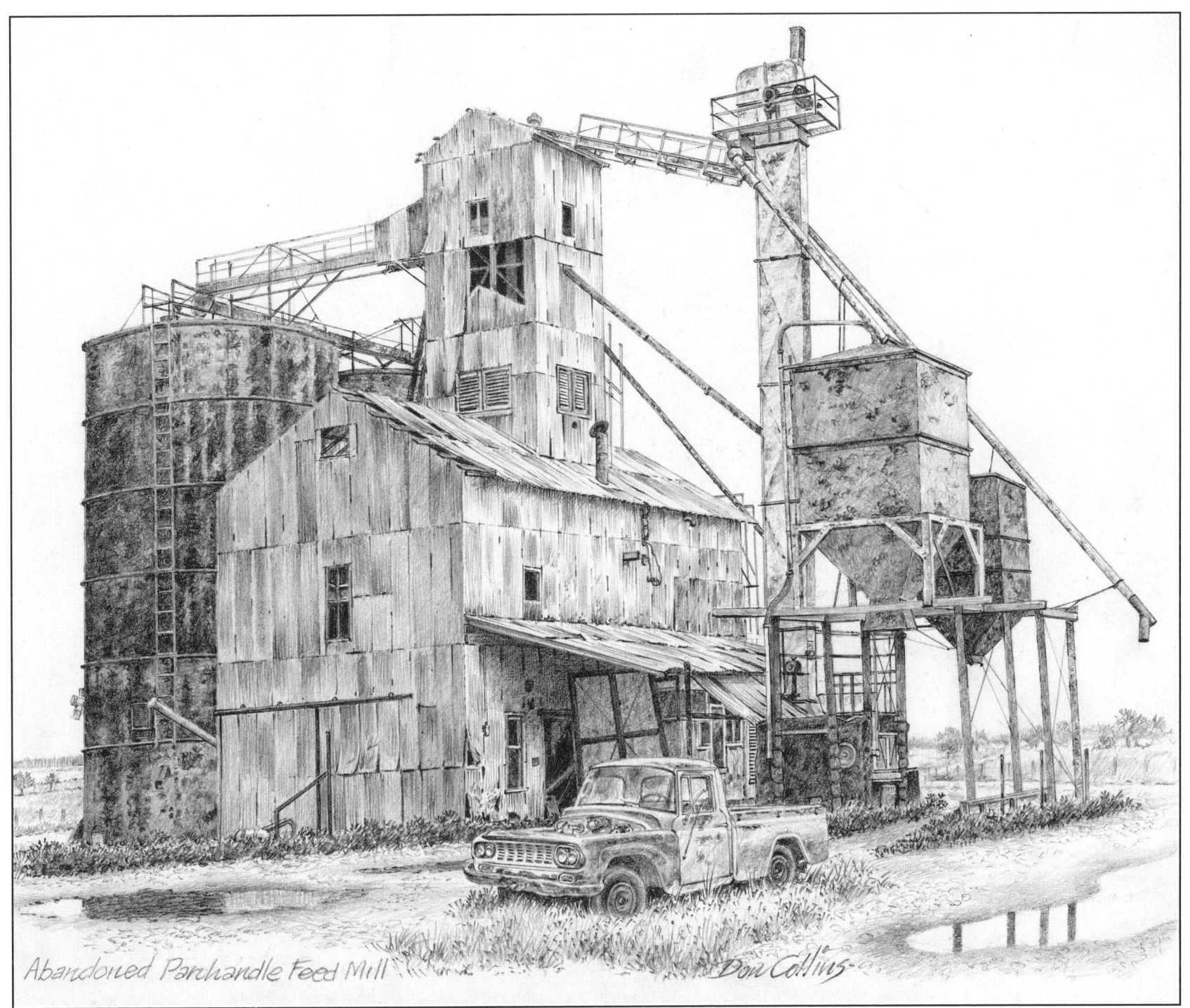

Abandoned Panhandle Feed Mill

Don Collins

PART FIVE

West Texas

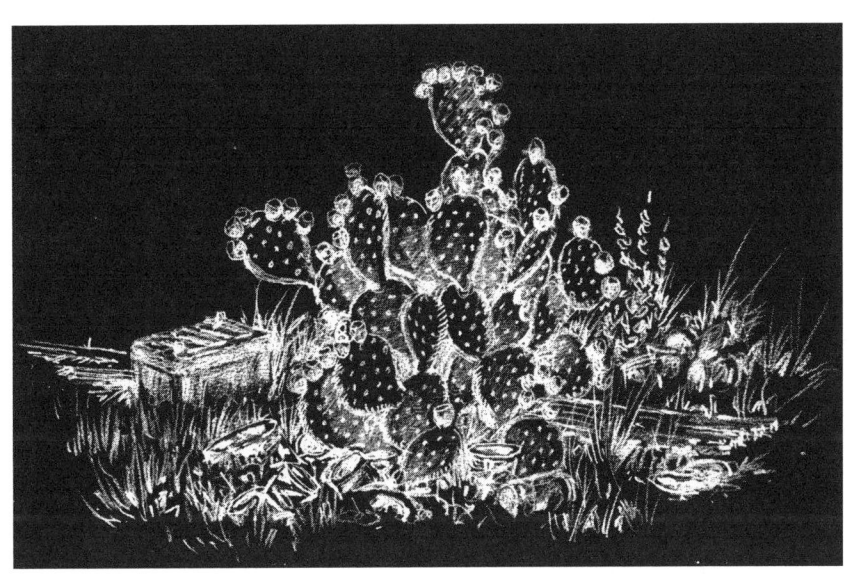

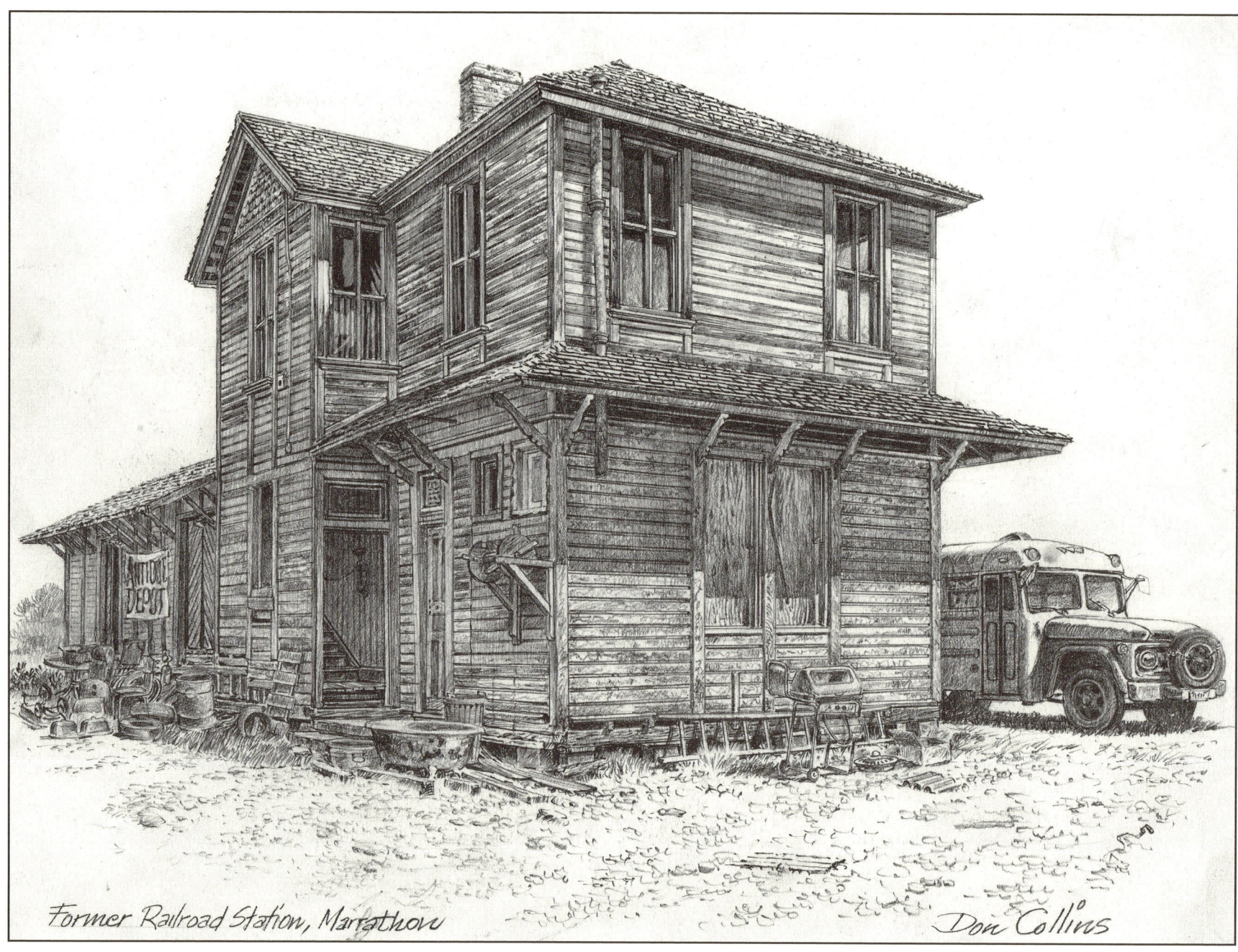

Former Railroad Station, Marathon

Don Collins

48. Former Railroad Station, Marathon.

The Marathon station has been moved up the highway perhaps a quarter of a mile from its original site. The owner, an amiable, bearded, shaggy individual, converted it into what he calls an antique store. I'd call it a junk store. The drawing eliminates two-thirds of the mass of stuff that he has assembled around there just so you can see the building. The proprietor was pleased to show us around, to take us to the old railway company apartment upstairs. It had barren, sparse living quarters up there. The other end of the building was the former freight depot, with the major doors. The loading dock has been stripped away. We are looking at the back of the station, the part that did not face the railroad. It's a common frame building, but typical of the railway stations in that part of the state.

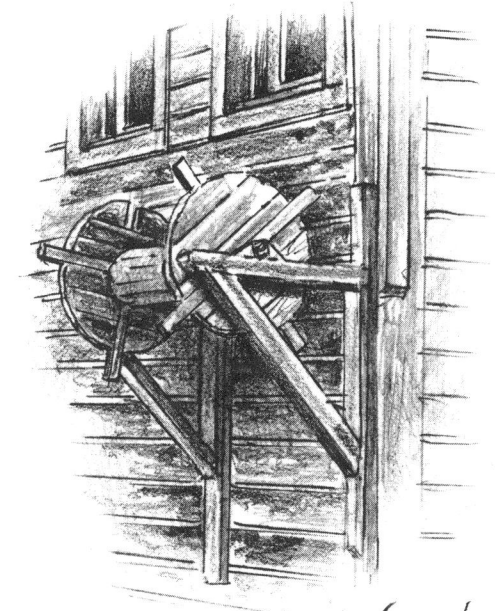

The old coal burning trains left a trail of sparks behind, so a convenient hose reel was a necessity.

49. Fort McKavett Ruins, ca. 1969.

Fort McKavett, northwest of Junction, is an interesting place. It kind of breathes of the Indian wars and what went on in that part of the state in the 1870s and 1880s. There are a lot of ruins out there. It has been taken over by the state and restored, but as an artist I don't find the restoration nearly as interesting as the former ruins.

This house appears to be an officer's quarters. There were barracks buildings there too, built much larger for the troops. Since it went to the lowest bidder, the stonework is not of the highest quality. You see irregular stones. They just fit them together without shaping them greatly. This place was way out on the far reaches of the frontier where danger lurked.

A number of my friends and I had a deer lease at Sonora. This was on the way, and a little off the road, but we would dodge off the road and go there on every trip. At that time there was a saloon operating in one end of a barracks building, and the keeper, a woman, had one of the early metal detectors. She spent all of her time out detecting things, and she had a vast collection of bullets and harness and belt buckles and quite a few weapons. It was a treasure trove of old things she had dug up all over the place. We always enjoyed that, stopping in and having a beer and looking at all the good relics.

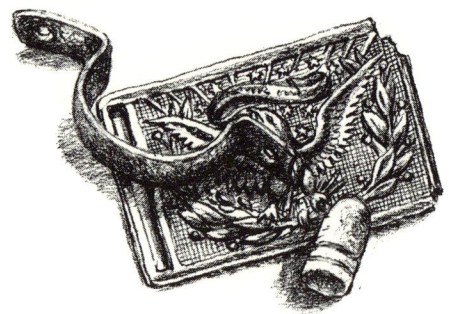

Before Fort McKavett was returned to government control and became a state historic site, the area was rich in artifacts from the Indian wars.

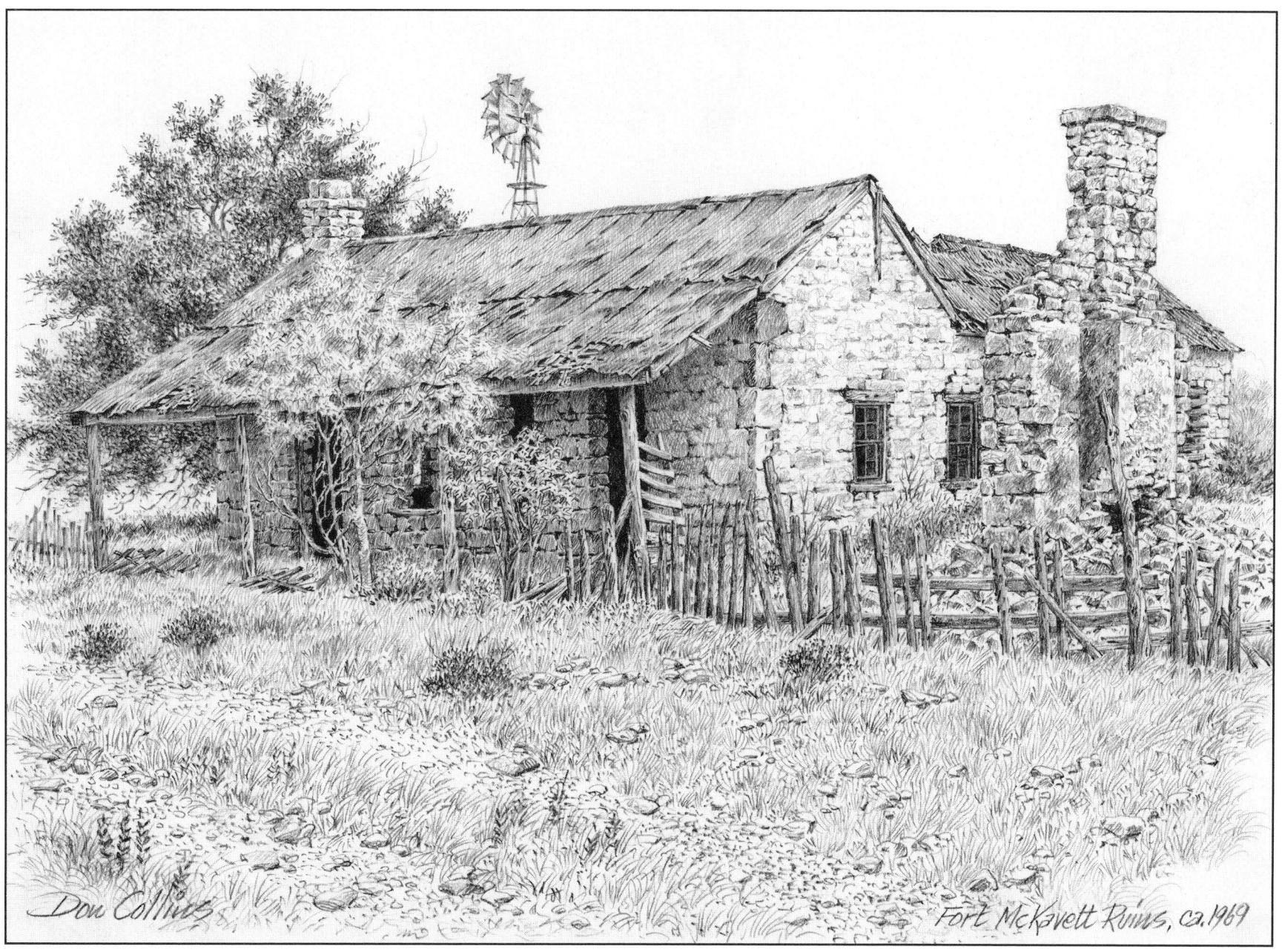

Don Collins

Fort McKavett Ruins, ca. 1969

Ifound Sherwood as a result of a search, a conscious quest for former county seats. The old town lies just a few miles southwest of San Angelo, and it has an absolutely beautiful old courthouse. It lost out in the voting for the seat of government after several years to Mertzon, which lies just down the road. I don't think the latter has any building of any consequence, at least that I can see. From an aesthetic perspective, they would have done better to stay in Sherwood.

The old courthouse remains as a community center and seems to be pretty well maintained. The clock and tower were probably bought off the shelf. That sort of thing was available at the time in that era in catalogs. You could kind of pick and choose your architectural elements. I'm sure that included the little finials on the gables and the odd little pieces on the corners of the building. They all appear to be stamped tin. But anyhow, everything seems to be holding together. It's a fine example of a Texas courthouse that, sadly, never was fully utilized.

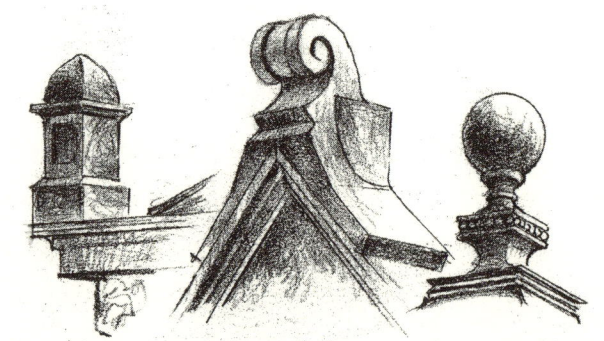

A little of this — a little of that! The embellishments on this imposing building appear to have been chosen out of a builder's supply catalog at random.

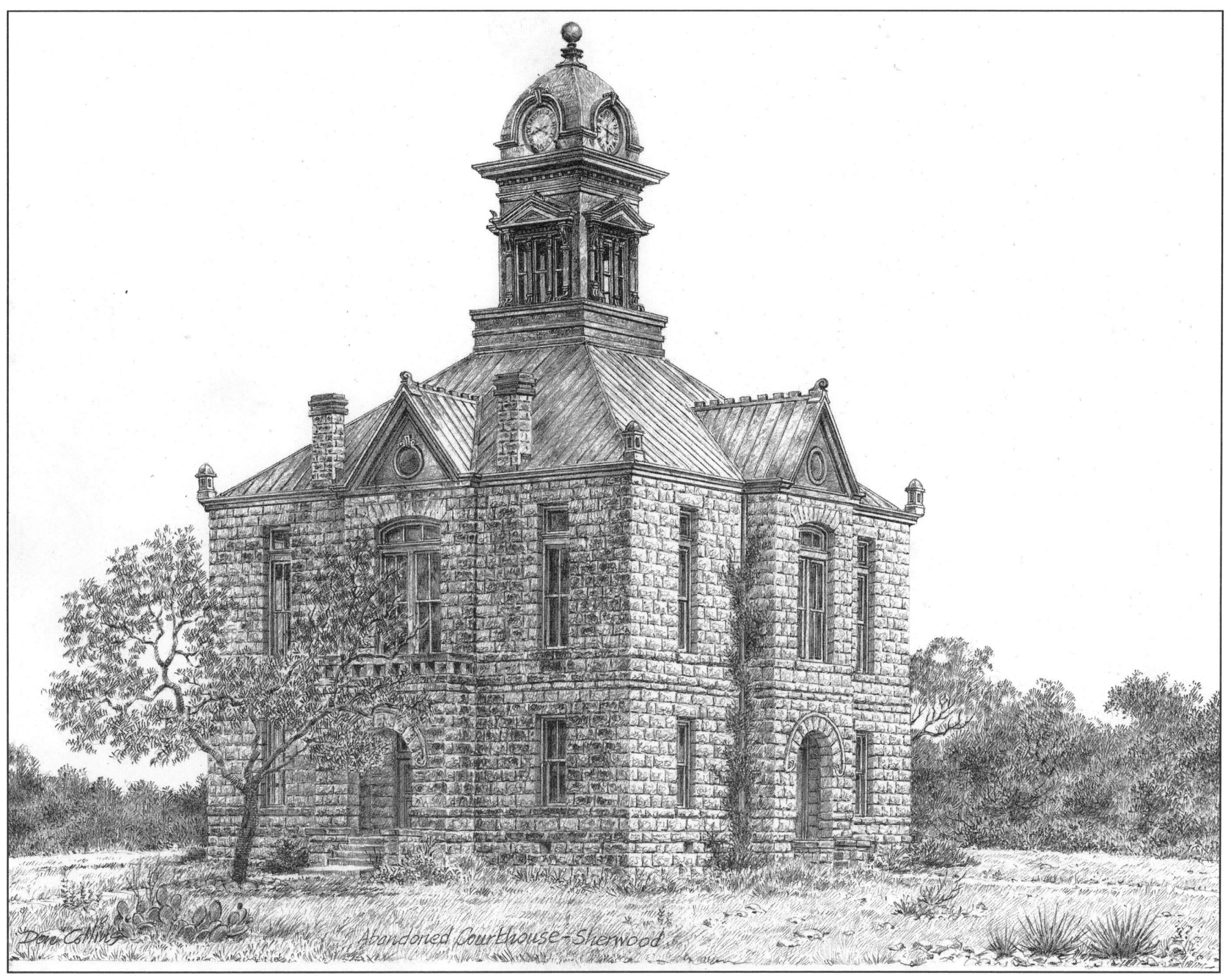

Abandoned Courthouse - Sherwood

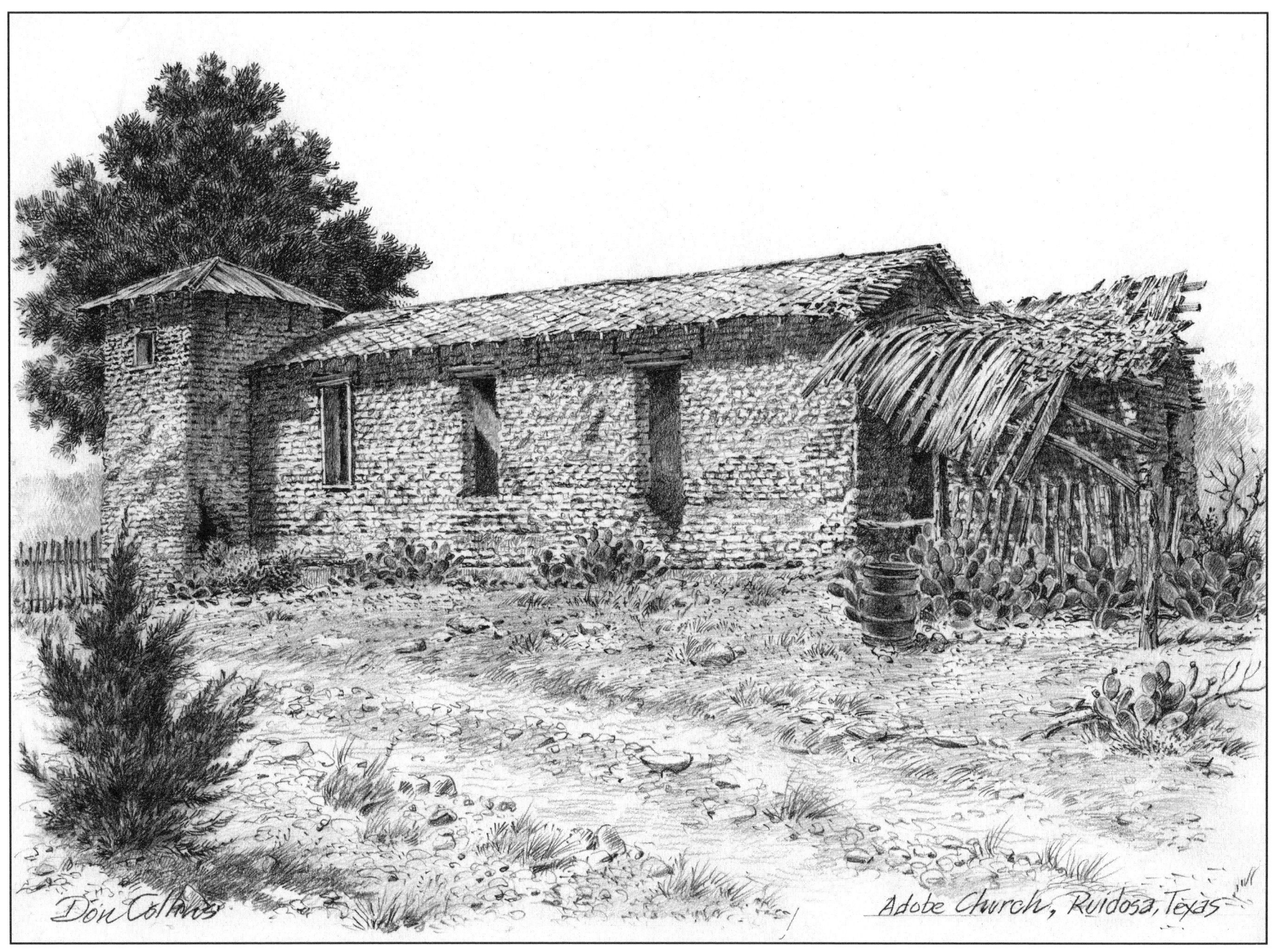

Don Collins

Adobe Church, Ruidosa, Texas

51. Adobe Church, Ruidosa, Texas.

Ruidosa, Texas, as opposed to Ruidoso, New Mexico, lies near the north end of the River Road that begins in Big Bend. About two or three miles past Ruidosa you end up in a guy's back yard at Candelaria. You drive right past this church. On the other end of the sanctuary are two graceful arches. The church is in very dilapidated condition, but I understand that of late there is a movement afoot to save it. This is an isolated building, representative of that part of the world with a really harsh climate and surroundings. It has the soft adobe color and altogether gives the viewer a good experience.

There is very little evidence of active habitation at Ruidosa, though there are plenty of signs that a great many people had tried to live there and given up. There are humble little one- and two-room adobe houses abandoned and melting away all over the place. It's a very hard place to live.

There's a little store adjacent to this church. The lady who runs the store is a trouper for staying there.

I don't see how anybody really quite makes a living at Ruidosa. There must be a lot of people out in the sticks there, enough at least to keep her going.

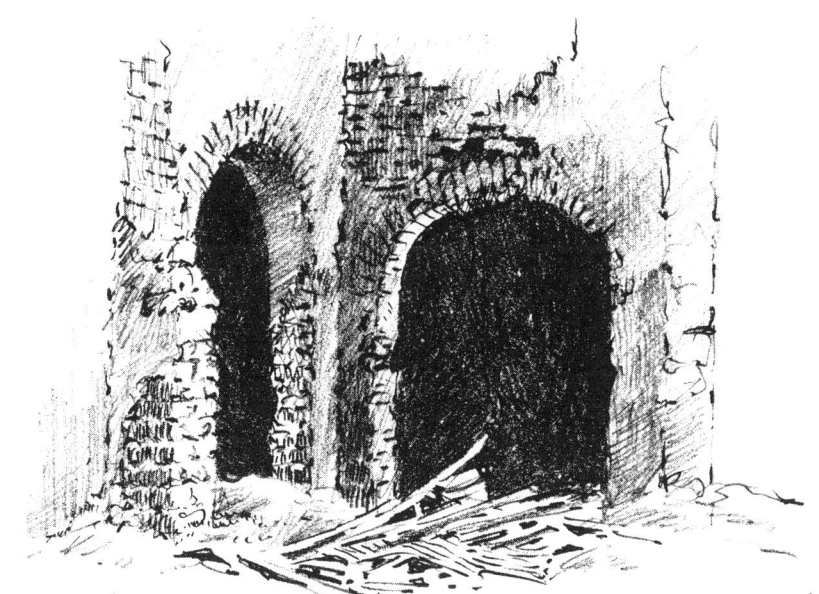

The adobe church at Ruidosa seems to be melting back into the desert.

52. Terlingua Mansion, ca. 1973.

In 1973 I went for the first time to the Terlingua ghost town in the Big Bend country. None of the so-called improvements that have taken place since had occurred. Everything was quiet. Terlingua now is a pretty lively place, and privately owned I think. The history of the quicksilver mining down there is well documented.

This, I think, was the mine owner's house. It has sort of an odd shape, but it's unusual for other reasons too: square columns and arches made of wood. It's striking in the way it's put together. I expect that even in its magnificence years ago this was a pretty tough place to live. The only cool spot would be under that big covered porch. I've since been back a number of times, and the last time the building was not nearly in this good a condition. So I'm glad that I got at least this much.

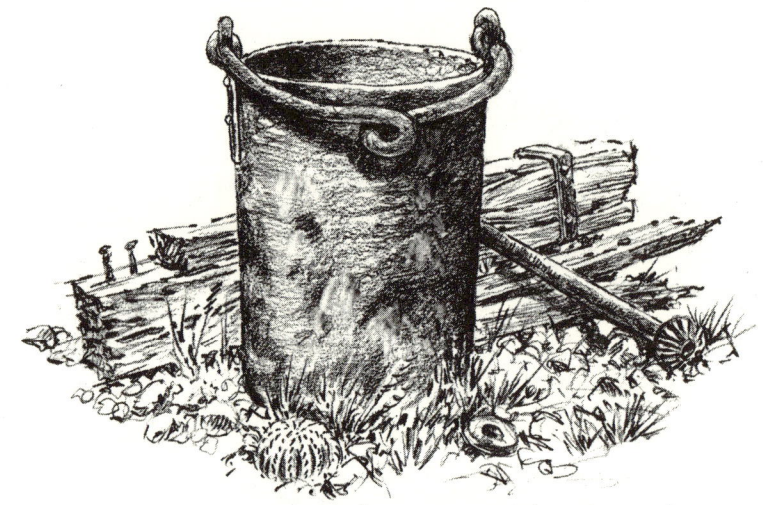

On my first visit in the early 1970's,
There was much evidence of the
mining activity in the area.

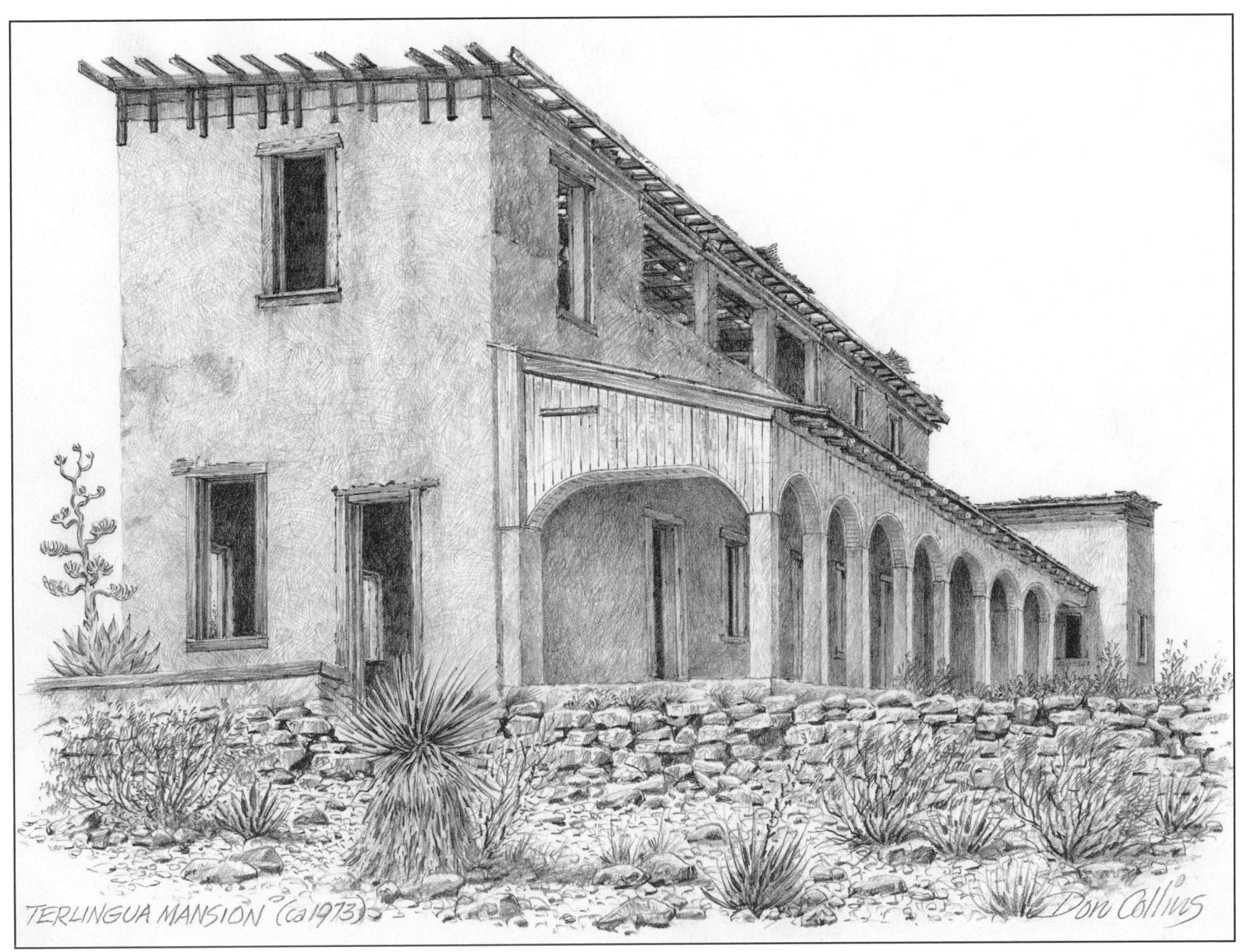

TERLINGUA MANSION (ca 1973)   Don Collins

53. Valentine Mercantile.

I was on a trip with Dwain and Billie Kelley when we stumbled across the mercantile store at Valentine. Dwain is a graphic artist from Austin, a really good one, but he doesn't generally like to get out of Travis County. We made this a little vacation trip in late September or early October and combined it with some serious searching for subject matter. None of us had ever been to Valentine before. In fact, none of us had ever been that far west by car from Austin. This is a place that has suffered from hard times.

When we drove into town, there wasn't very much left but this store. As far as we could tell, the mercantile was the major building remaining in the town. I really liked the pressed metal front. You know, they could order all of that from a catalog in those days. When we looked at this store, we imagined how once it had been a really lively place. For me this store is a marvelous example of the type.

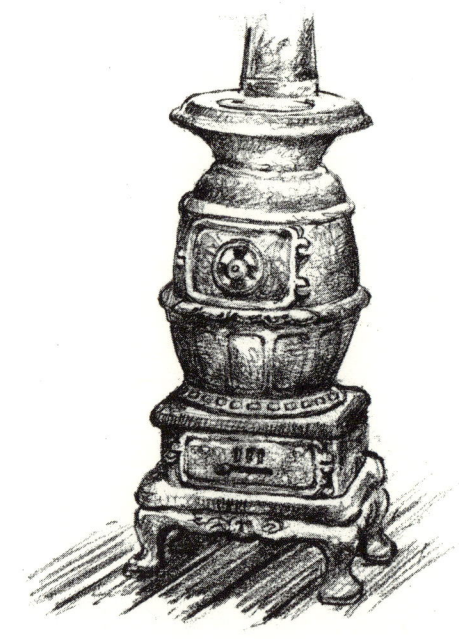

.The store at Valentine was just a shell, but I imagined the cowboys and oil men enjoyed one of these in an earlier day.

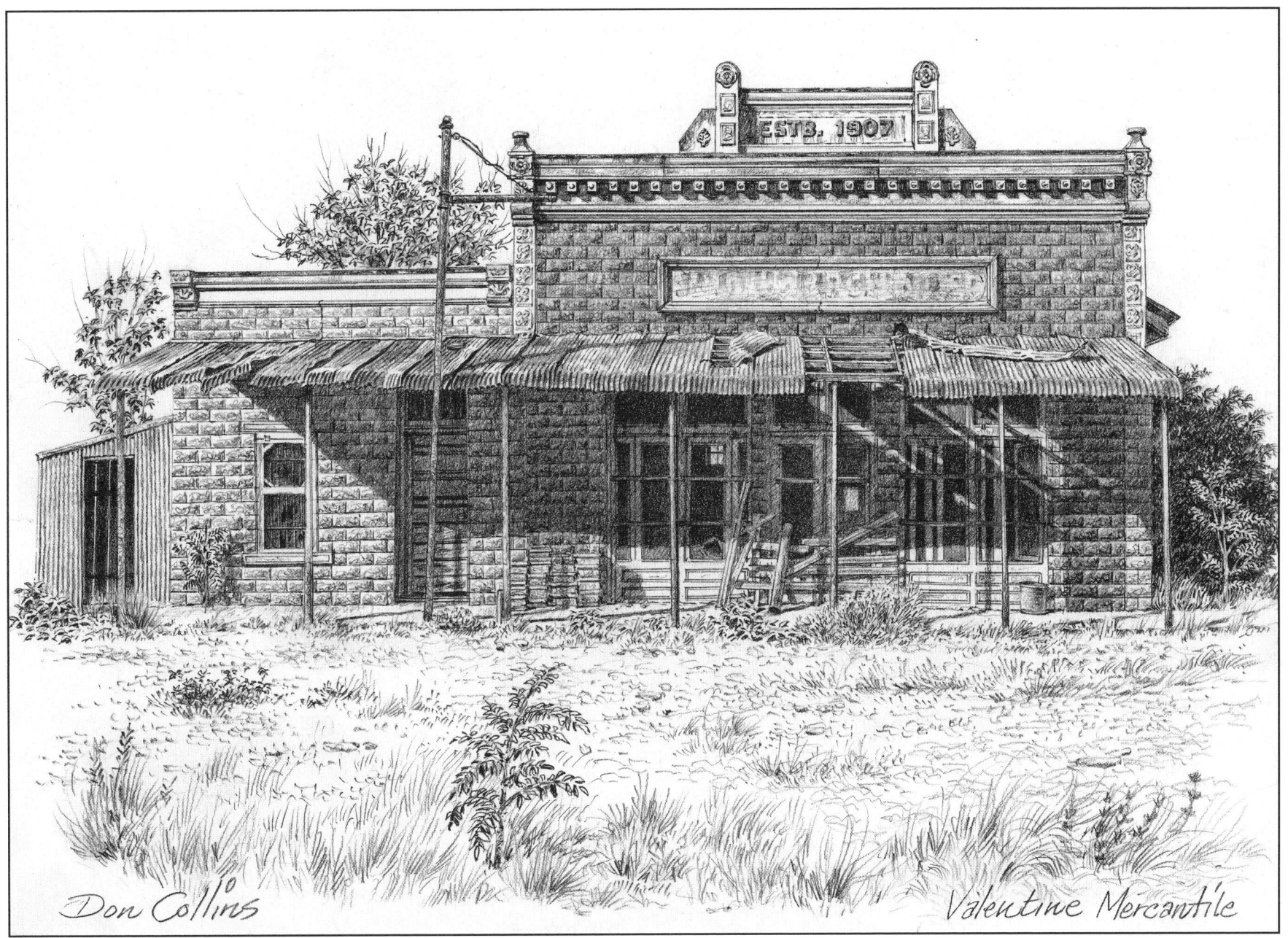

ESTB. 1907

Don Collins

Valentine Mercantile

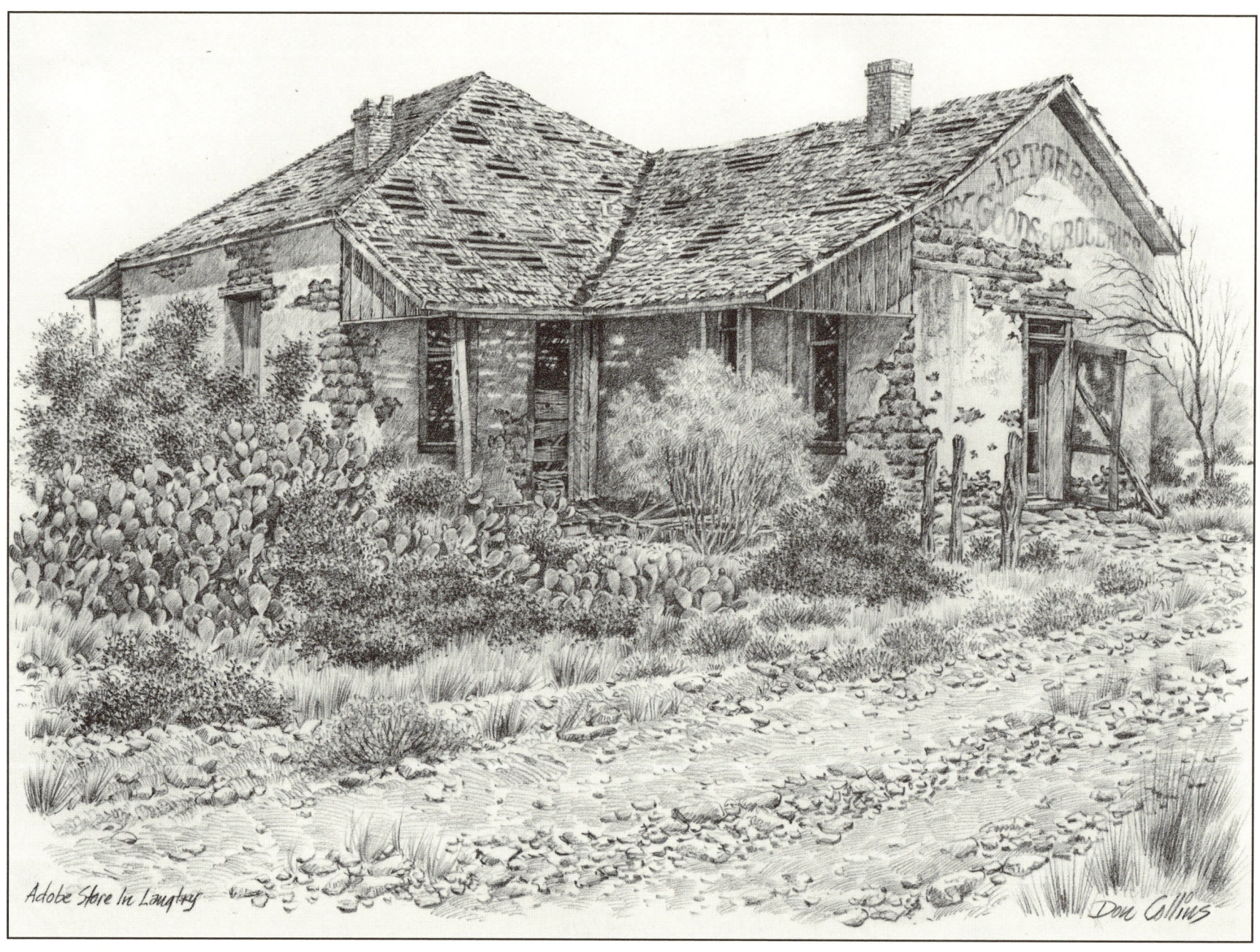

Adobe Store In Langtry

Don Collins

54. Adobe Store in Langtry.

This is a result of my first trip to the border and to Langtry. It's one of the very few buildings that I found still standing there. Today the town is known for Judge Roy Bean's saloon, which the state has preserved as part of a tourist information center. The Torres Store, just down the way, years ago sold dry goods and groceries, and is an interesting old adobe building. It is in a state of serious disrepair and is overcome by cactus and thorny brush. It has an interesting little design, two chimneys and an unusual roof. Torres obviously wasn't making it there, or his descendants, and it had been a long time since there'd been any activity at the store. In my more recent trips there to that area, I found almost nothing left.

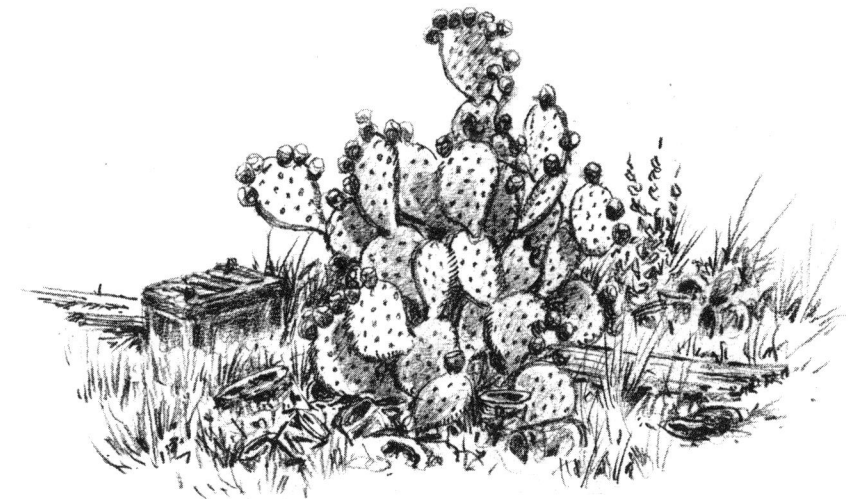

*On a follow-up trip many years later,
I found the adobe Torres store
was rapidly melting back into the desert.*

PART SIX

East Texas

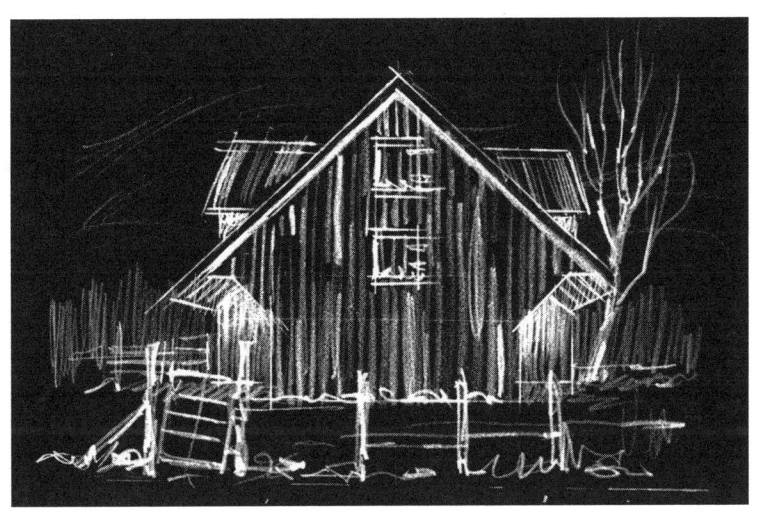

55. Hearne Station.

In my childhood, I used to ride the Rock Island Rocket past Hearne time and again, but I never noticed the railroad station. As I matured and got into the art business, I got very excited when I spotted this highly unusual triangular-shaped railroad station built where two tracks intersected at an odd angle. They built the station in a shape to use the space available. It comes almost to a point where the tracks come together. Additionally they built interesting shingle-clad towers on two corners. There are large wooden brackets that support the roof overhang. It is painted in traditional railroad colors, yellow with brown trim. Of course, it has been long since abandoned by its builders and the railroads.

When I first paid attention to this building, I saw no activity there at all. On subsequent trips it became various things: a TV repair shop once and something else. I've drawn a great number of railway stations, but I haven't encountered one of this shape anywhere else.

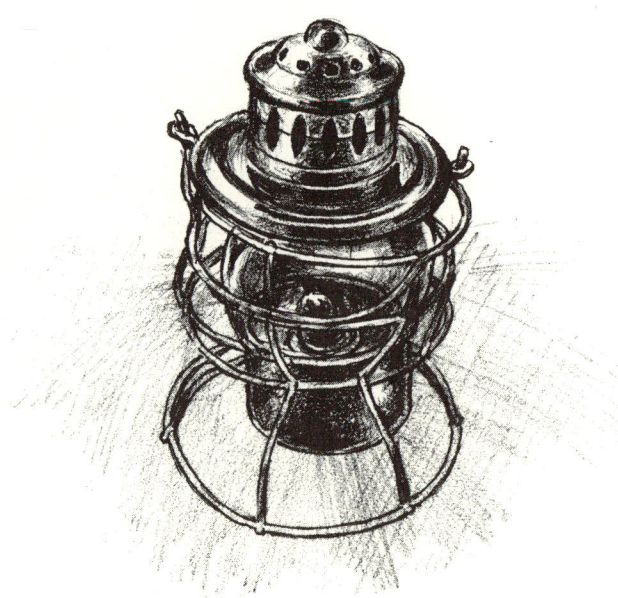

These great old stations are reminders of a less efficient, but a much more exciting and interesting era in the history of railroading.

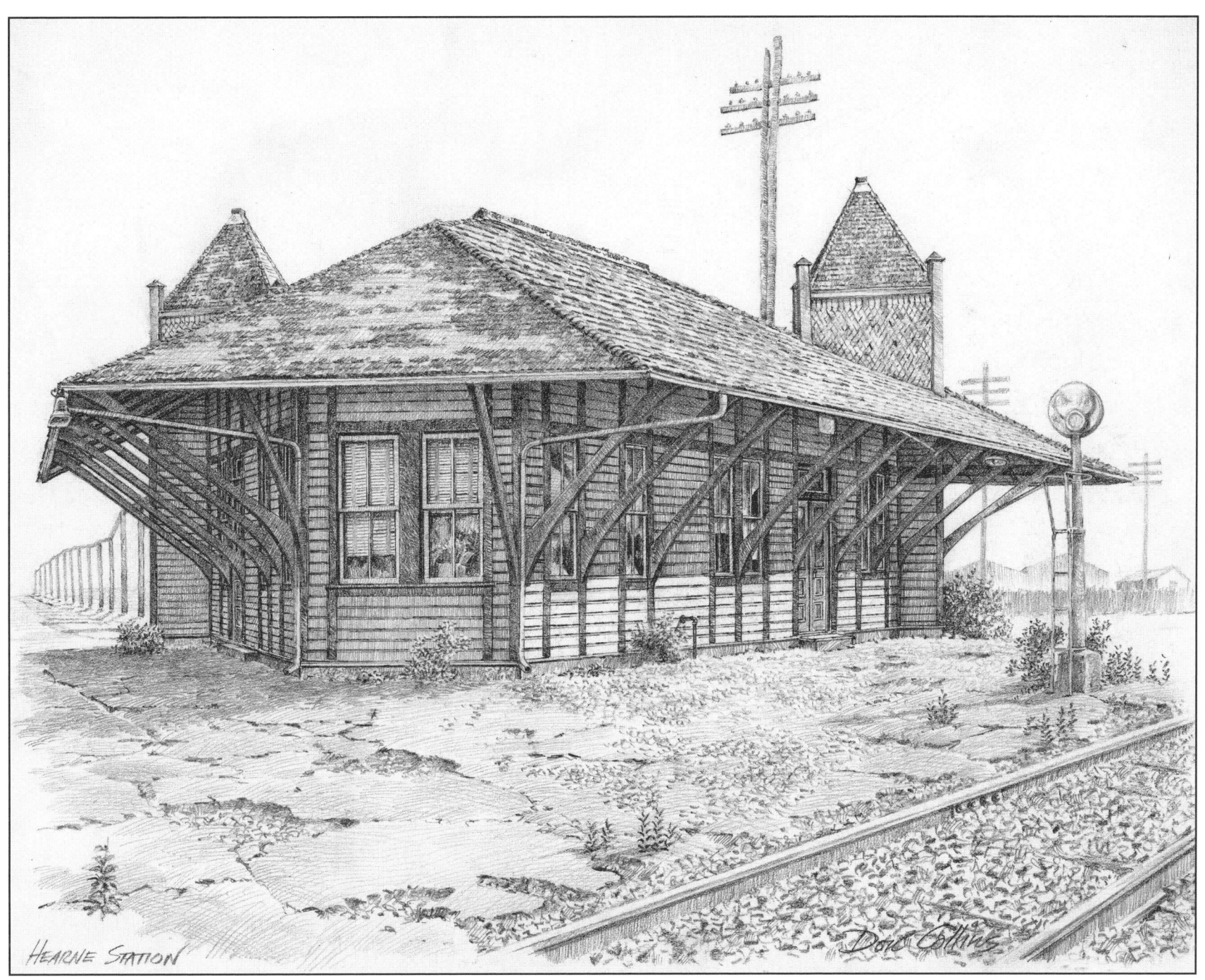

HEARNE STATION

This is a marvelous old building, a brick building in a very small town in the very poor
county of Grimes. Anderson itself is pretty
much melting away, like so many small towns in Texas.
There's not a lot going on there. Down at the far end
of the street stands an historic inn, the Fanthorp Inn.
These are the only two notable things that I found in
Anderson.

This great big, interesting brick structure domi-
nates the town, right at the end of the avenue on the
highest prominence there. The building has the unusual feature of a double exterior staircase. I never had
encountered a courthouse you entered that way to get
to the second floor. The building is well maintained,
still functioning as a courthouse.

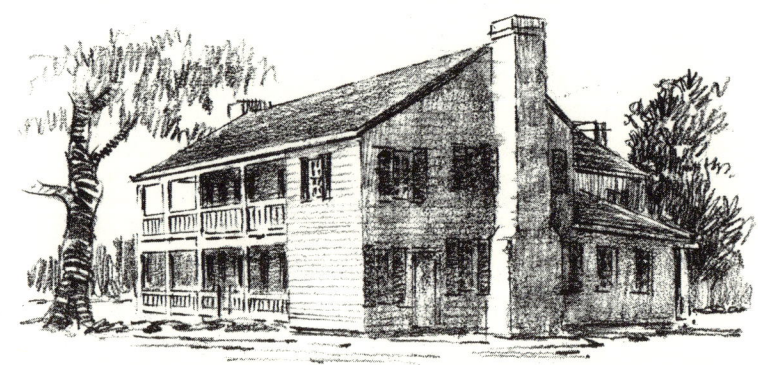

At the other end of Anderson's main
street is mellow old Fanthorp Inn, dating
back to the 1830's.

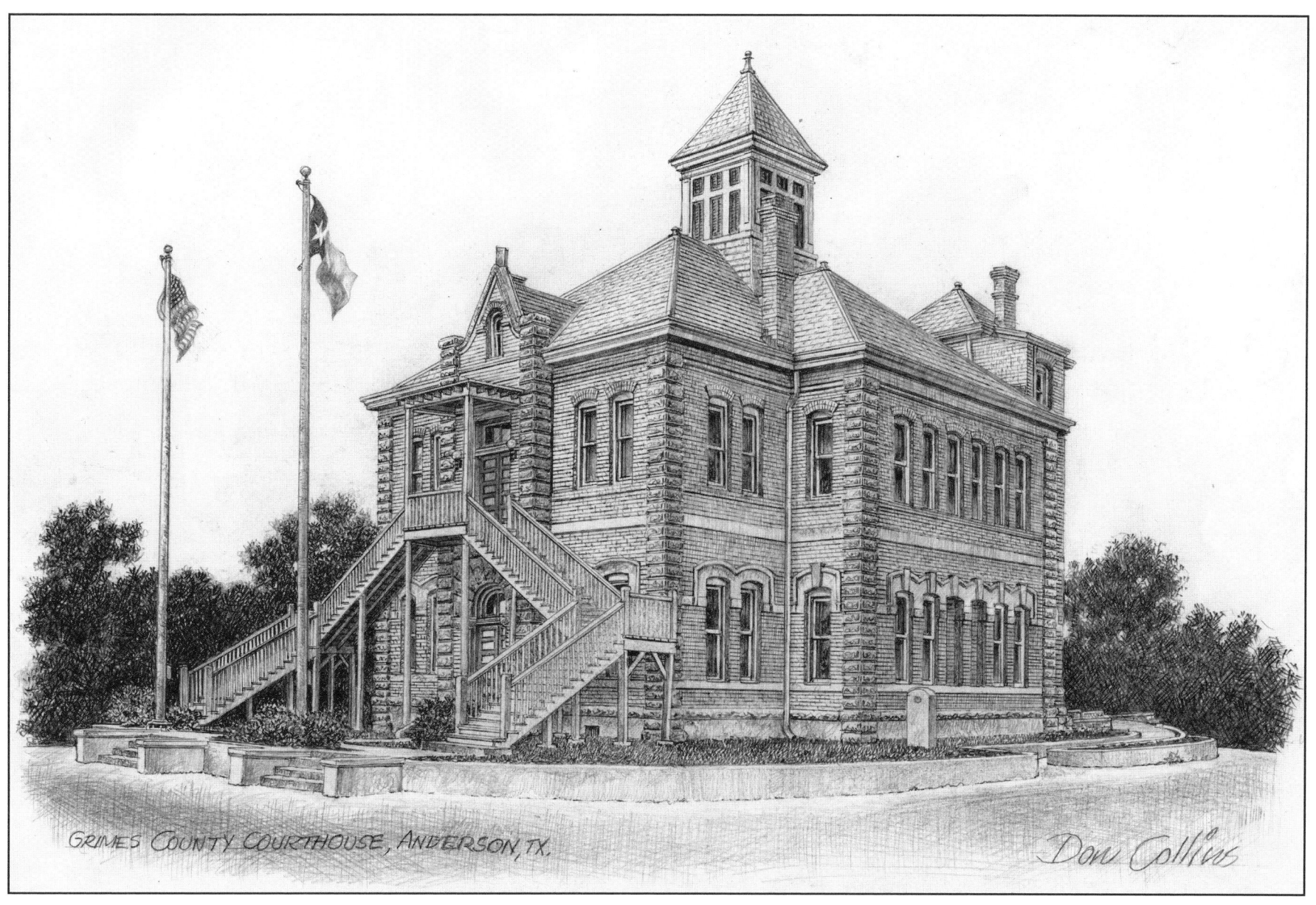

GRIMES COUNTY COURTHOUSE, ANDERSON, TX.

Don Collins

57. Texas & Pacific Depot, Marshall.

This beautiful, impressive red brick station signals the importance of Marshall as a railroad town in earlier days. There is still a good bit of rail activity here, even with Amtrak passenger trains twice a day. The white trim is carefully applied. I was attracted by the striking gables. A lot of little decorative touches. It looks like a railroad station of importance ought to look. They did a good job of it. It is still maintained as a museum.

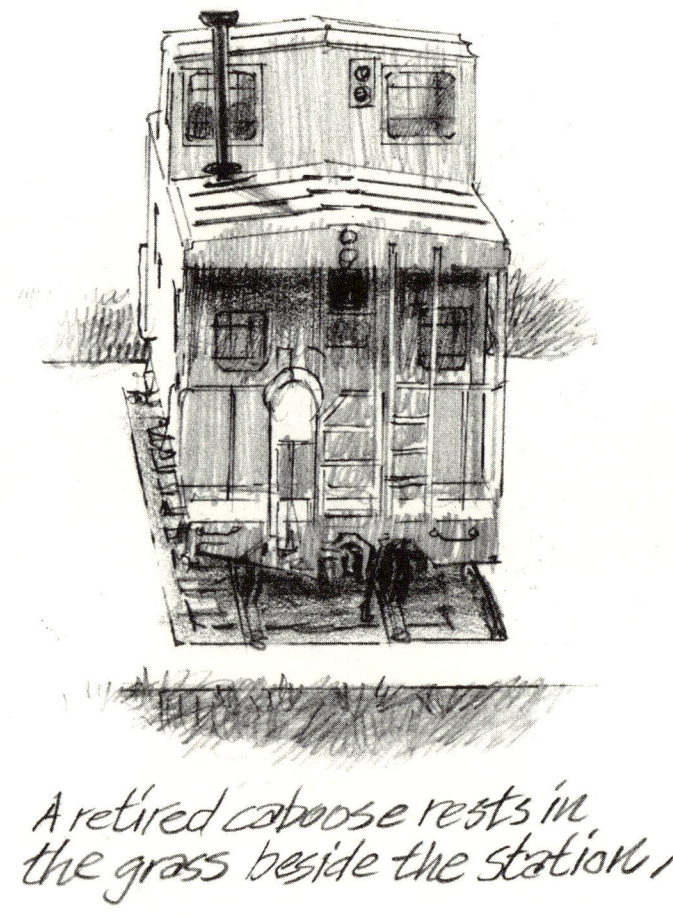

A retired caboose rests in the grass beside the station.

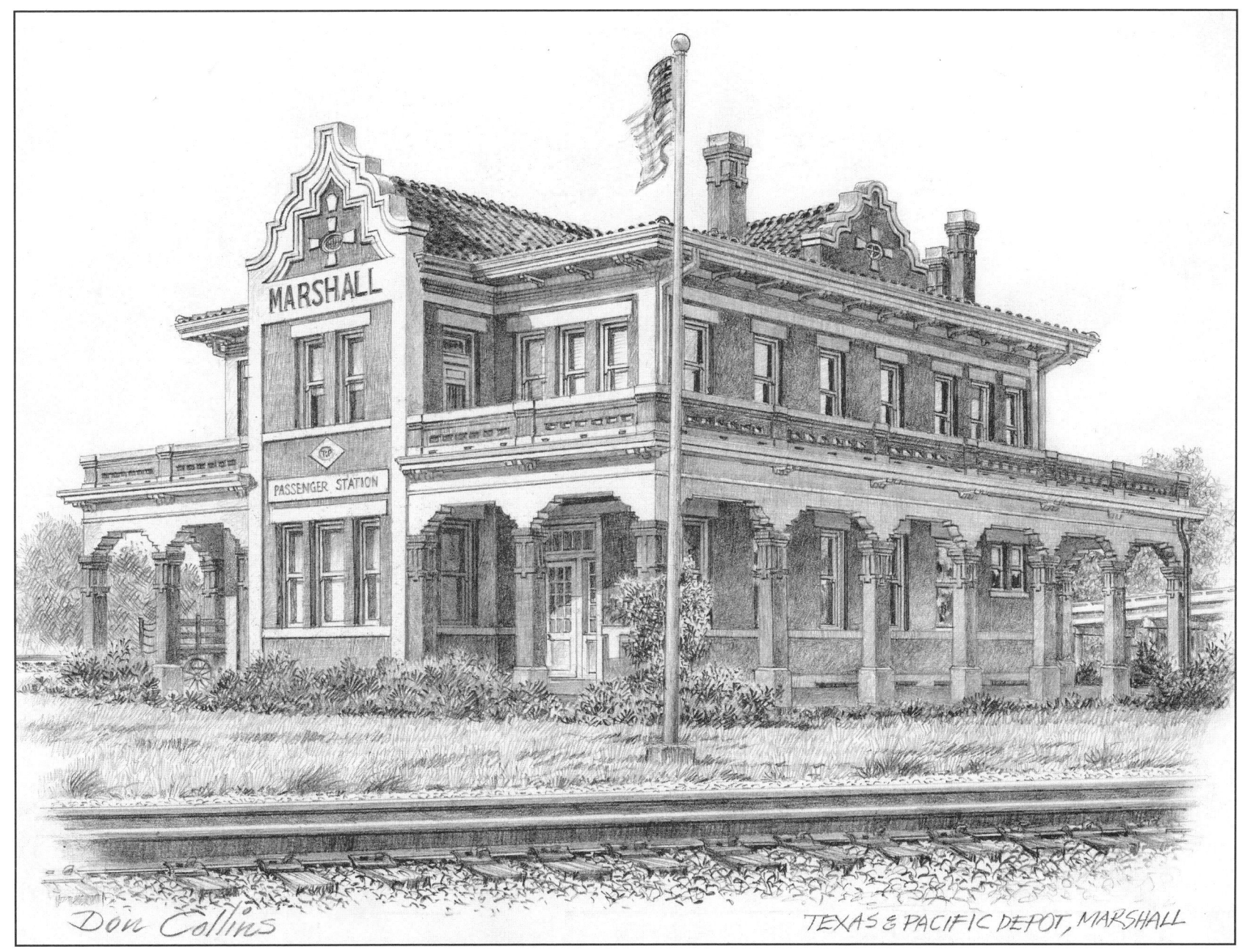

MARSHALL

PASSENGER STATION

Don Collins

TEXAS & PACIFIC DEPOT, MARSHALL

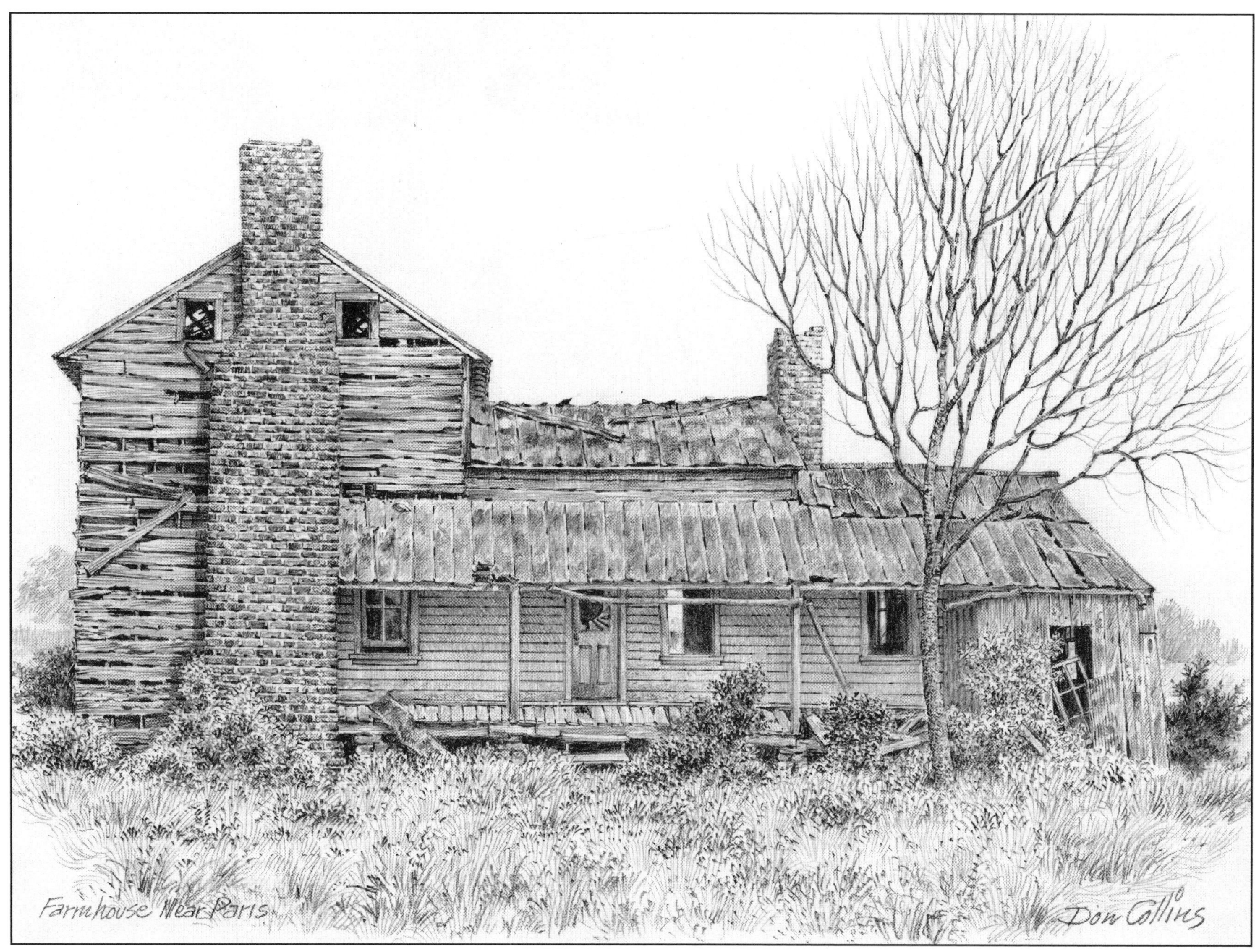

Farmhouse Near Paris

Don Collins

58. Farmhouse near Paris.

Iknow nothing whatever about this farmhouse, and I couldn't retrace my steps there if I had to. It was on one of those little drives when I started off on a road, I believe south of Paris, and I saw a road that I really liked, and I dodged down that. Then there was one over there that looked better, and I took it. Pretty soon I was lost, but I knew I was in Texas, but I didn't worry about it since I had plenty of gas and a lot of time. Now you know how I just ran across this fascinating old farmhouse with an unusual shape.

There was a big verandah across the side, a place to sit. Then they added a shed on the end of the porch. I don't know what the purpose for that was. It might have been a bathroom added at a later time. Obviously the building is in very bad shape, but the roof was interesting to me as an artist. It was a brilliant combination of colors because it was so rusted away. In proximity to abandoned fields, you can tell it was important at one time. It's very appealing from an artistic standpoint and also evocative. You know. Who were these people? Where did they go?

Somebody out there knows.

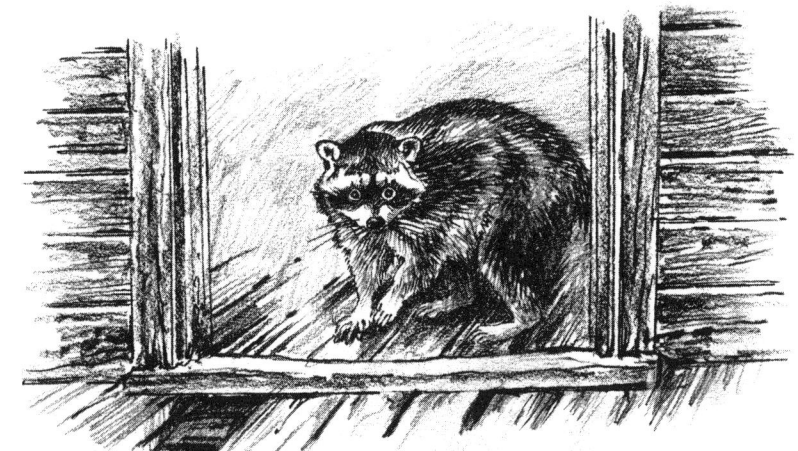

When old houses reach this stage of decay they often become habitat for a variety of critters.

59. Nacogdoches Station.

In my mind, this little railway station in Nacogdoches is a gem. It has a beautiful red tile roof and soft green painted bricks. It is not used any longer for trains, but somebody in Nacogdoches cares. The wrought iron brackets all the way around that support the overhang are really fine. The brickwork is good, the way that they handled the corners and all that. I like the exuberant touches, the spire on top of the miniature tower and the double chimneys. All in all, this is a really nice looking building. I only wish that more of the small railroad stations in Texas could be saved to that degree instead of just being ripped down.

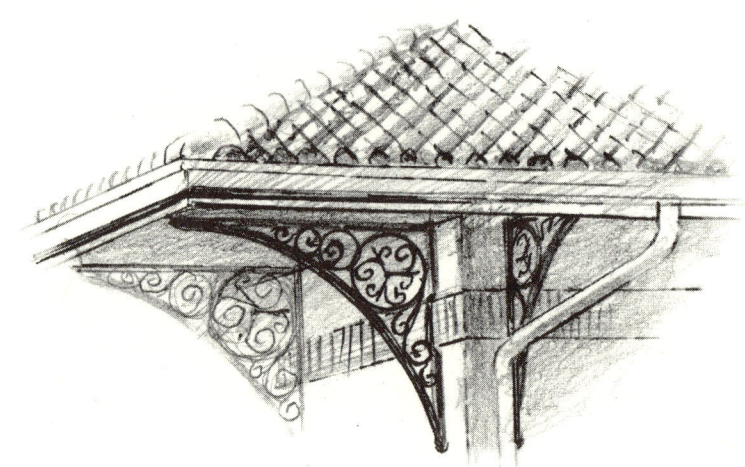

This beautiful little mint-green station has a lot of fancy iron brackets...I counted 35!

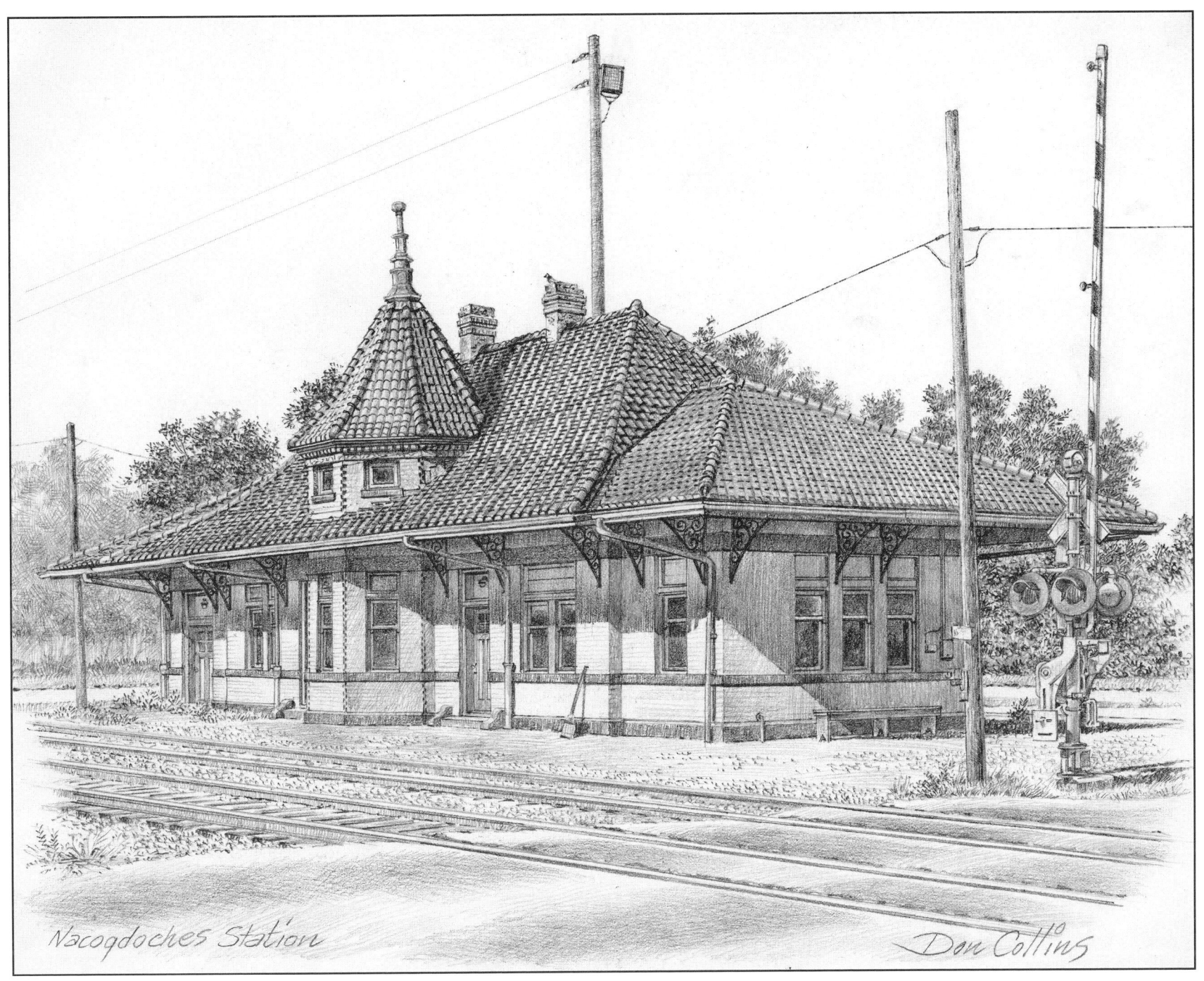

Nacogdoches Station

Don Collins

60. Barn at Teaselville.

The first thing you say, you don't know where Teaselville is? I didn't either. A friend of mine gave me a lead. An Austin friend told me that his daughter had met a boy from Teaselville and they were going to get married. He had visited the relatives in Teaselville, in the way that you do when you are breaking in two families, and that they had two magnificent barns. He said that I should get up there and take a look.

I have a good friend in Big Sandy who I visit from time to time, so the next time I was up there, I checked the map for Teaselville and found it. It's just southeast from Tyler, close to Bullard. Well, actually Teaselville just barely exists. It has a store and is more atmosphere than anything else. As I drove down the road, I saw two wonderful barns facing each other about fifty yards apart, built and owned by the same people.

They both have interesting double-tiered roof designs, with long sheltering stretches just below the upper levels. Of course, you've got the passageway for the wagons to pass through at the middle to load and unload. There is a major overhang on all sides, so much protective roof that the building is going to be around for a while. I believe I was told the original builder was English and was influenced by that in his design. This has to be one of the better barns that I have ever seen in Texas.

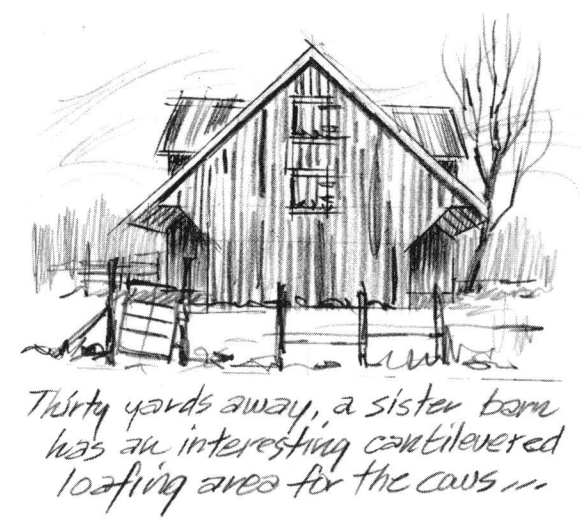

Thirty yards away, a sister barn
has an interesting cantilevered
loafing area for the cows ~

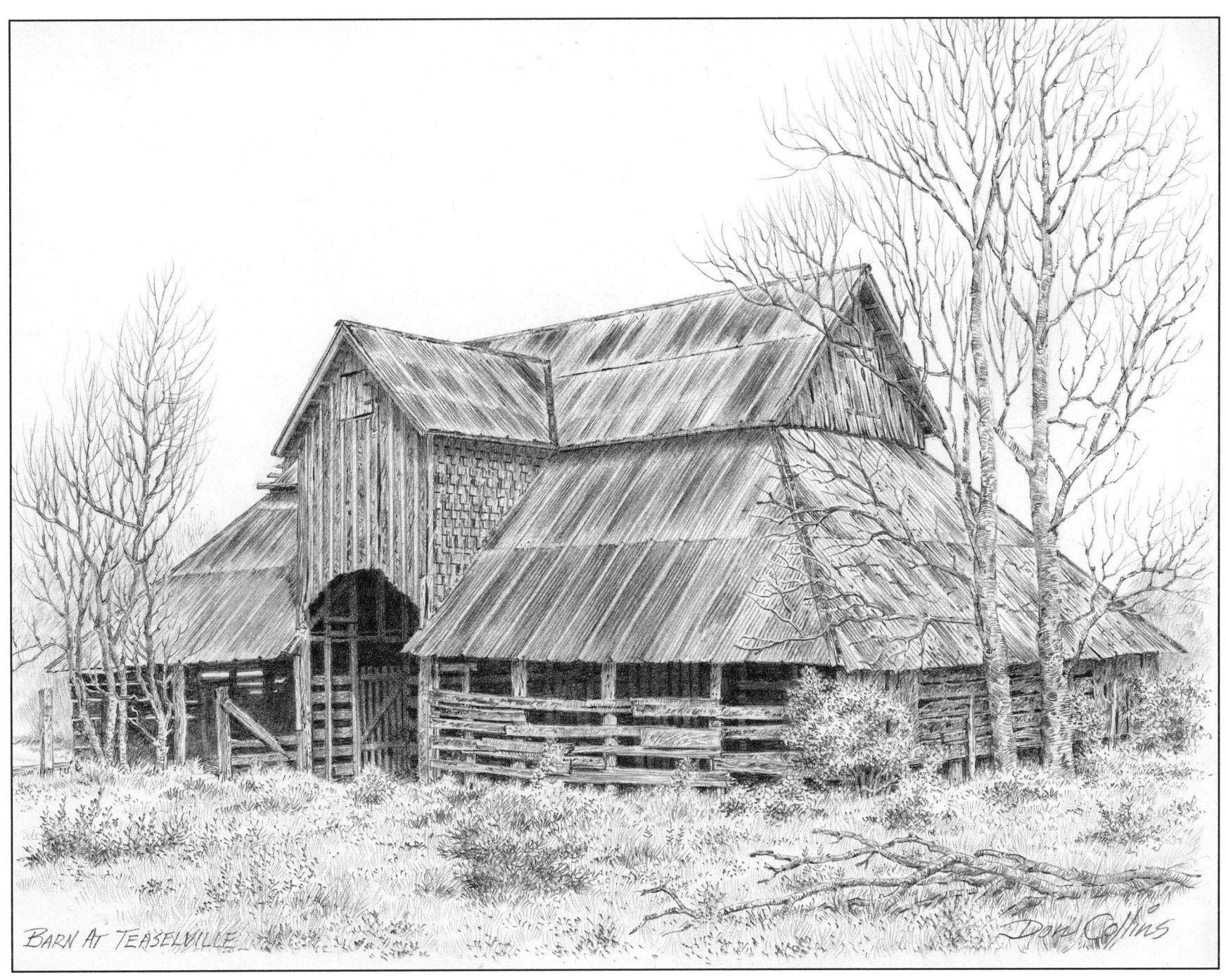

BARN AT TEASELVILLE

Don Collins

PART SEVEN

North Central Texas

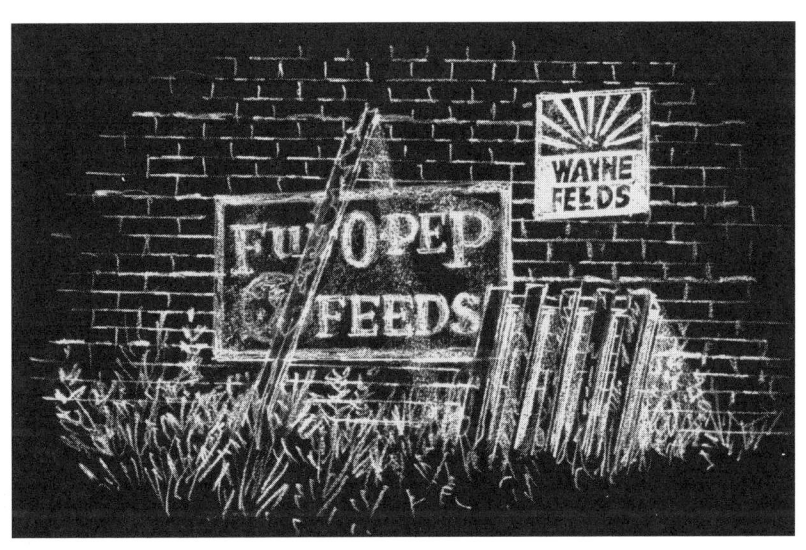

61. Interurban Car, Cresson, Texas.

I came across this old electric interurban car while snooping around in the very small town of Cresson, which lies astraddle U.S. Highway 377 southwest of Fort Worth. Cresson is like many of those many informal little towns. It is a mixture of out-buildings, gardens, houses, everything very irregular and nothing planned. Somebody had acquired an old interurban car and put it to use, apparently at one time as living quarters. No one was living inside when I got there, because it was already too far gone for that. They apparently were using it to store some stuff.

I remember as a small child watching the interur-bans roar up and down the line from Dallas to Fort Worth and from Houston to Galveston and from Fort Worth to Itasca. As a four-, five-, six-year-old, they greatly excited me because the interurban really got up and moved. They were the fastest things around. I expect they hit sixty or seventy miles per hour from time to time, faster than most cars of that day could go. This old car with the wooden sides is exceptional. It's got leaded glass windows that are a very fancy touch. I was attracted to the whole thing, the idea of salvaging and turning one of those things into a home. And, look at that giant headlight. All in all, it was a fascinating object, but it's no longer there. I don't know what the owner did with it, but the old car has been removed.

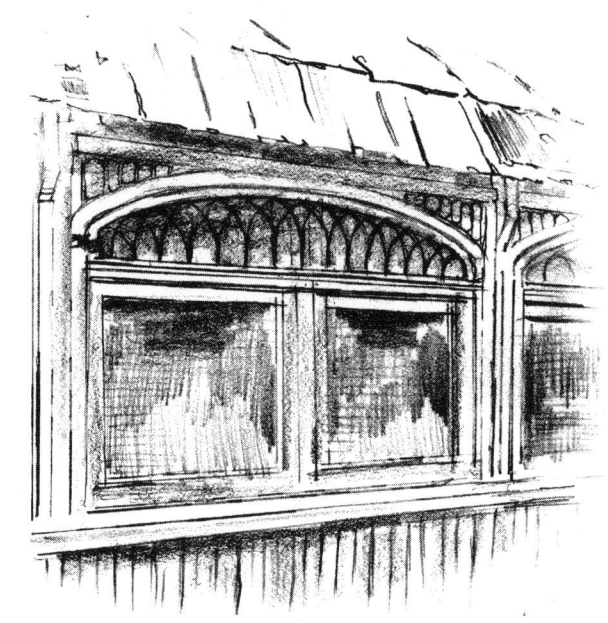

I was amazed at the fancy window detail on this old car.

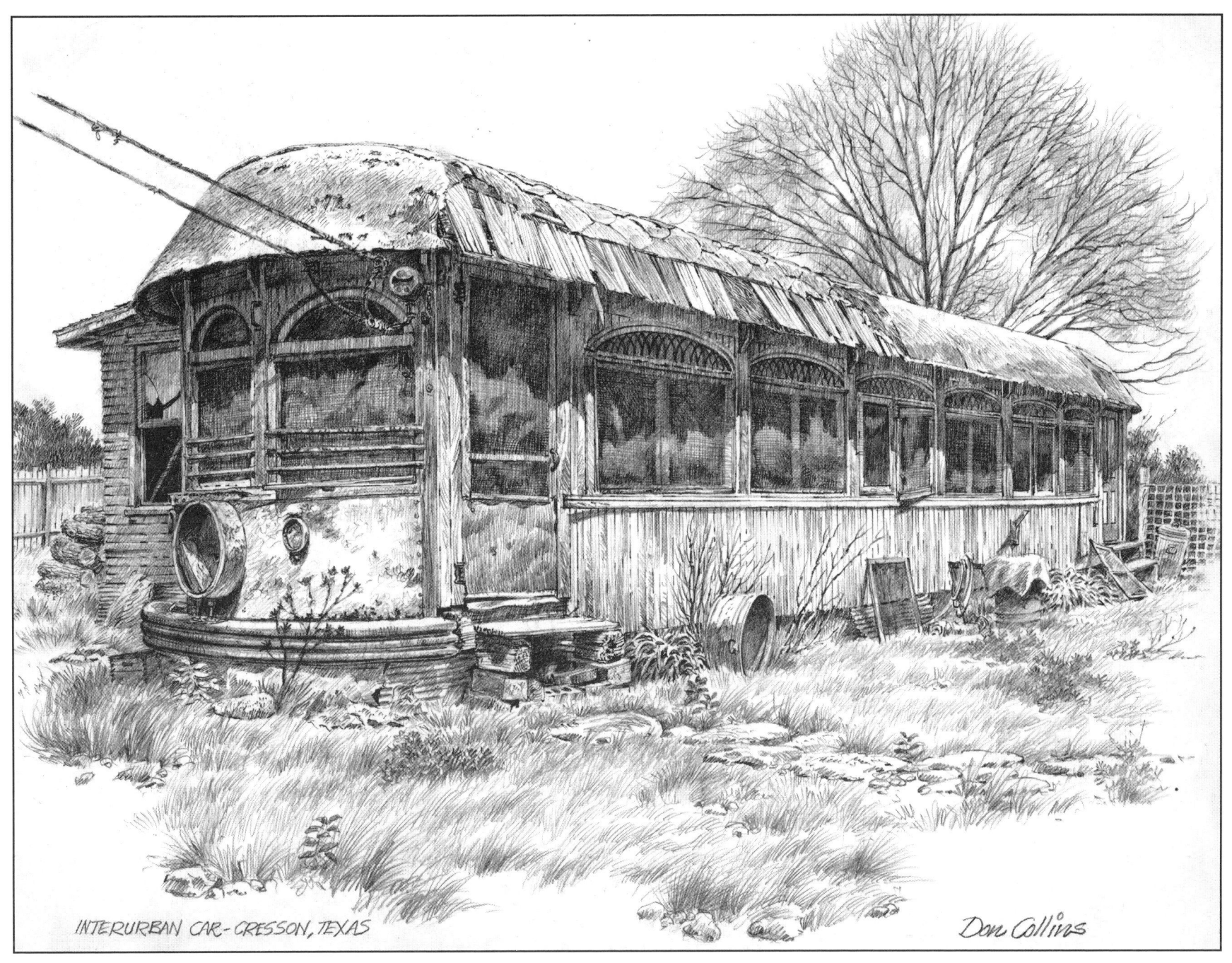

INTERURBAN CAR - CRESSON, TEXAS

Don Collins

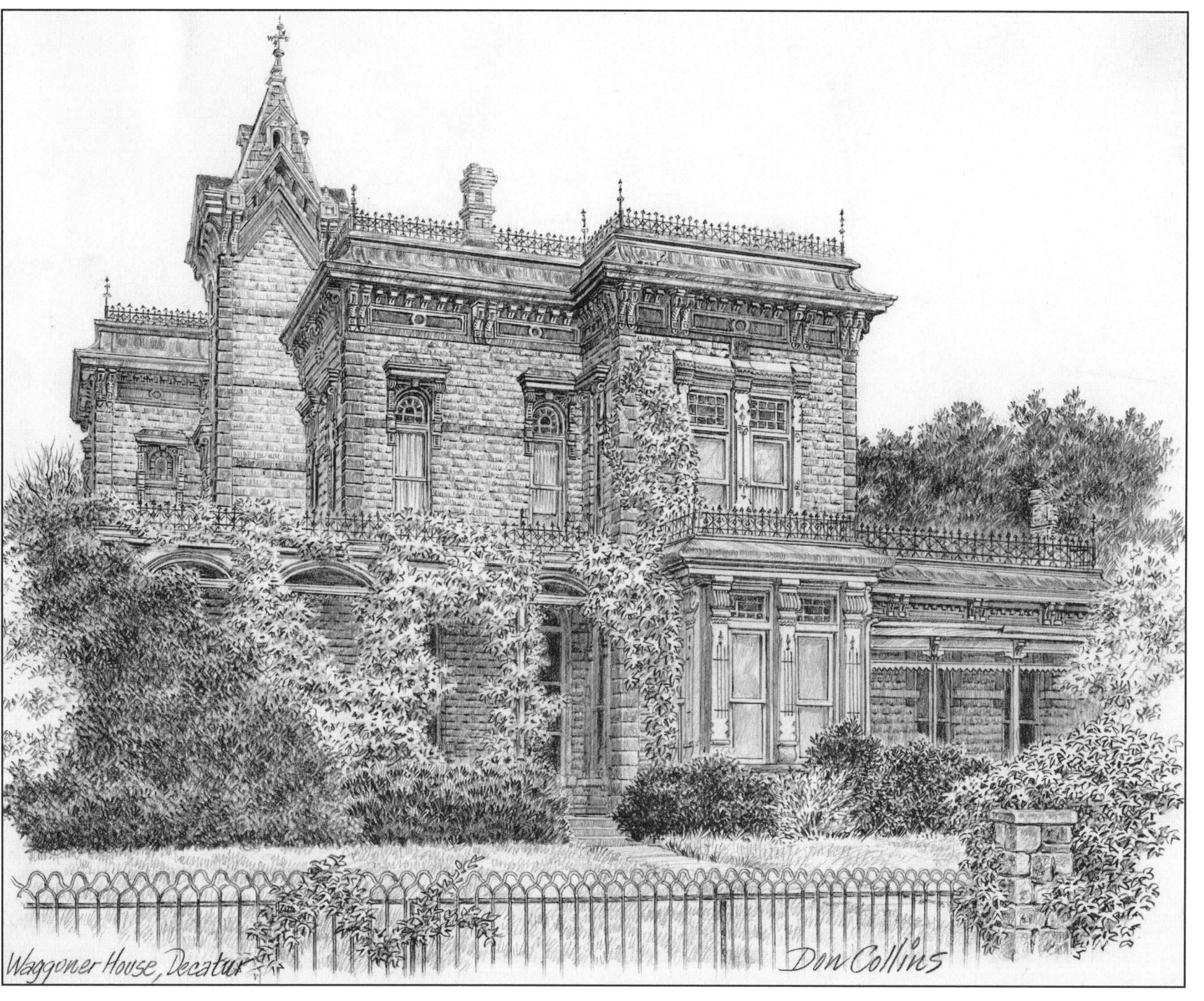

Waggoner House, Decatur

Don Collins

62. Waggoner House, Decatur.

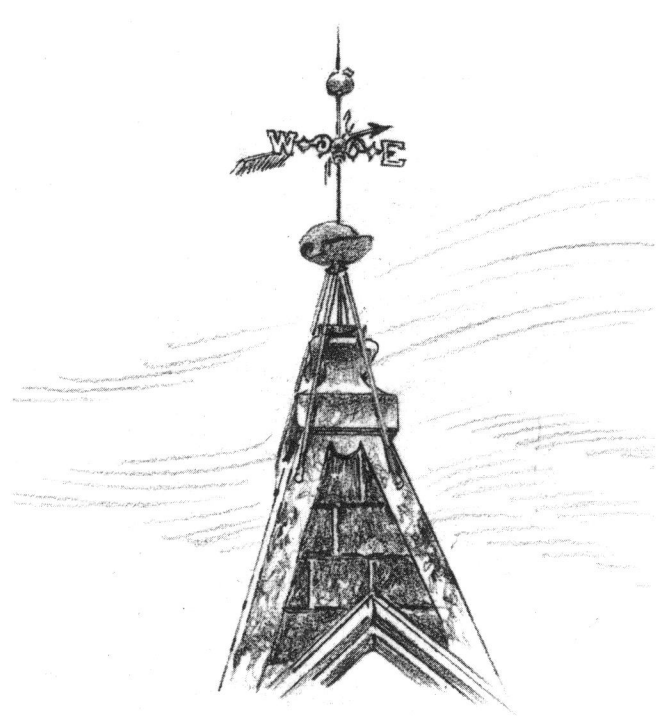

The Waggoner weathervane is attached to the steep tower by a spidery arrangement of thin rods —I wondered how it survived the strong North Texas winds for long over a century.

The Waggoner House has been very much seen, written about, photographed, and reviewed, but deserves it. Rancher Dan Waggoner built it on a rocky hill overlooking Decatur in Wise County in the 1880s. Drawing this place was a true challenge. "Can I really draw a thing like that?" I asked myself. It is tremendously hard to get all that detail. I guess such a house bespeaks the importance of the Waggoner family in that era. They pretty much dominated that part of the state. The old house seems in fairly good repair, although I noticed that there were things starting to happen to it. I didn't feel the same emotion here that I sense when I draw some of the more humble places, but I'm glad that I made the drawing.

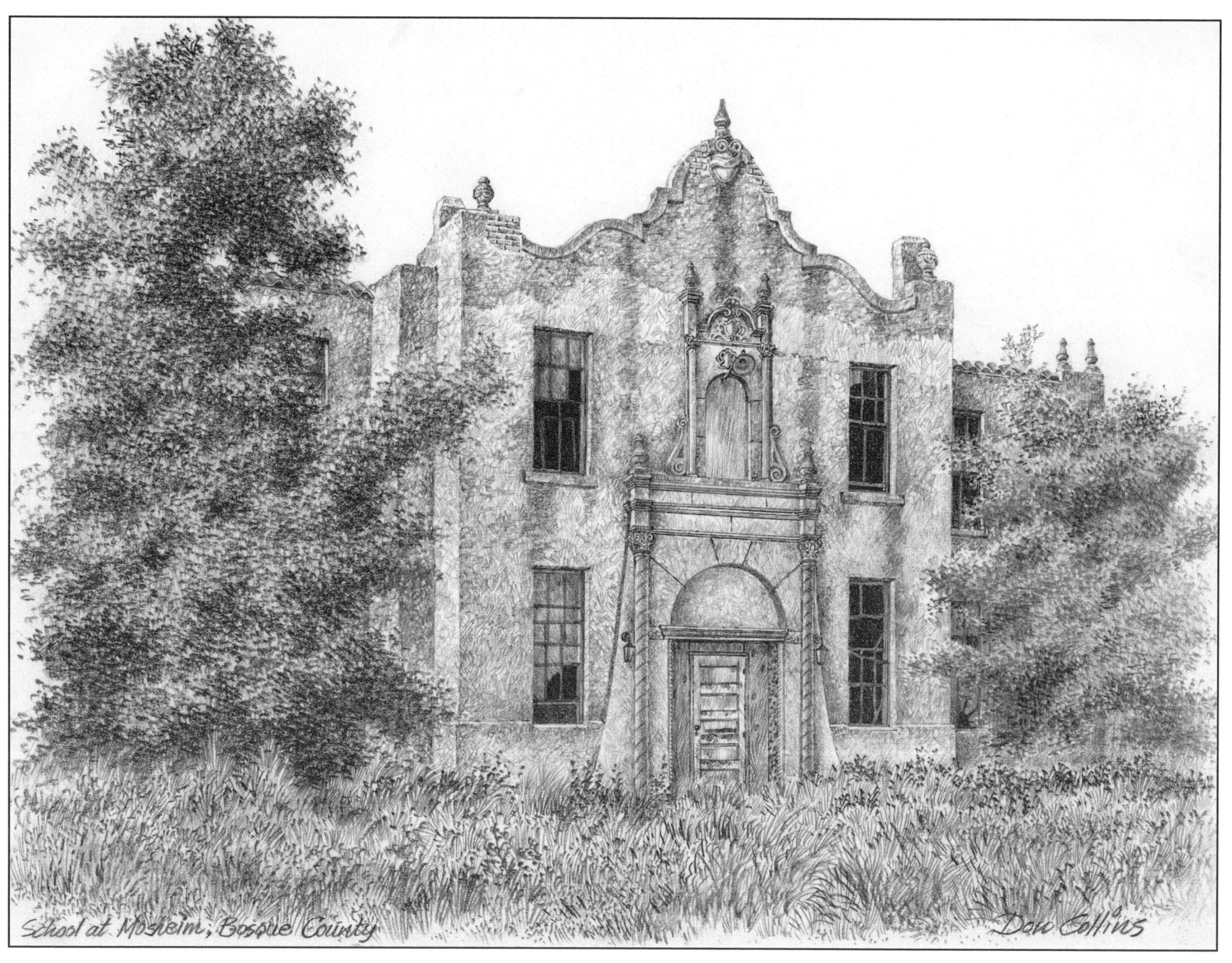

School at Mosheim, Bosque County

Dow Collins

63. School at Mosheim, Bosque County.

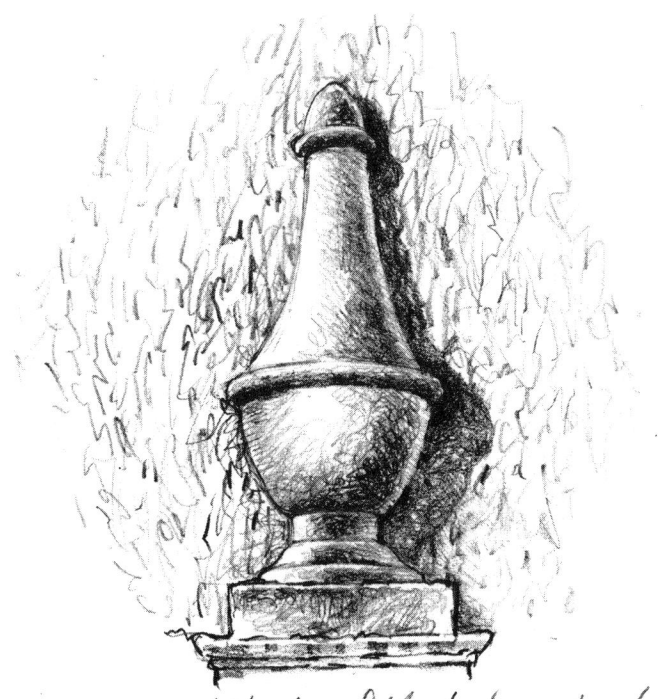

The architects of Mosheim school were fond of this decorative shape... there are at least 12!

Do you know where Mosheim is? Well, it is a little west of Valley Mills in Bosque County. There was a sign pointing toward Mosheim, but I didn't know what it was. So I went up there, and I was really struck by this abandoned school. It is just very attractive. I don't know what style that is, but it's Mediterranean-looking to me. It seems odd sitting out there in the middle of the cotton country. Somebody with pretty sophisticated tastes must have been sitting on the school board back at the turn of the century.

The schoolyard was kind of sad. It had empty swing sets and a little push merry-go-round sitting at an odd angle, grown up in weeds and abandoned. All in all it was an attractive place to draw. On a more recent trip through Mosheim, within the last year or so, I saw that somebody has gone in and removed a good bit of the underbrush and tried to clean it up. I don't think they've fixed the building, but I think there may be hope for it.

64. Old Mill, Dublin, Erath County.

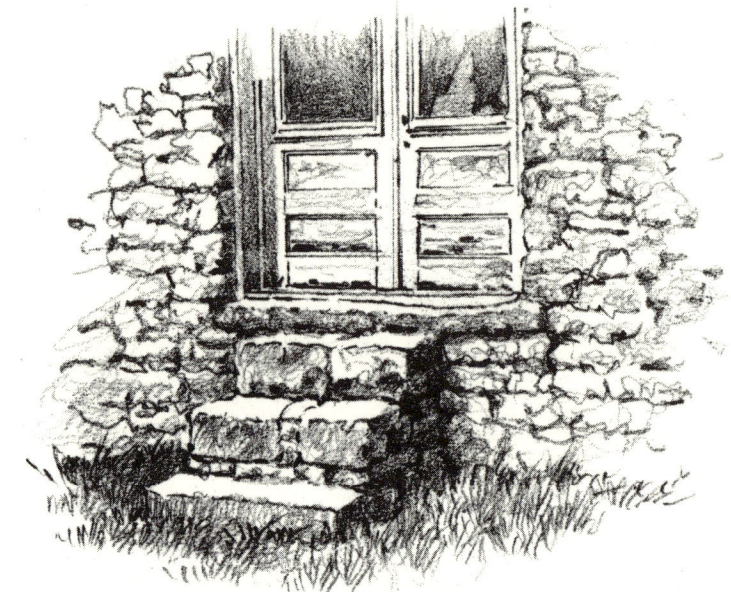

Proceed with care! The no-frills pre-OSHA steps lack a handrail and have 16 inch risers!

This old stone building stands just down the street from the original Dr Pepper plant in Dublin. William T. Miller erected it back in 1882 as a steam-powered gristmill for meal and flour. In 1926 his son converted it to grind animal feed and operated it for years before the family gave it to the local historical society. The mill doesn't have very sophisticated stonework, but it does have interesting quoins on the corners. They managed to do that. The rocks comprising the walls are of every description. It's a sturdy, business-like old place, still standing strong and tall. I wish I knew more about it.

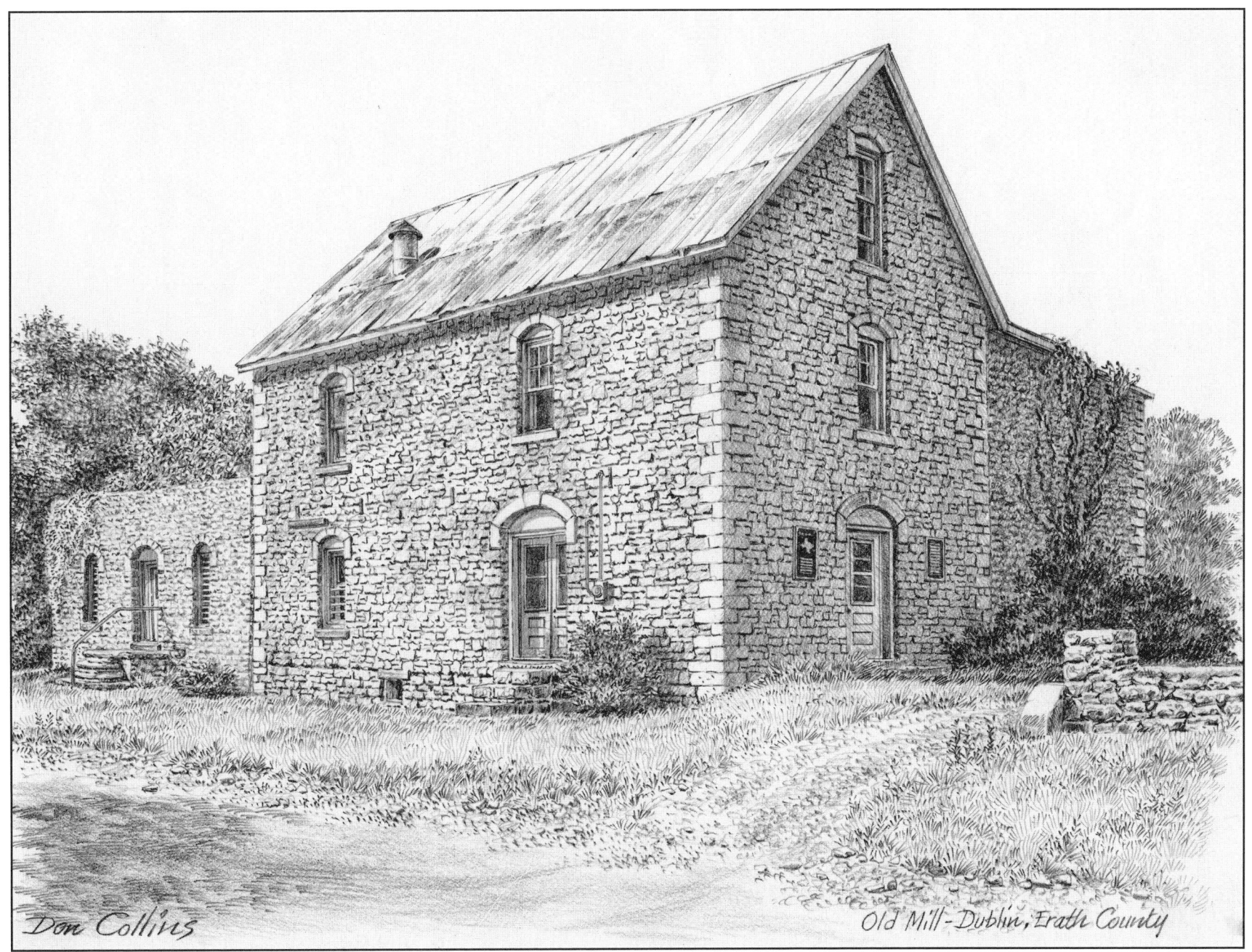

Don Collins

Old Mill – Dublin, Erath County

147

65. Bank Building, Granbury.

Granbury has many interesting things, but this building just yells, "Bank" at you. It's exuberant. Everything about it informs the world, "I'm important and this is where the money is." It really does. It's got all sorts of inventive and in some cases very odd architectural touches. The protuberances on the corners of the tower are something that I have only rarely seen. I saw a similar thing on the courthouse at Center. Maybe that was a fad at one time. There is no doubt that they stand out and grab your attention. It has some handsome leaded glass windows and interesting bulbous arches above the tower windows. The building is in good shape and is in use.

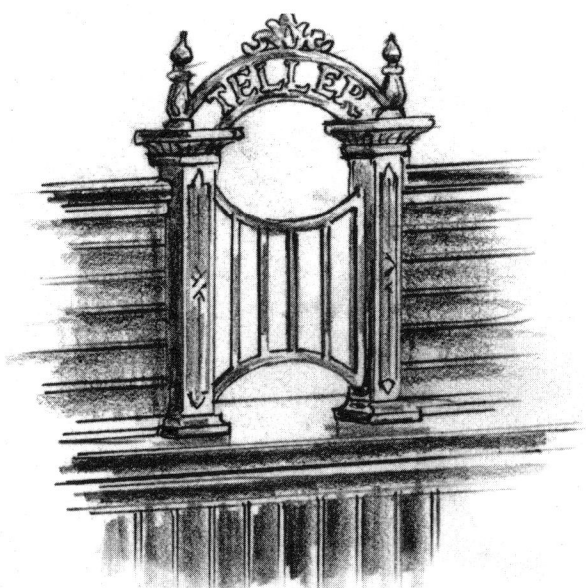

In these 19th century banks, the flourishes continued into the interiors, with lots of polished marble, varnished hardwoods, and even gleaming brass spittoons!

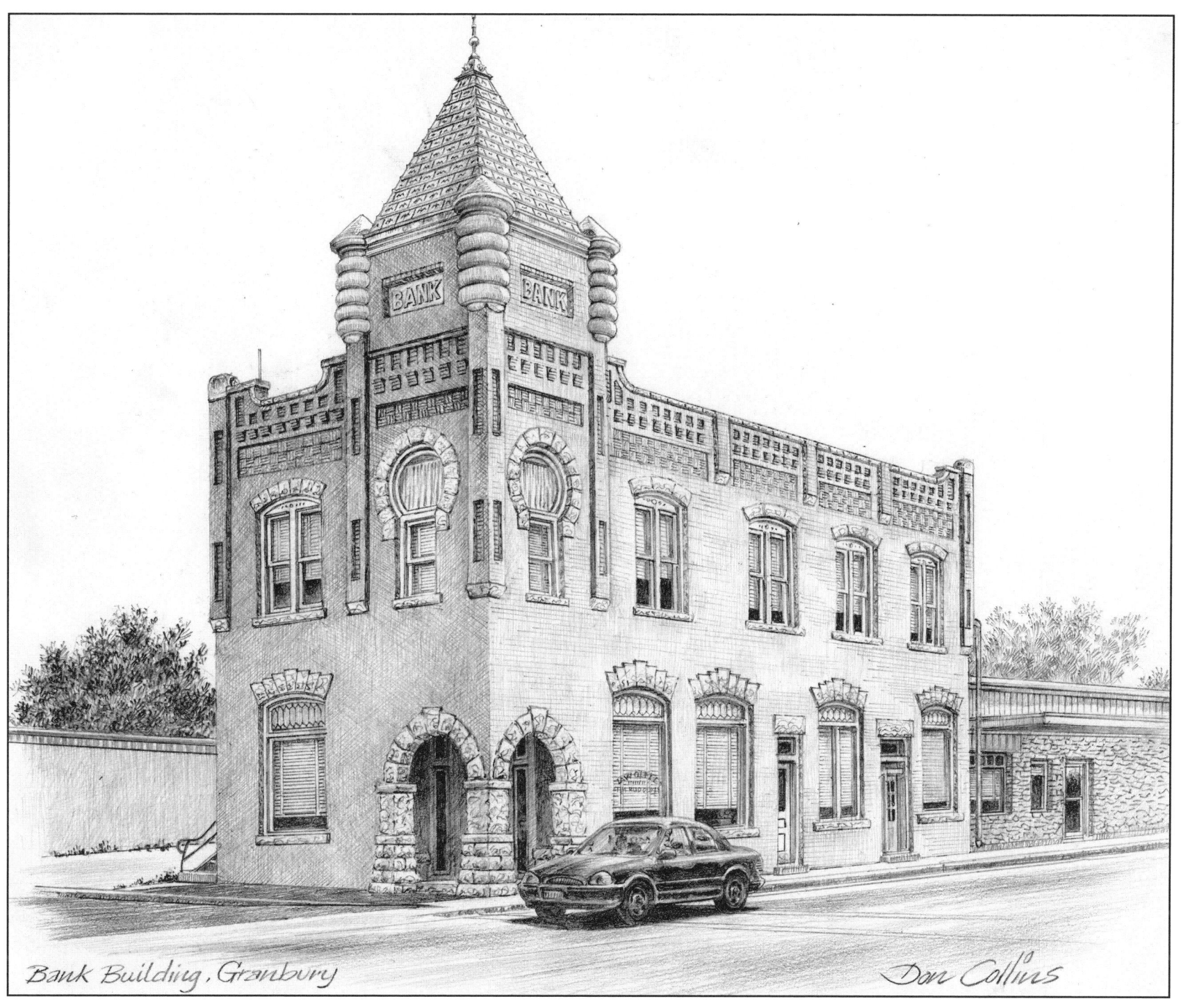

Bank Building, Granbury

Don Collins

66. Hildreth Ranch, Iona.

This is near my own old stomping grounds. The grand old house was erected by a rancher named Hildreth who was the grandfather of a rancher I knew in my youth, Volney Hildreth. He had a son named Volney, Jr., who was nicknamed "Juney Bug." We were contemporaries and went to school together.

Anyhow, the house in my days looked like it came from the set from *Giant*. It sits out on a totally bald prairie between Fort Worth and Aledo all alone, a large house in a spacious setting. You can see it for miles. It was by far the most important house in the neighborhood. I remember that the Hildreths had a Cadillac. Everyone else had a Ford, at that time in the Depression. I was occasionally invited to attend birthday parties in the back yard there. When "Juney Bug" had a birthday party it was a big deal. As an eight-year-old, you felt very honored to be invited to "Juney Bug's" place.

This old house is in sad repair. You can look on the right-hand side and see the water has gotten into all the face boards above the portico. It is now owned by a large corporate ranch and serves as a tenant house. Its glory days are all gone. The guy that lives in it said you can't live in the upstairs because the roof leaks too much and they keep buckets downstairs.

Making this drawing stirred my emotions because of what I recalled from my childhood.

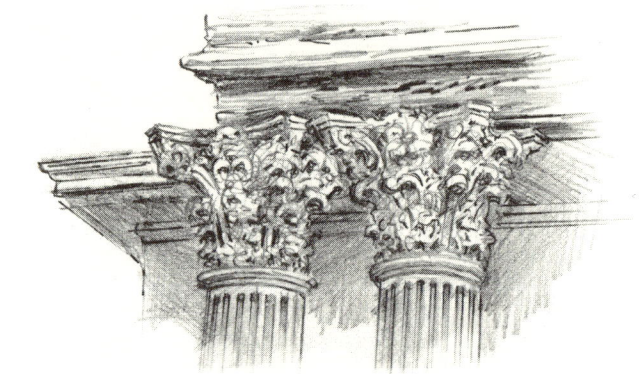

The elaborate plaster capitals on the Hildreth house have deriorated beyond repair.

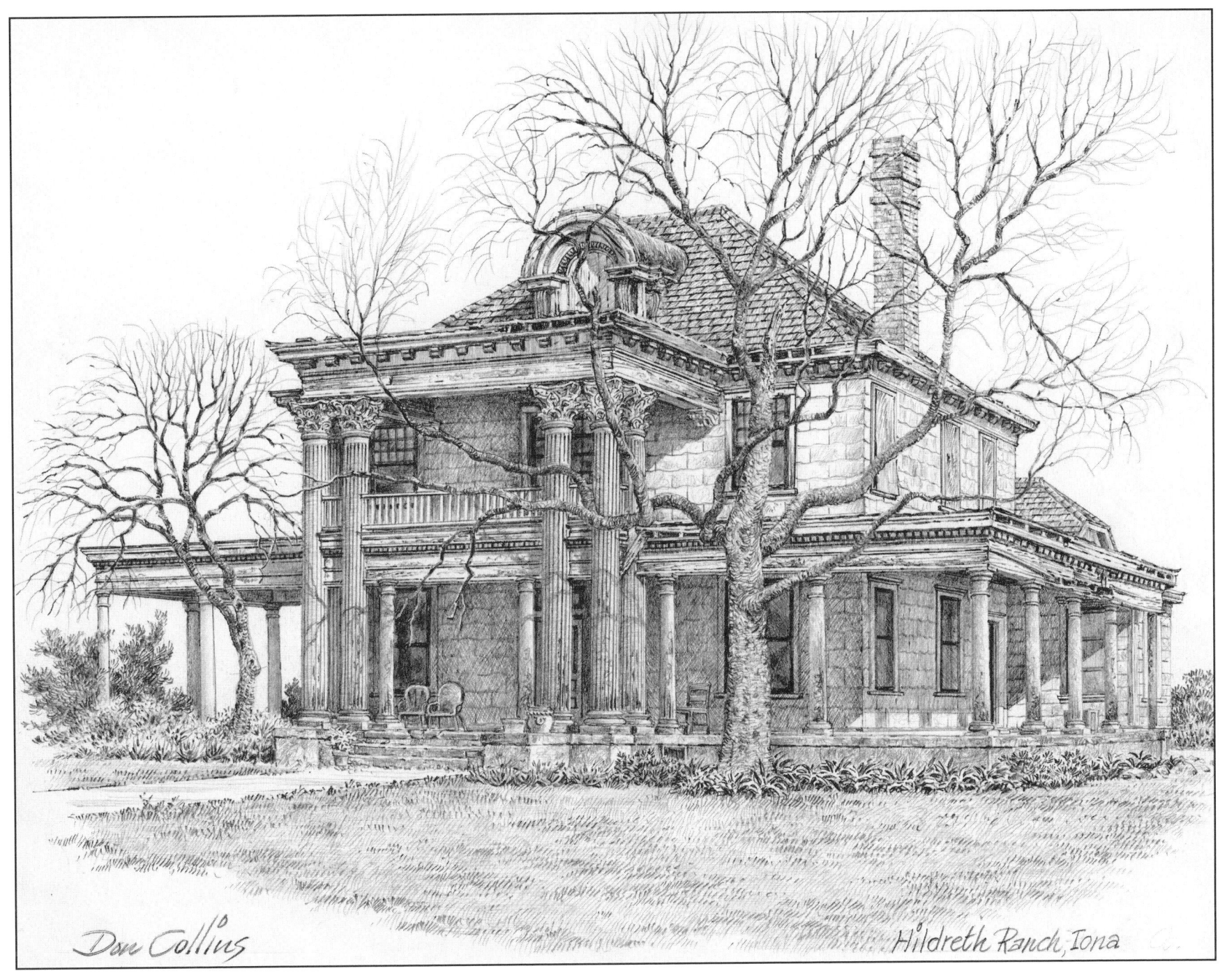

Dan Collins

Hildreth Ranch, Iona

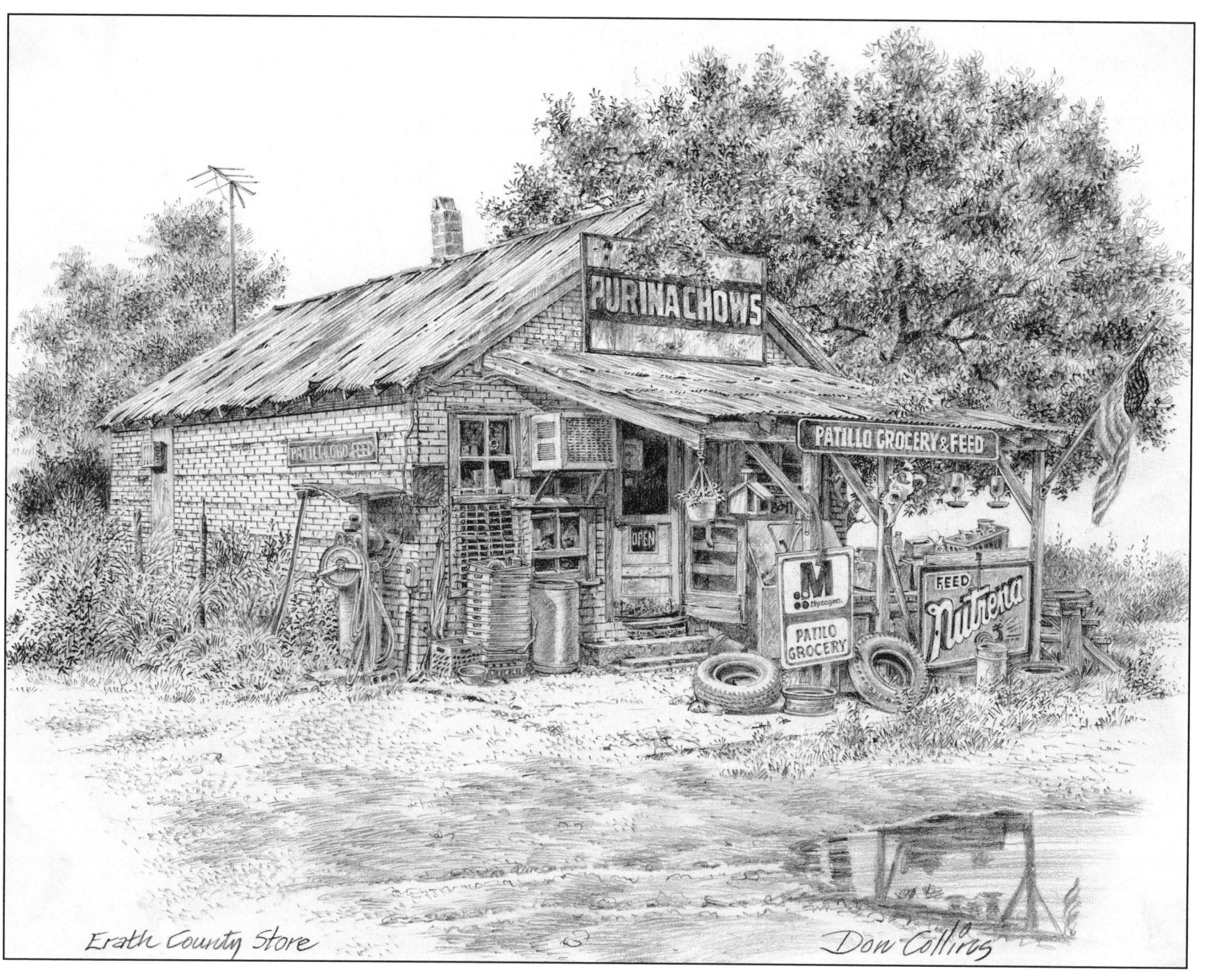

Erath County Store

Don Collins

67. Erath County Store.

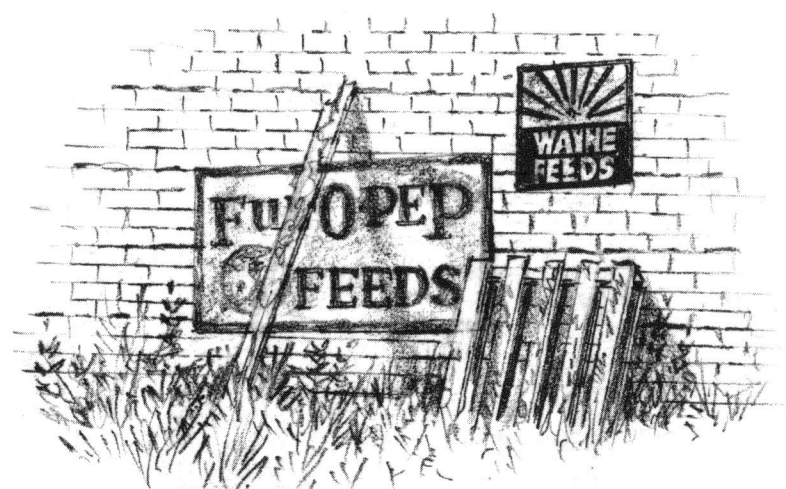

If someone gives you an advertising sign, you might as well put it up!

My brother, Neil, a favorite cousin, Alex, and I were wandering through the world north and west of Glen Rose and losing ourselves in that neighborhood when we stumbled across this place in northeastern Erath County—Patilo's Grocery and Feed. If it's in a town, I don't know it. It's at more of a crossroads. I was simply attracted by the variety of things going on out there. You know, the signs, and the fact that they spelled their name differently in two different places, Patilo here and Patillo here. It's typical of the old country stores that you used to encounter. It was an active store. You could go in there and get a Coke or an ice cream. A very humble little place.

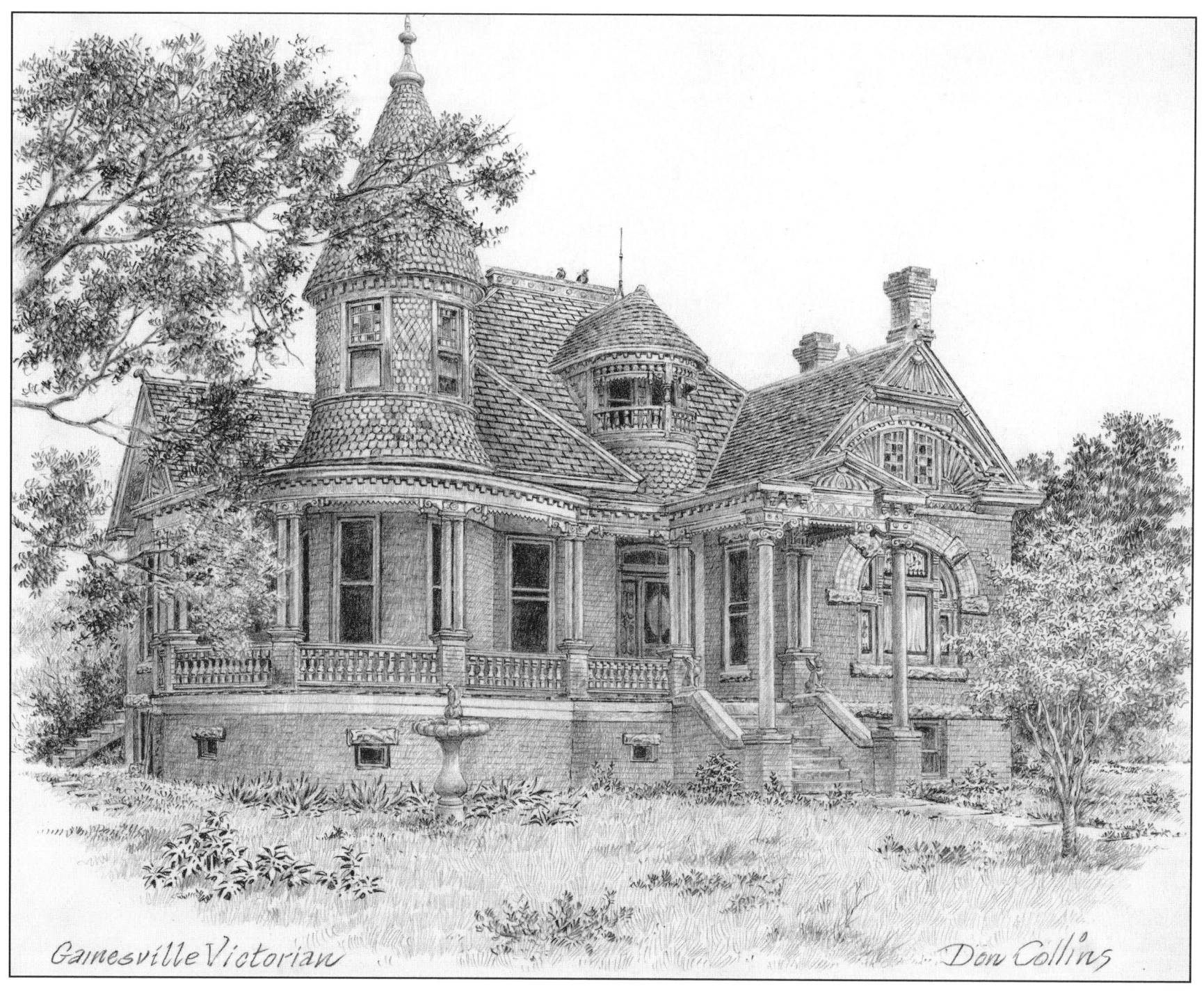

Gainesville Victorian   Don Collins

68. Gainesville Victorian.

This is actually a rather small house, but it's my favorite Victorian anywhere in the world. It's a tremendous little house with a palette of different features and touches everywhere. There is no place you can look without finding something to see and admire. It has absolutely beautiful stained glass and tremendous carpentry detailing in the gable. And, of course, all this stuff around the circular lookout and the tower. I mean everything about that house is just terrific. It's even got a pair of griffins guarding the entrance there, and they're part of the house.

The house was in questionable condition, lived in and not falling down, but with quite a bit of decay showing here and there. I went back last year, I guess, and they were working on it. So I was very encouraged. I liked it so much at the time I found it that I asked myself, "How much money do I have?" then "How much is that house going to cost?" and finally "Would I really want to live in Gainesville?" I mean, I just thought that was a great little house.

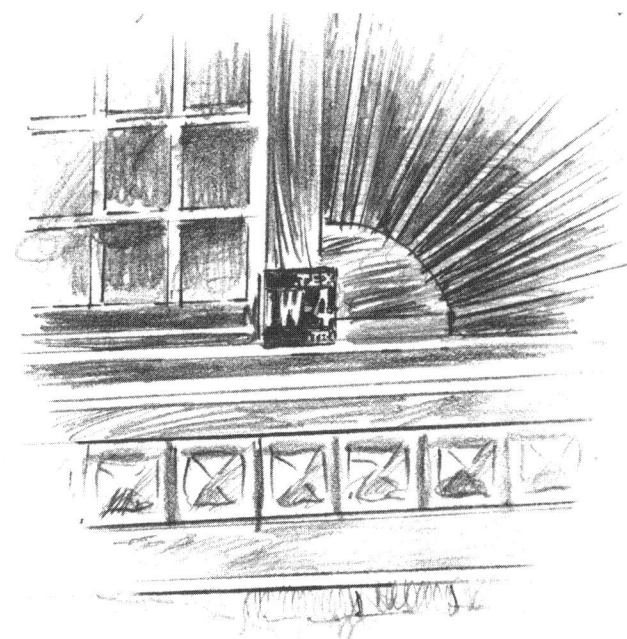

Way up there above the fantastic stained and leaded glass windows, someone had sealed a leak with a piece of old Texas truck license plate!

69. Lindbergh House, Norse Community.

This is one of the early ones. I expect I collected this in '65 or so. We're looking at the south side of the house. The east side of the house was caved in, stood very open, and they had some sheet metal and lumber blocking it up.

While I was there elderly Mr. Lindbergh tottered out to see me from the house next door. His current house was probably eighty years old, but that was the "new house." He explained that his grandfather had come over from Norway and had built the old house in the style that he was accustomed to. There is a full basement under it, and that's where his cattle lived. Sure enough I looked down there and saw stanchions and feed bins. Lindbergh was very proud of the place. He was probably in his eighties at that time, and that was, you know, thirty-five, forty years ago. I've drawn this house from three angles I think. There's something to see everywhere you look.

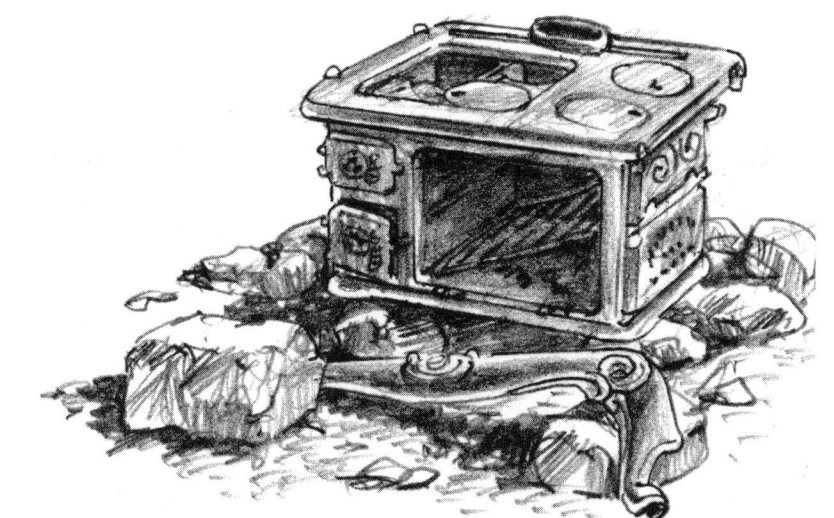

Around the corner of the house was this veteran of generations of delicious Norwegian meals.

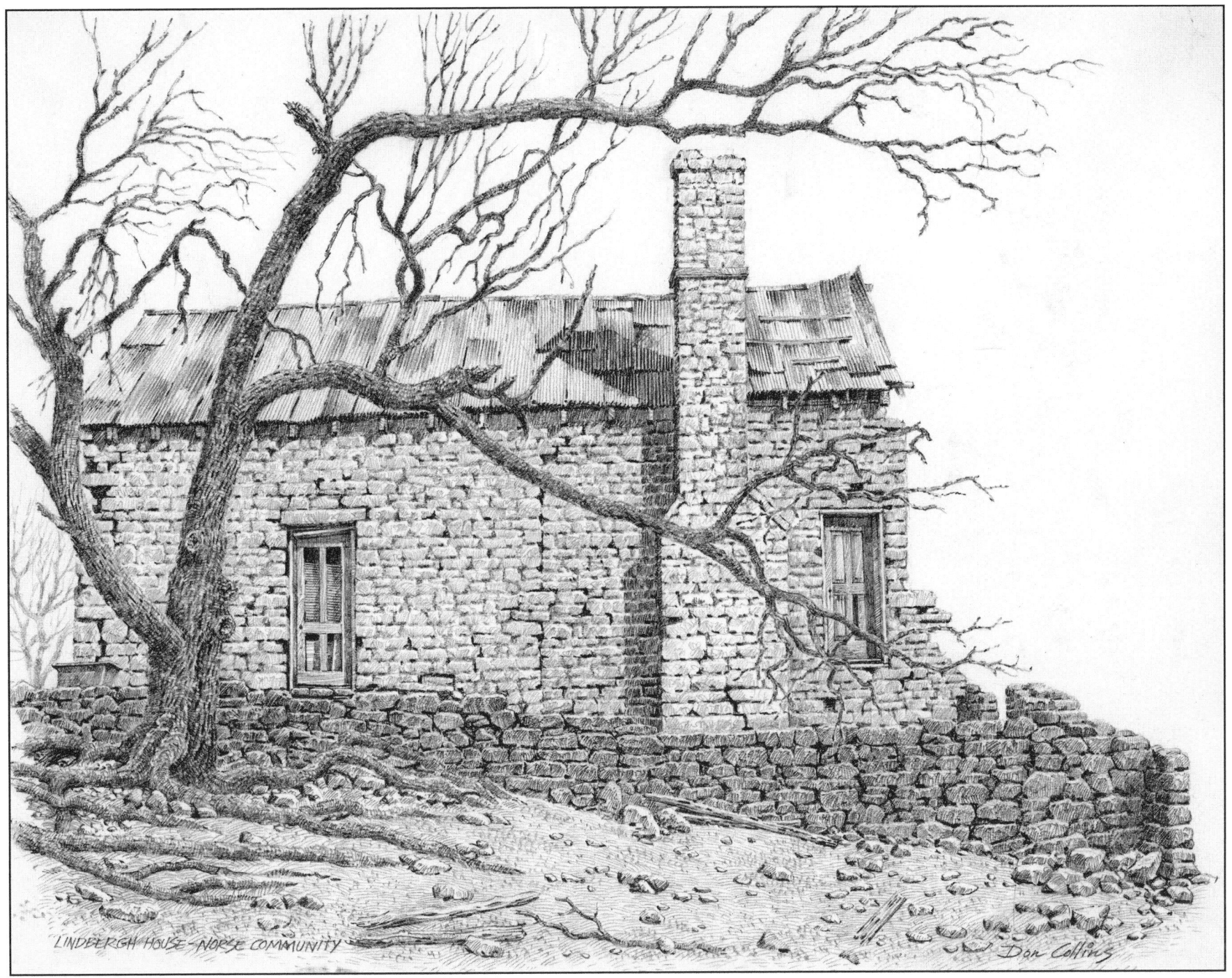

"LINDBERGH HOUSE - NORSE COMMUNITY"

Don Collins

70. Little Brick House near Aledo, Parker County.

This is one of my favorite places. This is two-and-a-half miles up the road from the family ranch where I grew up, and I have been in it many, many times.

I don't walk much anywhere now, but when I was a boy, my cousin, my brother, and I would walk up to Aledo six miles if we felt the need for a Coke in the summertime. We'd spend a nickel, and then we'd walk back and think nothing of it. We'd go twelve miles to spend five cents. Almost invariably when we'd go up there, we'd dodge in to look at this house. It was already abandoned.

The interesting thing about the house is its bricks. They were made from clay that was dug up at the site and fired with hardwood right there on the site by a man named Brown. The water came from a beautiful little branch just below the house. The building is actually about two rooms down, two rooms up, and a kitchen addition that is collapsed. According to the family, who still live in the area, all this was done by one man in 1856.

When it started to decay in the way that it did, I got alarmed and appealed to the state historical commission to urge the owner to take steps to preserve the house. They sent letters to that effect, but nothing was done, so the deterioration continued. It is sad to say, but now the roof is totally gone and about half of the walls have fallen down.

It is a very early house and possibly one of the first in Parker County. And the whole thing was made out of the water and the wood and the clay that is right on the site. I've never encountered that anywhere that I know of. And Brown did a neat job.

Near the Brown house, rural thrills in the 40's...an antique bike frame suspended from a towering cottonwood over a deep small creek.

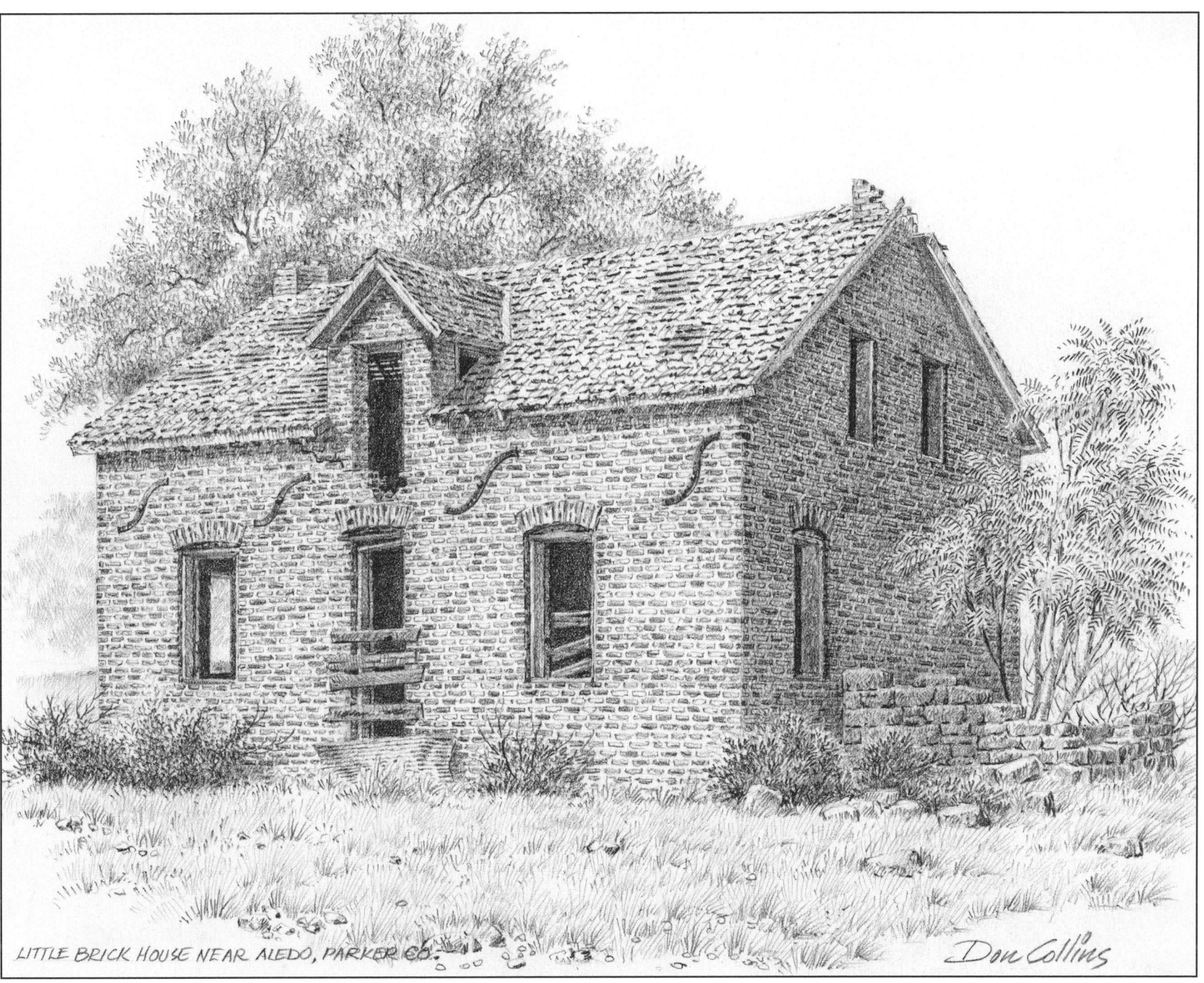

LITTLE BRICK HOUSE NEAR ALEDO, PARKER CO.

Don Collins

List of Plates

PART ONE: Central Texas.

1. View of Waller Creek, Austin. / 8
2. Cottonseed Oil Mill, High Hill. / 10
3. Ranch House near Evant. / 12
4. Comanche County Jail, Comanche. / 14
5. House at Hunter's Bend. / 16
6. Gin at Burton. / 18
7. Possible Code Issues, Austin. / 20
8. Bastrop County Barn, with Privy. / 22
9. Mt. Zion A.M.E. Church. / 24
10. Austin Mansion. / 26
11. Dime Box Ferguson. / 28
12. LaGrange Jail House. / 30
13. Farmhouse near Adamsville. / 32
14. Two Tired Trucks. / 34
15. House at Burton. / 36
16. Barn at Shelby. / 38

PART TWO: South Texas.

17. School at the John Ruckman House, Old Helena. / 42
18. Mid-Nineteenth-Century House of Sillar (Limestone Particulate), Guerra, Texas. / 44
19. 1880s Courthouse, Frio County. / 46
20. Noah Cox House, Roma. / 48
21. San Rafael Chapel, Randado Ranch, Randado, Texas. / 50
22. Little House near Cuero. / 52
23. House on the Rio Grande. / 54

PART THREE: The Hill Country

24. Central Texas Barnyard. / 58
25. Barn on the Little Blanco River. / 60
26. Little Log House at Leon Springs. / 62
27. Palisado House near Quihi. / 64
28. Garage/Water Tower/Chicken House, Boerne. / 66
29. Pioneer Ruin, Mason County. / 68
30. Smokehouse and Icehouse in Boerne. / 70
31. Barn near Castroville. / 72
32. Castroville Service Station. / 74
33. House in Southern Gillespie County. / 76
34. Pioneer Home at Quihi. / 78
35. Morris Ranch School, Gillespie County. / 80
36. Water Tower and Wash House, Mason. / 82
37. Dance Hall, Sisterdale. / 84
38. House near Liberty Hill. / 86

39. Camp Verde Store. / 88
40. Barn at Burnet. / 90
41. Old Bank at Comfort. / 92
42. Barn at Riomedina. / 94
43. Truck and House, Spring Valley. / 96

PART FOUR: The Panhandle Plains.

44. Former Courthouse, Rayner,
    Stonewall County. / 100
45. Panhandle Farmhouse. / 102
46. Railroad Station, Quanah, Texas. / 104
47. Abandoned Panhandle Feed Mill. / 106

PART FIVE: West Texas.

48. Former Railroad Station, Marathon. / 110
49. Fort McKavett Ruins, ca. 1969. / 112
50. Abandoned Courthouse, Sherwood. / 114
51. Adobe Church, Ruidosa, Texas. / 116
52. Terlingua Mansion, ca. 1973. / 118
53. Valentine Mercantile. / 120
54. Adobe Store in Langtry. / 122

PART SIX: East Texas.

55. Hearne Station. / 126
56. Grimes County Courthouse, Anderson. / 128
57. Texas & Pacific Depot, Marshall. / 130
58. Farmhouse near Paris. / 132
59. Nacogdoches Station. / 134
60. Barn at Teaselville. / 136

PART SEVEN: North Central Texas.

61. Interurban Car, Cresson, Texas. / 140
62. Waggoner House, Decatur. / 142
63. School at Mosheim, Bosque County. / 144
64. Old Mill, Dublin, Erath County. / 146
65. Bank Building, Granbury. / 148
66. Hildreth Ranch, Iona. / 150
67. Erath County Store. / 152
68. Gainesville Victorian. / 154
69. Lindbergh House, Norse Community. / 156
70. Little Brick House near Aledo,
    Parker County. / 158

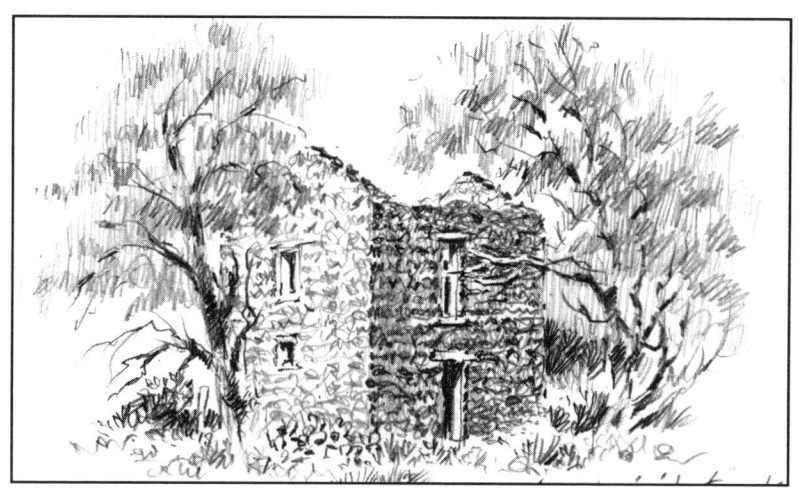

Traces of Forgotten Places

designed by Barbara Mathews Whitehead

set in Centaur type

1250 copies printed by Versa Press, Inc.

2008

ISBN 978-0-87565-361-7

Traces of Forgotten Places
by Don Collins
edited by T. Lindsay Baker
ISBN 978-0-87565-361-7
Paper. $19.95